PUTTING THE **SOUL** BACK INTO BUSINESS

A ROADMAP OF SOCIAL CHANGE

To Sam,
Best wishes

Dr. Tamara Howard

Tamara Howard

Author Biography

Dr Tamara Howard is a Harvard Graduate (AB 75). She started her business career in the early days of Biotechnology after gaining her PhD in Physiology from The Sackler School of Biomedical Sciences at Tufts University. Her business experience spans the USA and Europe and includes startups as well as large multinationals. She has worked for *IBM (UK) Ltd*, *Digital Equipment Corporation*, *The PA Consulting Group* and *Capgemini*. She now runs a small business consultancy focusing on growth, and caters to all sectors including not-for-profits, startups and large corporations. Over her distinguished career she has observed many shifts and changes in the business world.

Tamara also takes part in many voluntary activities. She helped to establish and acted as a trustee for *The Alison Wetherfield Foundation*, is a director of the *Harvard Club of the UK* where she works extensively in the Public Services Committee and elsewhere provides *pro bono* and reduced price consulting to small charities and social businesses.

Putting the Soul Back into Business is Tamara's third book. It follows *Who's Paying for Lunch - A Practical Manual for Maximising Sales in Small and Medium Enterprises* and *100+ Top Tips for Effective Sales Management.*

Tamara currently resides in Oxfordshire in the United Kingdom and may be contacted at: drtamarahoward@gmail.com

Published in the UK 2015 by

Verve Business Books Ltd
The White House
Mill Lane
Goring-on-Thames
Oxfordshire
RG8 0DD

ISBN 978-0-9929645-2-8

Design and artwork by Artefact Design, Godalming. www.artefactdesign.co.uk

Printed by Printwoks Global Ltd., London & Hong Kong

Contents

Foreword

PUTTING THE SOUL BACK INTO BUSINESS

"The Western mindset is changing when it comes to how we work. We are not content to work to just make money for ourselves, but also want to give back to our communities and those in need."

A young professional at Harvard Oxford Alumni Social Business Group

Businesses in the Western world are currently undergoing a significant shift. A new, more socially engaged ethos is starting to emerge. It has now become so widespread that even the educational establishment and governments acknowledge its existence. *Putting the Soul Back into Business* tells the story of individuals' experiences in driving this important change. In presenting these stories, this book aims to be a source of inspiration and provide potential routes or roadmaps, for those keen to implement social change within their working lives.

As a business consultant of many years, and having worked in organisations of all shapes and sizes, I began to spot a trend - a new behaviour among professionals and widely prevalent among the under 40s. Increasingly they were demanding a job in which they could personally contribute to the betterment of the world - whether by championing 'green' issues within their organisation and beyond, or taking personal steps to directly support local or international charitable or social support efforts. I asked myself: were my observations valid? How widespread was this shift, especially among those who will be our next generation of leaders? What is the impact of these motivated individuals?

Using my role in the *Harvard Club of the United Kingdom*, I decided to test the strength of this trend by working with an Oxford alumna and her contacts, to put on event entitled 'Putting the Soul Back into Business.' Panellists ranged from individuals within large organisations to founders of new social enterprises and charities. Each was asked to tell his or her story about wanting to make a personal impact on those in need, or on the environment. As the event drew near, I worried that I had misjudged the numbers and that only a few people would show up. The event was scheduled for after business hours on a week night in London, so 30 or 40 attendees would be counted a success.

In the end, we had to stop accepting attendees at almost 100, due to the limitations of the room. Professionals of all ages, hailing from a variety of educational backgrounds, crowded into the room. Surprised by the response, we agreed to run another event six months later and to our surprise, we reached capacity once more. Encouraged by those who attended, we now offer this event every six months in order to act as an inspiration and network for others who wish to bring this spirit to their own organisation. This event precipitated the formation of the *Harvard Oxford Alumni Social Business Group* (*HOASBG*).

So, after running a number of these events and speaking to all the attendees and panellists, what conclusions did I draw?

There is definitely a trend and it's growing and gaining momentum!

Attendees all loved the event because they could link with others of a similar mindset. Before the *HOASBG*, they felt like 'lone social warriors' in their organisations and, indeed, in the world at large. So, to expand the reach of the group, I decided to chronicle these stories so that their inspiration could be available to a much larger number of people and a wider audience, even those not wishing to enter the business world.

Putting the Soul Back into Business captures the stories of individuals who have embraced this spirit and struggled to chart their own paths to finding 'purpose' in their work. They are all social pioneers who have taken steps, great and small, to ensure that their organisations, businesses or business environments contributed and connected to important social causes. I hope this book will serve as an inspiration, and accelerate this important trend by providing a sense of connectedness to readers who share these aspirations.

Acknowledgements

First and foremost, I would like to thank those individuals whose stories are told in this book. In alphabetical order by first name:

Aaron Hurst
Adam Sampson
Alex Cole
Andrew Warren
Asma Shah
Ayesha Mustafa
Baillie Aaron
Béla Hatvany
Craig Dearden-Philips
Deap Khambay
Elizabeth Grier
Erika Uffindell
Gina Hayden
Jamie Ward-Smith
Jean Ward
Kay Allen
Laura Malone
Lucy Findlay
Maggie De Pree
Mark Brunton
Mark Stevenson
Maya Mehta
Neil Seligman
Paul Cheng
Paul Lomas
Peter Maxmin
Peter Ryan
Rob Symington
Roy Moëd
Steve Turpie
Warren Richmond
Vari McLuskie

I would also like to thank the following people who took the time and trouble to read my rough drafts and provide valuable comments and insights about the content and cover design: Tabitha Moses, Tony Bardawil, Steve Turpie, Kate Youll, Judy Friend, Maya Mehta and Vari McLuskie. In addition, I want to thank Ashley Smith for her insights as well as all those who contributed anonymously to the content of this book.

Finally, I would like to express my gratitude to the *Harvard Club of the United Kingdom* – the organisation that provided the infrastructure and support to run the' Putting the Soul Back into Business' events and Maya Mehta, my co-host who mobilised the support of Oxford alumni as well as other like-minded individuals.

A big 'thank you' to everyone!

Chapter 1

WHAT'S HAPPENING? - THE SIGNS OF CHANGE

> "You are not here merely to make a living. You are here in order to enable the world to live more amply, with greater vision, with a finer spirit of hope and achievement. You are here to enrich the world, and you impoverish yourself if you forget the errand."
> **Woodrow Wilson**

There's something unusual happening in the business world today, in fact in the Western world as a whole. Employees, particularly younger people, are beginning to demand more from their working lives. A good salary, an interesting role and a solid career path are no longer enough. Even those well-educated professionals tipped for the management fast track are not behaving the way they used to. These are not starry-eyed idealists. Rather, they are realists who accept the need to perform their professional roles. They understand their organisations' need to make a profit, but in tandem with this reality, they want something more. These professionals want to put 'meaning' back into their jobs.

This book has been written for these individuals. It is aimed at professional people who feel frustrated in their current jobs - whether in large corporations, professional bodies or government agencies - and seek a way to put meaning back into their working life. Each chapter focuses on different approaches and presents examples of how others have struggled to add a sense of purpose to their daily job. I hope that in providing the backgrounds and a variety of different histories, at least one example will strike a chord with every reader, and provide inspiration and insights. Of course individual stories contain unique situations, but what I hope they show is how these people overcame the obstacles they encountered and found a way forward. The varied stories provide a glimpse into the challenges and rewards of different routes to building a meaningful working life. There is no single, right pathway.

The stories contained within these pages will also help new graduates, about to step onto the career ladder, to understand the options available to them and what others have faced in the recent past. Finally, the book should also be enlightening for corporate leaders who are trying to understand what is happening to some of their fast-tracked future leaders, and why these individuals are dissatisfied, some to the point of leaving the organisation. The entire book documents the varied roadmap of social change that is occurring in today's working world as more and more people seek to integrate meaning into their daily jobs.

In essence, the purpose of this book is two-fold: to illustrate how a variety of individuals have managed to introduce a culture change into the businesses they work for, and how others have been able to transform this imperative for social change and meaning into a business or a career.

What exactly is this 'meaning' they seek?

Of course, 'meaning' denotes different things to different people, but in the context of this book, it involves making a difference to other people's lives or to the world at large. This difference doesn't have to be big (and it doesn't need to make anyone famous), but for the professionals under discussion, they need to feel personally involved. Some of those interviewed describe the impulse as 'doing good' while others use the phrase 'giving back'. Each wants to personally 'make a difference' and help to make the community and/or the world, a better place. From hearing their stories, it's clear that they describe the same, elusive quality - the desire to connect more fully with other people, and the world around them, and to make a positive difference as a part of their daily working life. These individuals want to feel 'connected' in a way that helps to make the world a better place, even if it is only a small contribution at the time.

Why is this trend such a big deal?

Well, first of all, it's new. While there have always been individuals who tried to incorporate social benefit into their working life, these were the exception rather than the rule. A generation ago, people who pursued higher degrees were happy to get a good job, move up the career ladder and try to balance their work and family life. They may have supported charities or local community efforts, but most of them didn't expect to do these 'worthy' activities while at work. To contribute to worthy causes was typically an individual's choice, usually performed outside working hours. In general, these people did not pursue a career in the charity sector - which, until recently, was typically not viewed as a viable career option. Work life and personal life, including charitable volunteering efforts, did not mix.

In recent years, there has been a shift. A wave of professional people are looking for work that is 'meaningful'; they seek a job or a job environment that aims to assist those in need, improve the environment and/or supports a social cause. They want hands-on activities that integrate into their everyday working lives, and as far as they are concerned, the tax-deductible charitable efforts of the Corporate Social Responsibility department are neither sufficient nor personally satisfying. These individuals crave personal involvement. Of course, there are people of all ages who share this approach and some of their stories will appear in the following pages. However, what is noteworthy is the number of younger people - those in their 20s, 30s and early 40s - looking for this element in their work life, and it is approaching epic proportions.

This trend has been confirmed by many senior managers at larger corporations who explain that it's getting more difficult to keep good people - high pay and a career path are just not enough anymore. Their staff want 'involvement' and to 'do something meaningful'. When this demand isn't met, staff leave, often for less well-paid jobs. These managers and executives are at a loss for what to do. However, there are some businesses and professional partnerships that have demonstrated creative responses to this trend and often the original business driver was to ensure the retention of good staff. Examples of such approaches kick off this book in Chapter 2. Other examples will be described in later chapters.

Today's young professionals are by no means the first to consider a more holistic business approach. There have always been pioneering individuals with convictions who bucked the contemporary attitude and trends in business culture. Chapter 3 will focus on some of these trendsetters and highlight their struggles to build and grow successful businesses which embodied their personal social values. Working many decades ago, these individuals received little support and had to go it alone. In order to be true to their own ideals and standards, they found it necessary to start their own businesses to achieve these results. There are also more recent examples of others who have chosen this route, which has now been termed 'for profit, for good'.

For some, the desire to give back came later in life after they had already succeeded in a more traditional role or organisation. Chapter 4 looks at individuals who turned to funding 'good works', social businesses and/or charities after leaving a successful career. The desire to 'give back' can strike at any age and can take diverse paths. While not everyone will leave a successful career to pursue socially beneficial activities, this approach does provide yet another path and options are vital.

Not all businesses lend themselves to a traditional approach, and some individuals have had to find a creative way to exercise their desire to add purpose to their job. They have, in fact, had to 'think outside the box'. Chapter 5 presents the stories of some of these individuals who pioneered activities in and around their places of work in order take part in activities that allowed them to give back to society.

In addition, the recent rise of what is termed 'social businesses' or 'social enterprises' re-emphasises this trend and illustrates one direction that these professionals' aspirations can take. Social enterprises are a rapidly growing business sector, capturing many bright individuals who would, in times past, have entered the traditional business world. Some social enterprises focus on the environment and some provide jobs and/or retail channels for disenfranchised or disadvantaged communities. Whatever the focus, the aim of these businesses is to be self-sustaining and to make money for the benefit of a selected constituency or cause. Stories of individuals who created social enterprises will be told in Chapter 6.

However, not everyone can or will start up a business. Others must carve their own paths. Some individuals have been creative and worked within the confines of their management roles to establish activities and programmes with a social agenda - truly 'putting the soul' back into their department or division. In later chapters their stories will be told in more detail. In all cases, there was a positive impact for everyone. But there are still more alternative routes that others have explored - one of these is the charity sector. Until recently, few business-minded people considered charity work as a career, so this path was not a common option. Creating a social business is another approach.

What choices are available for those who wish to solve social problems but don't want to enter the business arena? And how can individuals trained in the business or professional world add value in the third sector? There is no right answer nor is there a single route. Chapter 7 will look at the stories of social pioneers who blazed this trail, some starting their own charities and some who figured out how to deploy their professional training to add value to existing charitable organisations

Finally, some peoples' working lives take a wandering route, trying many paths before they find their way. Chapter 8 focuses on some of these stories. It is important to understand that in these times of change, the way forward is not always obvious or direct. Sometimes it depends on luck and often, persistence. The personal struggles chronicled in this chapter illustrate how, with determination, the professional can eventually find what he or she seeks. It isn't always easy, but, amazingly, most of the life experiences collected along the way contribute to the individual's eventual success.

And there are still other paths that these social entrepreneurs can take to satisfy their desire to give back. Many work in their spare time or build full-time jobs in order to create support networks. They seek to help and empower like-minded individuals who meet to discuss how these values can be incorporated into the traditional workplace. Over the past four to five years, a plethora of these groups has sprung up around the world, generating ideas, passing on success stories and acting as an inspiration to others. The *Harvard Oxford Alumni Social Business Group* (*HOASBG*) is now one of many similar groups in the London area. Chapter 9 contains many examples of individuals who have taken this route.

The source of most of the stories in this narrative is the *HOASBG*, based in London, England. But don't be fooled by the geographical bias.

This trend is not a 'British thing'; it's happening all over the Western world. The stories in this book are merely a snapshot in one place at one time and serve to illustrate the range of individuals involved and the methods they have used. The initiative has become so widespread that even the traditional businesses and educational institutions are now taking notice.

In fact, even the bastions of the business establishment - business schools - have jumped on this bandwagon and are offering courses of study in 'Social Entrepreneurship', and the terms 'social business' and 'social entrepreneur' have entered the mainstream. All the well-known institutions advertise courses, seminars and even degrees; Columbia, Harvard and Stanford Universities in the USA, INSEAD in Europe, and in the UK, London Business School and Said Business School at Oxford University are but a few from a long list of respected institutions offering studies in this area. The trend is big and continues to grow.

So what's going on and why?

It's difficult to pinpoint a single factor that explains why this is happening. Perhaps it is a reflection of the desire to make a personal impact in a world that is increasingly computerised, with correspondingly fewer face-to-face interactions between colleagues, businesses and customers. Today, even training courses are carried out online. In some organisations, employees will sit in close proximity to one another yet only communicate via email. Perhaps one strand of today's movement stems from a desire, or a human need, to interact with other people directly - a need that modern technology frustrates.

Ironically, this trend is enabled by those same technological advances that empower and inform the individuals via *YouTube*, *Facebook*, *Twitter*, and other social media. The rise of this social movement and the disproportionate involvement of under 45s in it certainly reflects the generations who have grown up with these electronic communication tools. It is now easier to become informed and then share this information with huge numbers of people. The rise of social media channels can make individuals feel both informed about what's happening in the world and, by facilitating widespread communication, personally empowered by being able to link with others to act upon issues that concern them.

Whatever the root cause, what is true is that a professional's job -

in fact, most jobs - generally take up more than half of a person's life and certainly more than half of one's waking hours. And the younger generation, the rising, potential corporate leaders of tomorrow, want to spend their life doing something that means more to them. Because they spend so much time in work, they seek to fulfil this need within their daily job. The obvious questions are: is this a realistic aspiration? Can it be done? These very questions are also those that these young professionals are asking themselves as they search for careers that satisfy all of their personal aspirations.

One individual who typifies this attitude and works in the corporate world today, thought long and hard about her aspirations and relayed her conclusions as follows. "There are some who say that 'doing what you love' is slightly elitist. That, in fact, only the empowered and well-educated have that choice, while others must work to put bread on the table. Whether or not this statement is true, it is true that those with the education and corporate position can make an impact and in small and large ways, can improve social conditions."

This woman clearly felt it was possible to effect change from within a traditional large corporation and her words echo the sentiments of many, many others in this movement.

Yet, the way forward for many is still unclear. The social pioneers creating new paths forward who are documented in this book demonstrate a number of options:

- Changing working practices from within a traditional corporate environment ('intrapreneur')
- Starting a traditional company with social values embedded in the fabric of the business
- Transforming an existing organisation
- Creating a social enterprise
- Carrying out social impact activities during personal time or instigating 'guerrilla movements' within an unsympathetic organisation
- Setting up or joining a charity
- Establishing a support organisation to help others become intrapreneurs or social entrepreneurs

Some observers don't understand why employees are making such a fuss and looking to these different career paths. Their logic is thus: that working for a charity is viewed as a career these days, so why don't all these social pioneers move into jobs in this sector? Wouldn't that solve the problem? If so, then things in the business world could carry on as before.

However, the answer is not so simple

While moving into a career in charity work or starting a social business may satisfy personal aspirations, these routes alone are not the answer to addressing all of society's problems. Think about it. If the best and the brightest of each generation leave their traditional careers in the corporate or political world, who will be left to run these institutions? There is no doubt that big business and big government are both here to stay for the foreseeable future and an exodus of highly educated, socially motivated individuals from these sectors could result in a serious social imbalance. There is no simple answer or solution.

What is certain is that neither big business nor government can afford to alienate the majority of these well-educated professionals and both of these institutions would suffer if everyone who wished to incorporate socially beneficial activities were to move to small social businesses or charities. Charities rely on the wealth of society in order to do their work, meaning there must be sufficient people toiling to generate this wealth. And government depends on tax revenues, which in turn are supported by a healthy economy and high employment. In fact, both depend on the commercial sector for their continued existence.

An economy composed of smaller social businesses could provide the answer, but these companies might find it difficult to compete in an increasingly global marketplace. Probably a better answer is exactly what seems to be happening at the moment. In other words, a little of everything: social businesses, well managed charities, newly-formed corporations that embrace these values, plus a slow transformation of the existing multinational organisations. If this last group doesn't shift, then they risk losing some of their most talented staff.

One example of how these talented workers feel alienated was illustrated by the tale of one young professional who sadly related, "When I told my manager about my evening and weekend charitable activities, he replied, 'Clearly we aren't giving you enough work!' And he wasn't joking, he was annoyed!" This individual - a well-educated, Harvard Business School graduate - was depressed by her manager's response and soon resigned to join a small social business, taking a drop in salary to do so. And others are following her example.

Unfortunately, in some business sectors, the example above is not an exception. There are some types of businesses - particularly financial services, and some business entities, particularly large partnerships - in which it is extremely challenging to carry out this holistic, values-driven approach within the existing culture. But things are changing. Chapter 5 contains stories of individuals who have successfully bucked the trend and made strides to introduce socially beneficial programs into daily business life. Regardless, the challenge of how to take part in socially beneficial activities while maintaining a harmonious work life is still a very big issue for many who work for large multinationals.

Sadly, many individuals within these traditional environments have good stories to tell, but didn't feel 'safe' committing their stories and names to print. This is an understandable response if it puts a career at risk, but a sad comment on the state of the bureaucracies involved. Doing good and incorporating activities with social impact need not cost a company more in terms of time or employee focus. In fact, it can improve employee morale and productivity, as illustrated by some of the stories in later chapters. However, such change does require a different attitude and approach from the corporations involved. Some individuals have had great success in shifting these attitudes, and much can be learned from their stories.

Today's experienced professionals and young people entering the workforce are not the first to pursue greater meaning in their careers, but they seem to be the first to be doing so in such great numbers. Everyone whose story is included in this book is intelligent and well-educated - whether traditionally or through life experience. They were blessed with the tools and the opportunities to 'get ahead' and to take well-trodden paths up the career ladder. Many have degrees from top universities and most have post-graduate degrees or professional qualifications as well. Why aren't they content to take a more traditional path? What's leading them to carve out their own route - often at the expense of personal wealth - in order to give back to society in some way?

The following chapters will explore the most common routes taken

- Intrapreneurs - or social pioneers who try to introduce socially involved programmes within a traditional business environment
- Social business leaders - individuals who create traditional businesses into which they incorporate and demonstrate strong social values
- Intrapreneurs in challenging environments
- Creators of social enterprises
- Creators or builders of charities
- Founders of support organisations which promote and support 'social pioneers'

Each person's story is different and each chapter will take the reader through a personal journey and provide an insight into the challenges and rewards of choosing a particular path. Most of these pioneers have felt 'alone' in their efforts, and lacking a 'how to' roadmap to show them where to go. Hopefully, this book will provide an outline of possible options - as well as anecdotes and insights - to others who are still struggling to find a more satisfying career path, and to organisations who want to do more to encourage this.

Chapter 2

INTREPRENEURS - SOCIAL ENTREPRENEURS IN LARGE ORGANISATIONS

"Even when I became more senior in an organisation, initially, I still thought of myself as more junior. I didn't feel 'empowered.' Then one day I realised that if something needed to happen, I couldn't wait for someone else to do it."
Anonymous professional from a traditional large corporation

The *American Heritage Dictionary of the English Language* (Third Edition, 1992) lists the word 'intrapreneur' and defines it as: "A person within a large corporation who takes direct responsibility for turning an idea into a profitable finished product through assertive risk-taking and innovation."

Within this book and for many people involved in the social business network, the word has taken on a narrower meaning, denoting someone who takes direct responsibility for introducing and incorporating socially or environmentally beneficial activities into his or her daily working life and, if possible, that of his or her department or division. For many, it is a risky business - risky to their own careers - and each must carry out this activity without impacting the bottom line.

Many of the social pioneers chronicled in this book found themselves working in large corporations, vaguely dissatisfied with their jobs, but not certain what to do to add a social contribution to their daily work. Ensconced in a hierarchical organisation, the natural tendency was to wait until 'word' came from above, providing new direction and enabling new activities. Typically, the 'word' never came, so many considered leaving prestigious and powerful positions to take up more socially fulfilling work in the charity sector. Indeed, that's one career option and often the first alternative that many of these professionals consider.

Gradually, some of these people realised that specialist skills within their businesses, deployed with appropriately focused corporate resources, could be used to yield a significant social benefit and do so in a way that didn't impact their business's bottom lines. These professionals developed into social intrapreneurs who sought to enact change in working practices from within their organisations in an attempt to add meaning to their work and purpose to their jobs. They developed strategies to provide social benefit while performing their roles. Although often quite senior, typically a social intrepreneur is not the boss. Often they are professional contributors or run a department or division, positioned a layer or two, or even further, from the top.

When these activities succeed, it's easy to assume that doing them was 'no big deal'. However, success is not guaranteed. What cannot be conveyed to people who have never worked in these organisations is the degree of personal risk involved in trying these initiatives within the work environment. Corporations tend to be very conservative. They have rules and most activities are measured by the impact - direct or indirect - on the company bottom line. These businesses are all risk averse, and it requires extreme bravery to go out on a limb and deviate from typical company behaviours and processes to do something that does not contribute to profits. For a senior manager to do so could well be a 'career-limiting step.' That's why the stories told in this chapter are so important.

When individuals have already attained a senior position, they need to feel very strongly motivated by the idea of 'doing good' to put their future career at risk. Personally, they have everything to lose and professionally, little to gain. For each of the stories that follow, the only payback was the personal feeling that each was 'doing the right thing'. A fine example is that of Peter Maxmin, who was a senior manager at *Microsoft UK*. For many years he toyed with the idea of moving from his well-paid role at *Microsoft* into the voluntary sector. He didn't have a particular charity in mind, he just felt he had been fortunate in life and wanted to help others who hadn't had his opportunities.

To explore this option further, Peter discussed his aspiration with a management consultant who was experienced in the charity sector and it soon became clear that Peter could actually do a great deal from within *Microsoft*. Furthermore, he wouldn't need to change jobs, he could start 'doing good' almost immediately. He could also involve his staff, many of whom expressed a similar desire to give back to society and who were also considering moving jobs to achieve these aims.

With the power of a large organisation behind him and the programming and web skills of those in his department, Peter began to fashion an approach that could be incorporated into the working life of those within his department and others who were interested. He was aided by the fact that *Microsoft* gives its employees a certain number of days each year to use for volunteering. The end result? A coordinated business effort that 'did good' in the local community and deployed the specialist skills of those at *Microsoft*.

Its sounds so simple in the telling, but the way forward was not immediately obvious to Peter. Like many of the professionals whose stories are told in this book, he struggled to identify the career path he should take in order to fulfil both his ambitions and his desire to 'do good.' His story illustrates very well his personal struggles to find the right balance, and his success in achieving personal satisfaction while working within a large corporation. Like many, initially he felt that working in a charity, or starting one, was the only way to achieve a feeling of giving back to society. However, after careful consideration he realised that he could both enrich his working life and make a social contribution within the context of his current job.

Peter's story - Thinking outside the box

The early years

Peter Maxmin grew up in England. Both of his parents had careers - his father was a businessman and his mother was a doctor. As a result of his upbringing he always had a sense of business and a notion that he should contribute to society, but the way forward was not always obvious. At university (Cambridge) he studied Sociology and Psychology as he continued to explore options for his future that satisfied both of his personal objectives.

After graduating, his future pathway was not clear. He seriously considered working in the public sector but finally he decided that whatever he did, management skills would be useful and that the best place to gain these skills was the private sector. He applied and was accepted to a graduate scheme at the *Financial Times (FT).*

It was at the *FT* that he got his first taste of volunteering, reading to underprivileged children as part of a scheme supported by his employer. However, as working life became very busy, Peter found it difficult to regularly commit to the reading sessions during office hours and finally stopped volunteering. He felt guilty but was also certain that he couldn't find the time to continue the volunteering in that way. It soon became a moot point when Peter decided to attend INSEAD, the prestigious European Business School situated outside Paris. He wanted to study and understand the impact of the internet and how it was changing society.

Combining work and volunteering at Microsoft

After graduation, a natural next step was to accept a job with *Microsoft.*

Although involved in interesting work at *Microsoft*, Peter was still concerned that he was not personally making a contribution to society. To that end, he began to investigate what *Microsoft* offered in terms of volunteering opportunities and spoke to friends and business consultants outside the company. He knew that the *Microsoft* culture supported this sort of activity because all employees were given three 'volunteer' days per year. As part of the *Microsoft* initiative, Peter obtained an email distribution list that contained a number of charitable organisation for which employees could volunteer.

Having chosen an organisation that interested him - the *Homeless World Cup* - Peter decided he could best use his three volunteer days by employing his skills to help the charity define its digital strategy and revamp its website. This activity made Peter 'feel good' and that feeling was important to him. Not only had he made a contribution, but he had also used his skills to help. Another plus was that he found the project interesting and intellectually challenging. As a result, he started looking for other activities promoted within *Microsoft*, which had an arrangement with a group called *Time and Talents,* a charity based in South East London. Among other things, this group focused on pairing up volunteers' talents with the needs of the local community.

When Peter spoke to a woman at *Time and Talents*, he was told that there was a high demand among very small charities for help with IT and web training, but that these organisations couldn't afford to pay for consultants or even to send volunteers on training courses. Now Peter was in his element. From within *Microsoft* he sought individuals who had the appropriate skills and, pooling everyone's allocated volunteer days, put together a team who could conduct a comprehensive workshop for these small charities. In the end, 60 to 70 people showed up for help at the workshop, which focused on things like:

- Digital marketing
- How to get the most from the internet

Lessons learned

The workshop was great for both the charities and for the *Microsoft* team, who felt good about themselves and their contribution. The effort pulled together individuals from different parts of *Microsoft* and agencies to deliver the workshop. It was so successful, and generated so much satisfaction within the organisation, that Peter realised there were additional benefits to these activities. Not only were his team (and himself) happier and more fulfilled, but *Microsoft* itself benefitted.

Peter explains, "I began to realise that it was true, people - that's both employees and customers - appreciate brands or businesses that 'do more.'"

Peter continued looking for more opportunities to make a difference. He started to pursue 'cause marketing'. Using the *BING* (a *Microsoft* product) homepage, he set up a campaign called *Help Your Britain*. Initially, in the UK the homepage of this application showcased (for free) a charity, on the last Friday of every month. This initiative had an amazing effect on both the charities and *Microsoft* staff.

Peter recalls, "Everyone knows *Microsoft*, so it didn't hurt the company. However, the benefit to the selected charity was enormous, gaining visibility for their cause and generating offers of support."

Today, if you go to this website you will find the following introduction:

"*Help Your Britain*

In Britain there are more than 187,000 registered charities - all worthy to get some attention and the chance to tell their story. Below are the charities that *Bing* has been highlighting as part of a long-term campaign in which the British public nominated the charities they would like to see featured on the *Bing* homepage. Please check them out and be sure to watch the charity videos by clicking on the images." (*Mircosoft website:*www.bing.com/explore/helpyourbritain).

Peter considered that, "This initiative was a win, win, win situation. It was successful if you measured the satisfaction of employees involved, the charities and the *Microsoft* brand."

Peter and his own team's efforts did not stop with *Help Your Britain*, they went on to get involved in other activities, one of which was to use their skills to support a local primary school in Paddington, an area of London. At this school, most of the children were new immigrants from a diverse range of cultures, speaking a huge variety of languages. The school asked Peter and his team to help them by working with the children to put together a language-blind prospectus for the school so that new pupils and their parents would feel comfortable.

Once again, the whole *Microsoft* team found the experience challenging but rewarding, and the feel-good factor added to the richness of their day-to-day jobs and helped to build a sense of community within the team. Peter has since moved from *Microsoft* and now works at *LinkedIn*, a company which also has a strong volunteering culture and this feature was important to him when accepting the new position.

Is *Microsoft* an exception? After all, everyone knows about Bill Gates and *The Bill & Melinda Gates Foundation*. Perhaps Peter was lucky in selecting an employer who was sympathetic to his aims. Even so, he still had no obvious roadmap for how to set up his programmes. He was truly a pioneer blazing his own trail and doing so in such a way as to keep his staff happy while not impacting the corporate bottom line. Such initiatives take courage and creativity even in a like-minded business such as *Microsoft*. So, was Peter merely lucky, or are there other similar businesses? Just how difficult is it for professionals within an organisation to initiate change in the way that Peter did?

The answer is that the way forward takes some lateral thinking and personal commitment, but it certainly can and has been done by others. Furthermore, determined individuals can even figure out how to do so without impacting the bottom line, and within the context of typical business activities.

At the time of this story, Steve Turpie was a senior executive at *Zurich Insurance*, a major financial services and insurance company. He was Global Head of Sourcing and Procurement and ran a department with more than 150 people located in 19 countries across the world. Steve also believed that helping people was important, and tried to incorporate this philosophy into his life, both inside and outside of work.

Steve's story illustrates his own personal awakening to these beliefs and provides an amazing example of how it is possible to incorporate community activities into ordinary working practices provided one has the determination and creativity to do so. The following story is one example of Steve's commitment to integrating 'doing good' into the everyday activities of his team and some of the resulting benefits. Before getting to the details of Steve's socially beneficial initiative, it's useful to start earlier in his life in order to understand what shaped his outlook on life and business.

Steve's story – Inspiring others

The 'ah ha!' moments

"There were probably three seminal events in my life that led me to where I am today in terms of my life philosophy."

Steve began his story with this statement and went on to describe the key events that have shaped his personal philosophy. He talked about how he started his career in a 'typical manner'. He worked hard and was ambitious. Coming from a working class background, Steve was the first in his family to go to university - The University of East Anglia - where he trained as an accountant. He was eager to get ahead and succeed. After university, Steve did all the usual things: got jobs, worked long hours, advanced his career, changed jobs and attained a management position.

When he was about 35 and working for *Aviva*, he met with a

business coach who began to challenge his notions about happiness and personal motivation. She kept asking 'what' and 'why'? Steve experienced an 'ah ha!' moment after a sequence of probing questions when his coach asked, "What makes you happy? And why?" She asked "Why do you work 60 hours per week?" and when Steve gave an answer, she kept probing - "Why? Why? Why?"

In the end, it dawned on him that his motivation boiled down to, "It makes me feel good!" Even with this realisation, the questioning continued, "What else makes you feel good?"

The process forced Steve to closely examine his own motivation, both in work and, eventually, in all areas of his life. In the end, he explored lots of things and eventually discovered that helping others made him feel good. "And I'm not alone," he asserts, "I know that helping others makes everyone feel good."

Coincident with reaching this conclusion, *Aviva* transferred Steve (with his family) to India to take up a new role. "In India", Steve explains, "there were lots and lots of opportunities to help people. There was poverty everywhere." He described how he was fascinated and surprised that his children too, learned about things like poverty and racism first-hand. Steve overheard them discussing these issues with friends in a matter-of-fact manner that he initially found shocking.

Steve was happy at *Aviva* and described it as a fantastic company with regard to 'doing good'. The company culture supported those employees who wanted to help others and enabled them to give not just money, but also time. In India, Steve managed about 60 people and he observed members of his own team making time and effort to help others. "For example, one guy took every Saturday to coach a local girls' football team." Living and working in India was the second big event and 'eye opener' for Steve.

The third life-changing event was more personal. At around this time, his daughter, who was very ill when she was born, was diagnosed with autism and eventually also with epilepsy. "While living in India opened my eyes to suffering in the world, having a child with a disability gave me a more personal perspective on suffering. It also enabled me to meet other parents in a similar situation and share their experiences and feelings.

"Together, it was these three things," declares Steve, "the coaching, the India experience and my daughter's health that changed my perspective on what is important in life."

Taking action

As a result of this crystallisation of his motivation, Steve set about in a committed way to do things to help others. When he was transferred back to the UK, he was lucky enough to become a non-executive director on a local hospital board. He wanted to use his business skills to be of service, and to get involved with and look after people in his own local community. He also supported the founding of the West Suffolk branch of *The National Autistic Society*, through a series of fundraising efforts.

Steve spoke of how he processed his daughter's condition. "First, you grieve for the child you never had. Then, you come to a position where you just hope that your child will be able to live independently. Finally, your expectations shift again."

He now believes, "She will meet her own potential and it's our job as parents to help her do so. We need to provide an environment where she will thrive." He adds, "I now view disabled children and adults differently."

"In fact, my whole approach to work has shifted. I am now less competitive and have a much broader view - at home and at work. Work is important, but my motivation has changed."

After six years with *Aviva*, Steve moved to *Zurich Insurance*. He liked the company, his new role, the business strategy and the culture. Like *Aviva*, *Zurich* had a socially minded ethos. Working for *Zurich*, Steve ran a global team of around 150 people. He saw it as his job to provide the people he managed with the best possible environment to enable them to perform their jobs well and to be happy to be at work. Steve confesses that this attitude and approach was, "...a sea change from my early days when work was just about money and advancement."

His business coach told him that many people reach this realisation, but few managed it as young as 35 years old. His early transformation has enabled him to take new and innovative approaches to working practices. One such example provides an excellent illustration of how an enlightened 'boss' can merge community involvement with standard business activities. It also demonstrates that involving staff in community activities need not impact a business's bottom line.

Applying his philosophy to his work life

As a manager of people, one of Steve's important objectives was to create a good working team - quite a challenge with 150-plus people, many of whom had never met each other, who lived and worked in many different countries and would continue to live and work in different countries after team meetings. Effective teams get more done and work more happily, so Steve was keen to start the team-building process. Knowing that the process was emotional as well as intellectual and that emotions 'take time', he opted for a two-step approach.

His first team-building event was traditional. This event was step one in his two-step process. The objective was for his team to get to know each other and he employed consultants to help him with some of the activities. He combined traditional business presentations and workshops with indoor and outdoor team-building exercises. Then, Steve decided that step two should involve a community event.

The aim of this second step was to further cement the team's identity as well as to help the individuals to understand what leading and working in effective teams involves.

Rather than setting a 'mock' business task for the participants, Steve devised a real task, with deadlines and objectives, which was outside a traditional business framework but introduced the same challenges that would arise within it. So what was the 'task'?

Steve decided to apply the *Zurich Commitment* to the team-building exercise. This Commitment states that, "*Zurich* Cares - about people, about shareholders, about customers and about the community in which it operates". Working closely with two of his colleagues, Mark and Kim, and assisted by a local charity, a number of local community centres for the elderly were selected and it was arranged for 100-plus individuals to be transported to a hotel where the team building session was scheduled. Steve also invited key suppliers to *Zurich* to attend (and contribute funds!) and these observers were also present.

His staff arrived from all over the world and as people came they were mustered in a hotel near the airport. The following morning everybody was bussed to a different hotel at 8am and the session began. Steve put them in a room with 'Zurich Cares'T-shirts and nothing else. The group was divided into seven teams, and each team received a task along with a briefing note. These teams included: Media and Comms, Entertainment, Catering, Transport, Customer Requirements, a Venue team and a 'take home' team. The teams then appointed an eighth team - Management - which consisted of four individuals who were given a set of instructions.

The Management team was told that in five hours, they were going to be hosting an afternoon party for more than 100 elderly people, some with mobility issues. In essence, the teams had to provide entertainment including music and dancing, prepare and serve a silver service tea, decorate the venue, arrange for transport back, present each attendee with a 'goodie bag', and create a record of the event for the internal *Zurich* newsletter, all by the end of the day.

The teams were left to get on with things and one hour into the preparations, there was chaos.

In order to mimic a situation that would frequently arise in business, a few hours into the planning process a number of key people were moved to another group and the entire budget was cut. Following noisy complaints came an acknowledgement that these sort of things happen all the time in business life, and the teams then rose to the challenge and put together an auction to make up the short fall in funds. In fact, the auction was so successful that it generated a surplus of funds that were later donated to the community group who helped to coordinate the elderly attendees.

In the end, the groups 'produced' successfully. One task was to 'sing a song' and the *Zurich* employees did so. But then, spontaneously, the attendees responded by singing *For He's a Jolly Good Fellow*.

The impact on the staff taking part was immediate. Of the 100-plus *Zurich* participants, some were in tears. One man decided to change his return flight so that he could visit his grandfather on the way home, and another changed his plans and left the next day to be with his father who was undergoing by-pass surgery.

This event was the first day of a multi-day business meeting and the next day, the group carried out more usual business activities. However, there was now a new depth to the teams that hadn't existed before the event. One of the supplier participants reported, "This was the best combination of community investment, teamwork and business learning I have ever experienced." Others echoed this sentiment.

Those positive feelings did not end with the event. Steve's team have recently taken the initiative to embed Community Involvement on a day-to-day basis, rather than something that only happens once a year at an away-day. In this scenario, everyone 'won' - the elderly attendees had a memorable day out, Steve's business and team-building objectives were met, even exceeded. His staff were inspired to change the way they work at the office and set up other community efforts and none of these activities had a negative impact on the *Zurich* bottom line.

In conclusion, Steve managed to bring more meaning into his work environment by designing his own 'business game' and doing something for folks from the local community at the same time. It took his personal commitment and creativity to design something from which everyone benefitted, and he managed to do so within *Zurich*'s business culture. Furthermore, he fostered a collective drive among his team to enable them to carry on 'doing good' within the business context. This story illustrates that, often, a single individual's actions <u>can</u> make the difference.

However, while things worked well for Steve at *Zurich*, sometimes such changes do not remain embedded in a company's culture. Returning to an earlier example, once Peter had left *Microsoft*, did his programmes remain? To this day, *Help Your Britain* remains on the *Bing* web page and showcases a number of UK charities, so it seems likely that some of his projects did cause a permanent change in the *Microsoft* culture. At *Zurich*, much of Steve's good work has now become institutionalised in the way his international team works, so it is likely that it would carry on in some way without Steve's ongoing support. But some company cultures seem impervious to permanent change, despite the efforts of individuals.

Jean Ward tells a different story - different from many points of view. Within *Capgemini UK*, she created a company-wide response to the 2004

Boxing Day tsunami disaster only to have the company culture return to its previous state when she retired a few years later. Another difference is that Jean is from an earlier generation, who did not traditionally mix social impact with business activities, and reading her story clearly illustrates this different background. However, circumstances inspired Jean to take action and, working within her organisation, she managed to achieve something significant and meaningful for many, many people - both those who took part in her project and its recipients. As with all of our stories, it's important to understand Jean's early life to fully appreciate her work.

Jean's story – Spurred into action

A traditional childhood

Jean Ward considers herself to be like many other women from her time. She was born and grew up in Wembley (part of Greater London) and went to the local Girls' Brigade from the age of seven. She was a very, very shy and introverted child but thanks to the Girls' Brigade she had many friends and considered the activities, in addition to Sunday school at the local Baptist church, as a social club rather than a religious education. This group of girls helped Jean develop good friendships, some of which have lasted more than 50 years.

"I was just your average child," explains Jean. "Very much a product of the times - the 1950s and 1960s. You know, today you hear about *The Beatles* and 'flower power', but none of that reached us. There was still rationing from World War II which wasn't abolished until the mid-1950s, but we never realised how austere life was at the time." She credits her grandparents with having a huge influence on her life. Perhaps her practical approach to religion stems from the fact that one set of grandparents was quite religious while the other was not. Because she respected both sets of grandparents, their divergent views may have given her some perspective on religious beliefs. Or perhaps it was her practical, Scottish ancestry - both parents had moved to the London area from Scotland.

Jean attended a girls' grammar school, describing her performance as average. In fact, Jean describes much of her life as typical and average for a young girl of her time. Her social life revolved around church events and she remembers her religious upbringing not as an indoctrinating, proselytising one, but more as a set of principles and guidelines by which to live one's life. Jean describes the religious instruction she received as being of the 'Do unto others as you would have others do unto you' type of advice and she has stuck to these precepts throughout her life.

As Jean prepared for A-levels (school exams taken at 17-plus years old), she chose an eclectic combination of subjects: Geography and Art simply because she enjoyed both. Her next step after grammar school seemed a *fait accompli.* Her family placed a great emphasis on learning. In fact, many relatives were teachers. So it was natural that, after grammar school, Jean trained to become a teacher.

But three weeks before starting the course for her teacher's certificate, her younger brother died while away on a school trip. Jean was 18 years old and about to embark on a new phase of her life, so it was difficult to process all the changes. However, she carried on and completed her certificate - learning during the process that she definitely did <u>not</u> want to be a teacher.

So what could she do with A-levels in Geography and Art?

Work was a means to earn a living

Jean began training as a cartographer for the *Department of the Environment*. At the end of two years spent drawing maps, she received her HNC and left to take a position in local government with the *Greater London Council* (*GLC*). The next ten years were busy ones for Jean. She worked full-time at her job, had two children and got an MBA. She was so busy balancing life, further education and family that she didn't have the time to look for 'more' in her job. She was busy and relatively content.

However, the status quo was not to last. It was the 1980s and there were big political changes afoot. In 1988, Margaret Thatcher abolished the *GLC* and as a result, the IT department was outsourced to an IT services company called *Hoskyns*. Jean was transferred to *Hoskyns*, where she helped set up the new Geographical Information Systems (GIS) division. This acquisition was a big change for *Hoskyns* because, in acquiring 350 people from the *GLC*, so the business suddenly increased its employee base by more than 30%.

For the next 23 years, Jean stayed with this organisation, which was to acquire various other IT businesses and by the mid-1990s became a part of the French group, *Cap Gemini Sogetti* (now *Capgemini*). When she finally retired in 2011, the company had grown to 10,000 employees in the UK alone! This growth led to many interesting job challenges and over time, Jean performed nearly every role in the business until, at the end of 2004, she was made a Board director of *Capgemini UK*.

Jean's promotion to the Board was a significant step because it was the first time in many, many years that she did not have direct responsibility for staff or a cost centre; she was given the role of Global Head of Delivery for all of *Capgemini UK*'s services. She was in a powerful position, but for the first time in her career, without daily management responsibility. By this time, her children were 'launched', so managing the home/work balance was less of an issue.

The scene is set

Up until this point, Jean's life was typical of a successful, intelligent woman of her generation. She worked hard, attained degrees and higher degrees, moved up the corporate ladder and broke through the 'glass ceiling' and onto the board of a major company. Her time was filled with both work and family and she exercised her brains and creativity regularly in meeting the ever-changing demands of both. She didn't ignore 'good works' - she sponsored friends and colleagues who tried to raise money for various causes - but she didn't go out of her way to find them. She helped people she encountered who needed help and she continued to live her life as her early religious education had taught her, to 'Do unto others…' However, this situation was about to change.

Around this time, she met her former boss, Nigel Fielden, for dinner. He had recently retired and Jean wanted to catch up with his activities since leaving *Capgemini*. The dinner turned out to be a turning point that launched her into a new direction at work. Nigel related the story of his daughter, Sally, and her boyfriend, Jonathan, who were caught up in the Boxing Day tsunami in December 2004. Jean listened transfixed as Nigel related what happened.

Nigel said that he had been out walking on the fells when his mobile phone rang and it was his daughter, calling from Thailand. She told him she was on the roof of a building with some other people, that she was hurt and that she didn't know where her boyfriend Jonathan was. After these words, the line went dead. At that point, information was scarce, the magnitude of the disaster wasn't known and nobody could tell Nigel what was happening. He immediately secured flights to Bangkok and then travelled to Phi Phi, the tourist area where his daughter was staying, and began his search.

Amazingly, amidst the chaos and destruction, Nigel found his badly injured daughter and arranged for her to be transported back to a hospital in the UK. He remained in Thailand to look for Jonathan. After searching everywhere and visiting nine make-shift morgues, Nigel finally found Jonathan's body. The body was in such bad condition that he could only verify the identity by means of a tattoo. When the tsunami hit, both Sally and Jonathan were in their room, Jonathan in the bathroom and Sally in the main part of the holiday accommodation. A wave vortex swept through, carrying Sally to the top of a nearby building. Sharp materials and debris cut and banged against her, causing numerous injuries. Her boyfriend, Jonathan, was just in the wrong place and was probably killed instantly.

Fortunately for Sally, there were five or six others huddled together on the top of the building, one of whom had the phone she used to ring her father. A Norwegian, who was ex-special forces used to dealing with people and harsh conditions, took charge and eventually led them to safety and thus, Nigel eventually found his daughter. Both Sally and Jonathan worked for *Capgemini* so, as Jean listened to the story, she wondered what *Capgemini* planned to do to help. Jean was very, very moved by Nigel's story. As she explains, "I felt terrible for Nigel and Sally - who I knew - but I also thought what many others thought, 'What if that had been my kids!' and felt that *Capgemini* should do something appropriate to commemorate Jonathan's life."

Jean's opportunity to make a difference

Capgemini is a large organisation and at that time (2005) there were over 10,000 employees around the UK. Jean made enquiries and discovered that Jonathan was based in Rotherham so she rang the director in charge of that location to ask if there were any plans to do something as a memorial to Jonathan. The reply - *Capgemini* planned to plant a tree - surprised her. "I became energised and thought, 'We have to do something more! A tree just isn't enough.'"

Jean went back to her former boss Nigel and asked him for suggestions for a *Capgemini* memorial for Jonathan. Nigel mentioned that he had been to Laos and discovered the need for a school, and he had already set up a charity to build a school in Laos. He explained what a great impact a school could make and how it could provide a lasting benefit. Jean thought about Nigel's recommendation and considered it a good idea. But neither she nor *Capgemini* wanted to establish a charity, so she began to investigate charities with whom *Capgemini* might work.

After further research, everyone agreed on the charitable partner, *Plan UK*, who in turn suggested that a school in Indonesia would provide the greatest impact, and Banda Aceh was selected as the target location. *Plan UK* could provide the infrastructure in Banda Aceh so it was left to *Capgemini* to raise the money. Jean insisted that this programme was personal and that she wanted hands-on interaction with the building process. In doing her part, Jean galvanized staff at *Capgemini* and began a fundraising process to achieve an initial estimate of £20,000.

The school took 18 months to build and the cost escalated to nearly £110,000 due to profiteering by building supply companies, but Jean and her team carried on and raised the required money. She also involved a great many *Capgemini* staff in her crusade, all of whom felt moved and inspired to see the school built. She deployed traditional *Capgemini* skills such as website design and creation, and project management, deploying staff who were not working on fee-paying projects to get jobs completed. As Jean recalls, "I was inspired to do something and I didn't ask for permission, I just did it and no one stopped me." The team ran a Black Tie dinner that raised £20,000, solicited customers' to donate items to a charity auction, and asked individual employees to give and to organise fundraising. In the end, around 150 employees took part and all felt committed to the cause.

The *Capgemini* fundraisers' approach to the project was inclusive and the head teacher and students all contributed ideas to the building's design and décor. In 2006, Jean went out to Indonesia to see the completed school. The head teacher of the previous school, which had been destroyed, survived the tsunami but she had lost her parents, her sister and her own four children. Of the original 130 pupils, only 40 remained to attend the new school. However, it was welcomed and considered a great success.

In the end, Jean was publicly recognised by the rest of the Board for the leadership she demonstrated in galvanizing this effort. Sadly, since Jean retired, *Capgemini* has reorganised and the hands-on, charitable momentum has vanished from the company. Jean remains in touch with the head teacher at the school in Banda Aceh and plans to visit again to see how life has progressed. Her story shows what the efforts of one person with determination and the appropriate skills and position, can accomplish in a large corporate environment. It also shows that <u>without</u> an individual's leadership and determination, things can quickly return to the status quo.

Although the momentum generated by Jean's project disappeared from the company culture, her actions continued to have an impact on some of the individuals who worked with her at *Capgemini*. From time to time, others try to resurrect the same energy and focus that Jean demonstrated to use company resources and skills to provide social benefit. For Jean, many strands of her life came together at just the right moment: she was in a position of power, she was senior and had many decades of 'track record' under her belt, her personal risk was less because she was near retirement - although she honestly didn't consider this last point because an overwhelming urge drove her to take action. Perhaps another factor was the death of her brother in a boating accident many years before, giving her a great empathy with those who had lost someone they loved in the disaster.

Whatever the reasons, Jean acted from her heart rather than her corporate intellect, so she took a risk and managed to use this feeling to engage and lead the rest of the UK business. Until this moment, she had never combined her work life with her charitable activities, but the death of a fellow employee in a huge natural disaster lead her to combine these two aspects into one great effort. In the process, she inspired and encouraged many of the younger employees involved in the project.

In this chapter, the stories of three different individuals illustrate that with sufficient motivation, direction, energy and the investment of personal time, the culture within departments or divisions of a large corporations can be changed. In these examples, each successful intrapreneur brought a vision and determination to the effort. Each needed to display the "assertive risk-taking and innovation" that characterises an intrapreneur and all three had to exert significant effort, beyond that which just 'doing their day job' would require. However, with this effort came some culture change and the engagement of others in the business.

While all three individuals held senior posts, none of them was the ultimate boss and all were accountable to others for their actions. These stories demonstrate that in some organisations, change can be initiated from 'the middle' and doesn't have to be led from the very top. What it took in all cases was the motivation and extra effort to take action within the context of the organisation. None of these individuals 'fought City Hall' or tried to change the organisation in one fell swoop - they managed their initiatives within the confines of the existing business structure and measurements, and they all succeeded in making a difference.

These three people stand as examples to others who wish to work within the corporate environment and demonstrate that they too, can make a difference. Such actions won't change the world, or even the whole corporation, but a single individual can add meaning to his or her own work environment, inspire others and contribute to a small shift in the business culture.

Chapter 3

PROVIDING LEADERSHIP

"Our chief want is someone who will inspire us to be what we know we could be."
Ralph Waldo Emerson

Undoubtedly, the right leadership does help and when the man or woman at the top of an organisation incorporates a social mission into the corporate culture, this mission can weave its way throughout the organisation. Obviously, there is a more fertile environment for social initiatives in businesses where the executives believe in the moral obligation of their company to its employees and community, as well as to customers and shareholders. Do these companies exist? The answer is 'yes', and actually more and more large companies are moving in this direction.

This chapter examines those leaders of businesses who developed personal, socially conscious philosophies and then successfully integrated them into their business culture. In fact, a powerful motivation to set up their own businesses was the desire to embed their personal values into the workplace. This approach too, brings with it challenges and so it provides a path for only a few. However, it is a path that some professionals attempt to follow in today's business environment.

Two of the examples in this chapter are genuine 'pioneers' in that they come from an earlier generation in which their approach and thinking were very, very rare. It was often as much of a struggle for these leaders to keep their businesses going while adhering to their values as it is for the professionals of today to carve a balanced career in the current business climate. These leaders' stories illustrate their personal struggles to create and grow companies while holding true to their values and fostering a supportive work environment.

How do these efforts differ from what most modern businesses do? There are many executives who would point to their Corporate Social Responsibility (CSR) departments and cite how much money they contribute to charities. However, it is fair to say that many contribute these monies without making changes to their fundamental business culture. The contribution through CSR, though important to the charities supported, is not the topic of this book and is not the social movement under discussion. For some organisations, charitable giving is pigeon-holed into a separate department and kept isolated from the rest of the workplace. Such giving is obviously welcome, but does not constitute a socially involved business culture. Rather it is a necessary 'tick in the box' and an activity which appears in the annual reports of all blue chip corporations. The act of giving is unarguably present, but it is also a combined 'balance sheet' and public relations exercise, behind which the involvement and the 'heart' are often absent.

Companies, especially international conglomerates, which genuinely incorporate social values into their business ethics are relatively rare. However, though uncommon, such businesses have, in fact, existed for a long time, particularly those companies that have focused on employee benefits. In the UK, two confectionery companies, *Rowntree* and *Cadbury*, were both established in the early 19th century by families who adhered to the Quaker philosophy. Despite some desperate times in the early years of the businesses, both companies possessed strong social values and, unusually for the time, set up housing and other benefits for their employees.

The *Rowntree* company was a pioneer of this business model and 'enlightened' company management. In 1885, when the business was struggling to survive, Joseph Rowntree started a library for his employees, paid for in part out of his own money. He provided dining facilities, connected to the factory via an underground tunnel, so that his 3,000 employees wouldn't have to go outside in bad weather to eat meals. The company was among the first in the England to provide a works dentist and to introduce a retirement pension. In fact, *Rowntree's* pension scheme anticipated by some years the introduction of a state pension in the UK.

Joseph Rowntree's actions were radical, particularly for a Victorian business leader. The company went on to found one of the first Widows Benefit Funds in the UK, and in 1918 it introduced a week's holiday with full pay. In 1919 the company set up a Central Works Council for its employees. These are only some examples of the *Rowntree* company's concern for the factory workers' welfare. And *Rowntree* was not alone in these efforts. (www.rowntreesociety.org.uk)

In 1900, *Cadbury* set up a trust, which purchased land in the countryside outside the unhealthy urban environment that surrounded most factories. On this land, the trust constructed modern houses with good sanitation for *Cadbury*'s employees. Around this time, *Cadbury* also institutionalised liberal working practices such as different working hours for women and, before women were given the vote in England, female workers at *Cadbury* had a voice on policies.

Both *Rowntree* and *Cadbury* have since undergone many changes and this business culture did not long outlive the family, but their history does demonstrate the idea that socially involved companies don't relegate 'good works' to a support function like CSR. These family-run businesses took direct action and integrated their values into the core of the company, often at the owners' personal expense. These businesses were led by strong-minded individuals who lived their own values, and ensured that their businesses reflected this behaviour.

A slightly more modern example is the department store *John Lewis* - again a UK company - which is well known for its partnership approach. When John Spedan Lewis, the son of the eponymous 19th century founder, inherited the business in 1928 he made some significant changes. He established a trust in which all employees owned a share of the company commensurate with their salary. All partner/employees were to share in the annual profits. In this way *John Lewis* served both its employees (partners) and its customers. He also devised and communicated the Partnership's Purpose and Seven Guiding principles, both of which are still used by the business today. The *John Lewis* purpose is today as it has always been:

'The Partnership's ultimate purpose is the happiness of all its members, through their worthwhile and satisfying employment in a successful business. Because the Partnership is owned in trust for its members, they share the responsibilities of ownership as well as its rewards profit, knowledge and power.'

(www.johnlewispartnership.co.uk)

To this day, the *John Lewis Partnership* makes every effort to adhere to its guiding principles. It makes profits, distributes them to its 'partners' (i.e. employees) and abides by its strap-line to customers 'Never knowingly undersold.' The company is respected and trusted by its customers, who hold *John Lewis* as a standard against which to compare other retailers. Never let it be said that running a socially involved business cannot also be successful. *John Lewis* regularly produces good profits even when its main competitors struggle.

In all these businesses, *Rowntree*, *Cadbury* and *John Lewis*, the culture was driven by the man at the top and reflected his personal values and beliefs. But does this sort of thing still happen now? After all, today's big businesses are larger than ever before, heavily automated and have a global reach. The answer is: it is difficult, but it *can* happen. However the personal journeys of these leaders are fraught with obstacles and challenges, and they do not all succeed at first.

Béla Hatvany's story is fascinating in many respects. It chronicles the history of the developing IT industry from the 1960s to the present day, and shows the struggles of an innovator who attempted to build businesses that enabled him to remain true to his personal values. It demonstrates that great personal sacrifice is often required to uphold such principles, a fact often not appreciated by the rest of the staff.

Indeed, in a case such as Béla's, there is typically twice as much work because in addition to creating and running a business, there is also the drive to ensure that employees adopt the founding philosophy so that the company culture reflects the leader's vision. In addition, the leader must perform all these activities within a business context. Employees must still work and undertake their jobs to a high standard.

As with most of these stories, Béla's begins with his childhood and it tracks the evolution of Béla's beliefs and his commitment to maintain them in the face of extreme business challenges.

Bela's story: For Profit, For Good

Origins of Béla's business philosophy

Béla Hatvany began his story by explaining, "I have tried to establish businesses that were 'for profit, for good'. By that I mean businesses that served all their constituents in a balanced way. I believe that businesses should grow in a way that serves all constituents equally. That is anyone who has anything to do with the business: employees, including the cleaning lady, customers, suppliers, even the environment. This belief is fundamental to my business philosophy and approach."

Why?

Béla Hatvany's business beliefs have evolved from his life experience. The child of parents who fled the deteriorating and dangerous conditions in 1930s Hungary and Spain, Béla grew up as an outsider during the austerity of war-torn and post-war England. His father had been a wealthy Hungarian Jew who married the young daughter of the Spanish Ambassador. The couple were on holiday in Romania when a friend tipped off Béla's father that he would be arrested if he returned to Hungary, a country that was preparing itself to align with the German Axis. They made their way to England leaving everything behind.

Soon after war was declared in 1939, and despite his refugee status, Béla's father was interned as an 'enemy alien' on the Isle of Man. One of Béla's first memories as a very young child was of saying 'goodbye' to his father from a boat. Béla still remembers the injustice in his father being placed in a prison along with just the sort of violent anti-Semites he had fled Hungary to avoid. It was a grim and difficult time for the family.

So it's no surprise that Béla describes his youthful self as an 'angry young man'. He saw himself surrounded by unjust and unacceptable conditions. These circumstances took their toll on his family and his parents divorced when he was 12. Acting out, probably in response to his parents' separation, Béla began to 'nick' (steal) things from his fellow students. He explains, "I did it because I could, and because my situation seemed 'unfair'". Raised a devout Catholic, Béla chose to confess his crimes to a Priest who discussed the circumstances at length. The Priest advised Béla, where possible, to give back the monies and stolen items and where he could, he did so.

Perhaps it started with this confession, but from this point Béla started 'giving back' and began to consider the world from a slightly different stance. He was still angry at injustices, but his responses took different avenues. While studying at University of St Andrews (Queen's College) Béla wrote an article for the college newspaper in which he described his view of the world and how he felt that individuals possessed different motivations. When asked what prompted him to write the article, Béla replies, "I think I was trying to sort out the world and to document what I saw. I genuinely wanted the world 'to work' and I believed I had a neat insight into the fundamentals of human behaviour."

Starting out on the career ladder

During his university career, Béla became involved with computers because his university syllabus included an apprenticeship in business. His work began at *British Petroleum* where he worked from 1956 to 1960 while attending the University of St Andrews. After graduation, Béla moved companies several times between 1960 and 1965, from *De La Rue Bull*, to *Burroughs* and finally *Honeywell*. As a result of these experiences, Béla determined that he wanted to be his own boss and to work for himself instead of taking positions in large, corporate businesses. He describes these businesses as "like penal institutions" in which people "attended work" because "they had to" and not because they enjoyed it or wanted to do the job.

Béla recalls, "Everyone had the 'isn't it terrible, it's Monday!' and the 'TGIF' attitudes, behaving as though work was a penance to be endured."

He remembers, "Whenever my boss's boss came in to my area, it was clear the he had no idea what was happening in that part of the business. I was determined that, when I ran a company, I would treat my employees better. From that moment, I began to develop my business philosophy. I realised that I would have to serve everyone who touched the business - including me. Even now, after all these years, my philosophy is still evolving."

Up to 1965, Béla's career gave him a range of experience in the new and growing computer industry. He started as a customer engineer, repairing hardware and then became a programmer. From there he advanced to technical analysis, then technical support and finally, to sales. Béla now had a well-rounded understanding of this new business area and wanted to get more involved in the industry and its potential applications, but he wanted to do so in his own company.

Branching out on his own

As a result of his employee experiences, he was determined that his company - whatever it was to be - would not be like the businesses in which he had worked. He knew that he needed more training and had to fill some gaps in his business knowledge in order to make this leap. So, newly married, Béla left *Honeywell* and the UK in 1965 to attend Harvard Business School in Boston, Massachusetts, USA.

After graduating from Harvard Business School in 1967, Béla left for Mexico at the request of a friend, to conduct a six-week consulting study on the feasibility of computerising sugar mills. This role eventually resulted in his moving his family to Mexico to start a business called *Comsisa* in which he developed the first turn-key system for sugar mills in Mexico by offering bureau services from a central location.

Everything was going well, both in business and in family life. But then, Béla's original investor, a personal friend, needed to sell his investment in *Comsisa.* After a series of financial transactions, the company ended up in the hands of a less scrupulous individual. This man employed sharp business practices that flew in the face of Béla's personal and business philosophies. *Comsisa* was Béla's first experience, outside of large corporations, of trying to work with someone who did not share his values and he quickly realised that it was a mistake. This experience led him to understand how important shared values are to a healthy business.

In March 1971, after three years in Mexico, Béla and his family moved back to the US where he began to plan a new venture. He asked himself: who would be the best customer? Who could benefit in a big way from computer services but was currently poorly served by IT? In the end, Béla and a university friend, by now business partners, decided to focus on libraries. The final decision was helped by circumstances, as they knew someone who ran a library in Cleveland, Ohio, and could speak directly to a decision maker. On April 1st, 1971 *Computer Library Services Inc* was born.

The business went from strength to strength, but needed more investment, which brought with it more shareholders and board members. Fighting amongst the board put the whole business at risk, and then promised funding was withdrawn causing the company's bank to foreclose on its debt and force the business to 'wind up'. It was fortunate that around this time, Béla's wife took up meditation and he followed her. He now credits meditation with helping him through this very difficult period. Both he and his wife continue the practice to this day. Meditating gave Béla perspective on the disagreeable activities around him and helped him to manage his personal stress.

Perhaps this experience helped solidify Béla's business principle: in order to serve all its constituents (investors, employees, suppliers, customers), and in spite of a desire to 'do right' by people, there are times when a business needs to be cruel to be kind. Everyone must perform and do a good job or the business dies.

At this point, Béla had a 'lucky' break. After investigating the bankrupt business, the bank realised that the only value remaining in the business was in its accounts receivable, so the administrators asked Béla if he would return to the company, on his old salary, to chase these payments while the business was wound up.

As Béla travelled from customer to customer, he found that they wanted to buy more things from *Computer Library Services Inc* - terminals and systems - so he sold off everything that remained in the bankrupt business's inventory. Apart from the debt and management conflict, there was nothing fundamentally wrong with the offering and the premise of the business was still a good one. The customers wanted the services, and more, from the company. As the inventory continued to find buyers, the bank soon became aware that the 'bankrupt business' was actually making money!

Given the positive outlook, Béla decided to raise money by selling his patent on a flexible screen so he was able to cancel the debt to the bank. And thus, the old company's services carried on under the new name of *CLS Inc.*

Success at last

CLS Inc created the first Online Public Access Catalogue (OPAC) for libraries. It also offered a Book Ordering Service and a Circulation Control System. The first year's turnover was $4.7m, as the business went from strength to strength with turnover rising to $23m by 1982. In 1983, when *CLS Inc* was sold to *Thyssen-Bornemisza (Thyssen)*, Béla negotiated the rights to the UK-based CD-ROM development. At the time, CD-ROM was just an idea; it was not a recognised standard as it is today. That was soon to change and Béla was to play a part in establishing CD-ROM's use in business.

With these development rights, in 1982 Bela used the money from the sale of *CLS Inc* to fund a company that would support startup businesses, and named it *INCubator*. Because Béla saw CD-ROM as a great business opportunity, the CD-ROM development team was formed into the first business to be funded by *INCubator*. The timing couldn't have been better.

Béla called together industry experts and within a few days, the various attendees hashed out a standard for CD-ROM. Every major player attended - they couldn't afford not to show up because their competitors were attending - and the output became an ISO-9660 standard. This standard enabled and gave birth to the CD-ROM industry in 1982-83 and CD-ROM became yet another area in which Béla was a recognised pioneer. The new business backed by *INCubator* was named *SilverPlatter* and Béla focused all his own efforts on this new business.

Despite these successes, it would be wrong to focus only on Béla's business achievements, however impressive. At this point Béla also fulfilled his promise to his family and moved back to Europe, and even though he did invest in *SilverPlatter*, it was based in the UK and not the USA. 'Between businesses' he focused his efforts on personal giving while he devised his next business venture. He chose to use his money to promote his personal ideals.

By now a committed meditator, Béla and his wife Ellen used some of their funds to buy land so that they could donate it to the Christian Meditation Centre for a facility in London. They also set up a charity called *The Mustardseed Charitable Trust*, which distributed monies to a wide variety of good causes, particularly those offering opportunities for disadvantaged girls around the world. Béla and Ellen also invested in a number of other charities as he worked to get *SilverPlatter* off the ground.

Throughout the 80s and 90s, *SilverPlatter* grew rapidly and became a success. Béla personally won many awards and was recognised for his work in both technology and information services. During this time his family grew to six children and was based in London, where Béla and Ellen continued their daily practice of meditation. Béla continued his involvement with *SilverPlatter* until the business was sold for $113m to *Wolters Kluwer* in 2001. Many letters from staff and archived business letters confirm that he maintained his business values and integrated them into the company throughout this period.

Applying his philosophy as an investor

After the sale of *SilverPlatter*, Béla's involvement shifted to that of an investor/board member in a variety of technology-based startups. Throughout, Béla ensured that the aims and philosophical values of the entrepreneurs involved were in line with his own. The right relationship with management and the ethos of the companies he supported became increasingly important to him as time progressed. He strove to build and support companies that served all their constituents. Béla's ethos meant that all activities were performed well and in a holistic and balanced manner so that everything and everyone that the business touched was properly served. But it wasn't a free ride for the idle - poor performance was as unacceptable as it would have been in any successful business.

Béla explains in detail, "Although commercial behaviour can seem ruthless, one needs compassion - like a surgeon. A surgeon must ruthlessly chop out injured or cancerous parts of the body. To do so causes pain and localised injury, but in performing the job, the surgeon aspires to save the whole body. A surgeon shouldn't hesitate to cut out diseased tissue - even so, he or she proceeds with great care. This example is a good analogy of a holistic business approach."

Over the years, Béla has pondered, "How do you measure the holistic performance of a company? How can you tell if it's serving its constituents in a balanced way?" The details of 'who is served' do vary from business to business but today, Béla has a process. A third party, appointed by the board, conducts an annual audit to assess whether all the business's constituents are being well served. Separate specialists are hired to assess the different functions. And part of establishing the right balance requires a change of mind-set with regard to money. Of course, money is important, but money and profits are not the only measure. In addition, employees must enjoy working and doing their jobs, in contrast to the experience of Béla's early working life.

Customers should be delighted with the offering and trust the company. The culture of the company should be one where everyone feels that they are doing something meaningful and valuable.

Béla's combined business and personal philosophy - his holistic approach - exemplifies what many of today's professionals seek. His experience in the mid-1960s doesn't sound very different from that of many professionals working now in large, multinational corporations. Not a lot has changed in some organisations - although it seems that today, more people refuse to tolerate it and are looking for alternatives. It took Béla years of hard work to achieve a position from which he could create and practise such a business philosophy. It wasn't easy, but it was possible. Today, he funds and guides a number of businesses that embody this approach. He is working, still learning, still on his journey.

There are many important lessons to be taken from Béla's story; perhaps the most obvious is that success stories tend to look easy in retrospect, but, in fact, are marked by failures and seemingly insurmountable challenges along the way. The truly successful person carries on, despite the setbacks and often at great personal cost, until success is achieved. During this arduous process, Béla never took his family for granted and kept his promises to them even at a cost to his role in the business. He gave back to employees who helped along the way. He also learned that he had to work hard to keep everyone involved and committed to his corporate values and he also had to become firm, even ruthless, with those who were not performing. Finally, he and his family kept the bigger picture in mind and contributed to causes and movements in their community, trying to maintain a holistic approach, not just to the business environment, but to all of life.

Béla is not the only executive to create and grow a successful and ethical business in the midst of what tends to be a soulless environment. Erika Uffindell started out in the 'cut and thrust' world of advertising and brand consultancy in the early 1980s. At this time, making money was the Holy Grail of the business world, and financial services and advertising sat at the heart of this movement. Erika's journey illustrates that an individual with sufficiently strong values need not become trapped by the different values and ethics of others. It also demonstrates how one leader managed to 'bring along' her employees, through good times and bad, never losing sight of the business culture. However, this leadership didn't 'just happen' - it took a conscious effort and Erika, too, learned through some mistakes along the way. She was in an especially interesting position because her own business was all about the genuine transformation of a large corporation into a more values-led organisation.

Erika's story – Living her values

The Motivation

"At heart I've always been a communicator," explained Erika as she began the story of her personal journey. She was awarded a degree in visual communications, which led her into a career in publishing. At this time, the late 1970s and early 1980s, there were many new magazines appearing in the marketplace and Erika worked for the first five years of her career launching new titles. She credits this time and her experience with enhancing her ability to present new ideas to people.

Eventually, Erika sought new challenges and applied for a number of different jobs, and, over the next few years, she ended up working for a number of brand agencies. During this time (the 1980s), she experienced a number of management/leadership styles that didn't sit comfortably with her. "Many of these individuals led others by using 'control' and 'fear'," Erika recalls. "And I just didn't like it or feel that this behaviour was necessary."

She went on to explain that everyone worked very hard, and long hours, regardless of the management ethos, and the threatening, bullying style added nothing and didn't sit well with her personal values. "I have always had a sense of fairness, compassion and integrity," she elaborates. "So trying to incentivise people by fear and finance alone didn't feel right to me." As time went by, Erika finally had the opportunity to set up her own brand transformation company, providing her with the chance to test her own management and leadership styles.

Teaching her Values

In her company, Erika worked with large corporates across many sectors including healthcare, property and banks. She worked with senior leadership within these organisations and helped them to focus on business strategy, brand strategy and culture - all key components of a brand. Her approach was to work with these leadership teams to distil everything to enable them to answer the question 'What is the business's higher purpose?'

"The main way I have integrated the values into *Uffindell*," explains Erika, "was by living them myself. Our core tenet in the business is 'family' and the way this is lived out is by everyone really caring about each other - not just in their working day - but really interested and caring about their overall wellbeing. We have a very flat structure and an open plan environment - so there are no 'offices', no closed doors, and we try and ensure everyone feels they have a voice and can make a difference in the firm. The office environment is designed to create a sense of family - so through layout and style we have tried to reflect more of 'a home' than 'an office'."

Erika described how these values were inherent from the early days of the company, when it was very small, but they were not necessarily articulated as such. At one point in *Uffindell Consulting's* history, her employees sat down as a team and discussed what they felt was important to them as leaders. They then aligned it with what their clients (via a survey) considered to be the company's strengths, and with what employees said they valued about the business. From this exercise they clearly distilled and spelled out their culture into four values: integrity, inspiration, intelligence and intuition. The business looked for these attributes in the people they hired and in what they tried to bring to life in all of their projects and interactions with people.

When asked if the business ever 'stumbled' along the way, Erika replies, "I think if anything (on the mistakes front), many of us have been in the business for a long time so we tend to take the values and culture for granted and we were not always as quick to communicate that to new people as we might have been - but that is now part of the induction process. Whilst people would hopefully say our culture of 'family' and our values are inherent in the DNA of the firm, you do of course have to share with new people joining the firm what the values are, and provide feedback if people's behaviours do not align with the values and culture."

Learnings

Uffindell Consulting is now 25 years old. Clearly, Erika's business approach appealed to enough companies to allow her to prosper, grow and evolve her own style. Indeed, she asked herself the same question, 'What is my purpose and role in the world?' Erika sincerely works on answering this question and returns to it regularly to re-assess her life's journey. But are the executives with whom she works equally sincere? When pressed she agreed that many organisations just 'tick the box' - many leaders know what they are supposed to do, but just go through the motions and are not genuinely committed. But this lack of commitment eventually impacts company performance.

"The most successful organisations, and those with the most committed employees, are those that genuinely embrace this approach," reflects Erika. "One of the reasons I have personally followed this philosophy is that, over the years I've seen so many companies set up 'on a promise' and then management's actions didn't follow these beliefs and employees became disenchanted."

"Also, sometimes growth means taking risks and large corporate environments don't provide many safe places that allow this kind of growth. However, there are exceptions and these exceptions depend on the business leader."

"I am pleased that we have created a firm that has employed and developed many talented people over 25 years and many have gone on to run their own businesses and employ people." Erika concludes, "To that end I hope we have played our part in the ecosystem of business and helped provide an enjoyable and fulfilling place to work. A number of people have left *Uffindell* to explore other areas of their career and have returned, and it is always satisfying to know that they enjoyed the experience first time round and came back."

From the very beginning, Erika's goals have been about creating a business:

- where people enjoy working and feel fulfilled
- that does great work for clients and helps them positively transform
- which creates profit and is sustainable so we can reward our people and invest back in the business

Erika believes that an increasing number of leaders today are awakening to the fact that running a successful business should be a balancing act between the pursuit of profit and the needs of people and the planet. A leader should also ask the questions 'What does it mean for me?' and 'Am I prepared to take this journey?' Erika adds that many top executives are further inhibited by concerns about the judgement of their peers.

Shareholder-driven companies typically provide the greatest challenge. The strong emphasis on ever-increasing profits blinkers the leadership team to the needs of other constituents such as customers and employees or the environment. Shareholder pressure drives them to focus on profits to the exclusion of all else. In these businesses it is far more difficult to balance the financial drivers with human values because executives are usually fear-driven themselves and under constant scrutiny from their quarterly reporting regime. To counter this pressure, *Uffindell Consulting*'s purpose (and Erika's!) is to help business leaders achieve this balance without impacting performance and to help them 'put the soul back' into their businesses.

Erika describes the evolution of her own business and its beliefs as 'her journey'. "Running a small business can be wonderfully rewarding," she explains. "But there is a huge learning curve - both in business and personal development. To be successful, a person - in this case me - needs to commit to a process of self-enquiry, to consistently undertake a practice of reflection, learn from mistakes and act on this learning."

Coping & evolving

When asked if she experienced any 'ah ha!' moments Erika immediately pinpointed a time about 15 years ago, 10 years into her new business' life. At this time a number of strands of her life came together. She had a son who was three or four years old and dependent on her. Her business too, demanded her energy and attention. Suddenly she felt an overwhelming sense of responsibility and, at the same time, she developed an extreme fear of flying - an unavoidable activity in her line of work. The solution? Erika found a guru for personal development and embarked on a serious practice of meditation. In time, she learned to recognise the ego aspects that were creating the fear, let go of her need to control things around her and gradually, her fear of flying diminished.

During her 'crisis' Erika realised that her own energy was blocked and that such blocks led to energy imbalance and illness. This perspective led her to view organisations as living systems with their own energy; systems that could also suffer from energy fluctuations, imbalances and blockages, resulting in 'sick' companies. She got in touch with a team in Spain who were interested in the same thing - envisioning organisations as living organisms and treating them as such. Erika liked this approach. It mirrored the same process she had explored for treating herself, and she believed that it worked.

Erica explained her belief that businesses don't remain static and neither do individuals. To grow and accept more in life, one needs to let go of things that are no longer essential. "Transforming a business is as much about transforming the leadership," Erika says. "And I have taken my own medicine and followed the process." While Erika explored new business options that reflected her personal journey, she held tight to her core business values and beliefs.

Letting go of *Uffindell Consulting* a little bit, she was able to clearly define the role of her business in her life and in the world. She clearly established the business's objectives as 'strategic consulting' and as she did so, passed on some of the control to others in the organisation. At the same time, she joined with four other individuals in Spain and other countries, to work in *PINEA3*, a business that focused on organisational transformation.

Erika has learned a lot over the past 25 years. She explains how *Uffindell Consulting* survived three recessions and, each time, tested her core values and added to her learning. She has worked with leaders and leadership teams in many large blue chip organisations and realised that a key step - both for herself and for the other leaders - was to let go of ego and move from thinking about 'me' to thinking about 'we'. This shift in attitude plays a key role in underpinning a rewarding work environment.

So Erika, like Béla, was able to create a business that satisfied her personal life philosophy. Also, like Béla, her philosophy developed alongside her business experience, and continues to grow. In her own business Erika practiced the principles that she espoused for others, developing a holistic and balanced company which provided fulfilling employment (exactly the sort of environment that many of today's professionals seek) as well as excellent customer service and a solid business performance. It was hard work, but over the past 25-plus years Erika has built a company that models her beliefs. Like Béla, she discovered that a journey of self-inquiry, meditation and mindfulness helped her through the challenges of running a growing business and enabled her to create greater balance in her life.

Unlike Erika and Béla, Warren Richmond didn't start his business with strongly articulated corporate values. He started his business because he had to earn a living. Early on in his working life, he realised that he was very, very good at presenting and selling branded products to consumers, but he did not feel adequately rewarded for his efforts when he worked as an employee in a large company. Therefore, he took the logical but risky step of starting his own business.

Regardless of his initial motivation, Warren is also a strongly values-driven person and he has managed to incorporate these values into his business, *Retail Marketing Group*. Warren's story demonstrates that setting up a profitable, entrepreneurial business can also incorporate a holistic approach - 'giving back', as appropriate, to employees and society without endangering the bottom line profits. Such an approach, when sincere, can also lead to a positive company culture and a good place to work.

Warren's story – Building a values-driven business

Responsibility started early

To understand Warren Richmond, his life view and motivation, it is best to start at the beginning. His mother was just 16 when he was born and living with her parents. This experience shaped his childhood and teenage years, and even after his success in business, he has not forgotten his early years.

Shortly after Warren's birth, his mother moved out of her parents' home to raise her baby on her own. Needless to say, money was tight and at the very early age of ten, Warren started washing cars outside a hairdresser's shop in order to contribute to the meagre family income. He would also go inside the salon and 'sweep up' to earn tips. Throughout his teenage years, he was always looking for any legal opportunity to contribute financially to the household.

Growing up, Warren felt that he had a different perspective from most of his peers and he enjoyed exercising his creativity. At school he chose to study Art until a kindly teacher pointed out that his talents might be more suited to studying Design. Heeding this advice, he studied for and was awarded a Design degree at university. However, unlike many of his friends, he needed to support himself financially as a student, so he took a job with *Epson*, a PC printer company, at a *PC World* store.

Warren soon discovered he could combine his creativity and design expertise in a business environment. By reconfiguring the *Epson* display and redesigning its presentation, sales success soon followed. Graduating from university in 1999, he went to work for *Epson* full time. The pay was low but Warren did well and *Epson* subsequently prospered from his efforts, rewarding him with full control of the Southern UK sales team. After a while it was clear to management that under his control the Southern team was significantly outperforming the Northern team, so Warren was given both areas to manage.

Despite Warren successfully running a UK sales team of more than 20 people, *Epson* declined his request for a pay rise. Warren decided this setback was a good opportunity for him to start his own business. So, in 2004, with nothing more than a 'vision' of what he wanted to do and a domain name, he set up *Retail Marketing Ltd.* This business would draw on his skills and experience from selling to customers, but he would offer these skills as a service to other retail businesses.

Setting up on his own

Warren also wanted his company to be different from anything he had experienced himself. He wanted it to be 'the best' at what it did, but without sacrificing values. He aspired to create a company with sense of family and a values culture that made employees look forward to coming to work. A measure of the success of Warren's vision was demonstrated by his business winning the 'Best Company to Work for' in the Thames Valley 2013 and 2014 as well as a place in the *Sunday Times Top 100 Best Companies* to work for in 2015.

But staff engagement was not his only measure of success. Warren also aimed to include a number of other company values:

- Delighting the customer (his customers)
- Sustainability
- Brand recognition

The company's mission was, and still is, to show consumers the same passion that the brand owners display.

Warren's philosophy is, "We don't do what we do for the money. We earn money to allow us to do what we want to do!"

So, what exactly do his employees do? *Retail Marketing* employs teams of people who engage with consumers all over the UK on behalf of brand retailers. The work involves training, merchandising and selling on behalf of these brands and providing the brand retailer with data generated from this consumer interaction so they can better understand their consumers. Warren continues to exercise his creativity, not only through presentation and design, but also through new and innovative ways of approaching the consumer marketplace. He sees opportunity in every aspect of daily life, keeping notes to capture his thoughts and creative ideas whenever and wherever they occur.

An example of this constant creativity is the formation of *DECODED Solutions*, a bespoke software development company. In the course of getting IT help for *Retail Marketing Ltd* Warren encountered a talented individual who needed help in establishing his own business. Warren provided that help.

Ideas can come from anywhere. Warren is also interested in the decline of the traditional retail market, and while walking through shopping malls and high streets he was concerned by the increasing number of empty shops and boarded up storefronts. With over 49,000 empty shops in the UK at the time, Warren came up with a creative solution to use this empty space and encourage passing shoppers back into retail. He established *NEXUSEngage* to drive a shift of customers back to the bricks and mortar retail environment.

"I want to help lead this shift," Warren says. "My biggest struggle was getting people to understand the business opportunity."

And this business opportunity was built on Warren's own expertise. If there was one thing he understood, it was how to display a branded product to engage potential customers and he knew he could use these shop windows to do so. However, to 'sell' this opportunity he had to interact with a different buyer from within his traditional customer base. A 'window display' came under 'advertising spend' so it required a different sales approach.

Warren soon discovered that these empty windows were a win/win for everybody - the shop owners, the branded retailers and the new company, *NEXSUSEngage*. His business proposition moved from strength to strength and he engaged a new managing director to take the business forward. Although *Retail Marketing* remains Warren's main focus and passion he is always prepared to consider new opportunities and driven by the desire to help, he is happy to allow others to continue the day-to-day running of his newly-established companies.

Living his values

Does Warren want to see *Retail Marketing* grow? The answer is an emphatic 'yes!' but he qualifies, "Although I am very driven, I am keen to ensure a balance between my business and home environment." Warren believes that his own behaviour contributes to the harmony surrounding him. "If I make a mistake, I admit it - and I expect others to do the same. I admire grit and determination. Equally I respect and encourage openness and honesty." He summarises his work ethic as follows, "I take personal responsibility for everything in my business and treat my employees as I would customers and I make the organisation chart very flat to encourage open and easy communications."

In addition to his businesses and family life, Warren has started a personal philanthropic journey over the past 18 months and believes that social responsibility will start to shape business in the future. This journey started with a conversation about how to get *Retail Marketing* back to thinking about people, not only within the business but in society. He created the 'love incentive', which was about acknowledging someone in the company who really understood and showed the true *Retail Marketing* spirit through their actions.

Colleagues nominated one another, each with the chance to win a variety of prizes over the course of six months. One of these was a once-in-a-lifetime trip to Tanzania with a small charity that works in impoverished communities. Warren and his wife accompanied a group of four *Retail Marketing* colleagues on a ten day trip, learning and experiencing what life can be like there. The business followed their journey every step of the way.

Returning from this trip, Warren - never one to do things by halves - decided to set up *The Retail Marketing Foundation* to raise funds to kick start change in communities, in the UK as well as in Tanzania. Throughout his journey Warren has been totally involved in the world of charity, understanding that charity should complement business rather than be separate from it. In August 2014 he undertook a nationwide bus tour to meet the 120 full-time *Retail Marketing* strategic team members. Part of the purpose of Warren's road-trip was to teach the team about the *Foundation*, but the main focus was on their individual experiences during their time working for *Retail Marketing* and ensuring that they were informed and engaged with the business aims and goals.

"At its most fundamental, these activities and values are critical to the culture and values of the business to ensure its long term prosperity," Warren explains.

As a final strand to his efforts, Warren actively encourages succession planning to allow the business to function independently of him. His belief is that, "If I can achieve that, then I know it will have been a success!"

Thus far, Warren has leapt from one success to another and even set up subsidiaries in South Africa and Australia. While doing this work, he discovered and articulated an interesting challenge: how to encourage employees to take the initiative in charitable activities. He has created an environment to enable them to undertake charitable activities, and publically expressed his support for these efforts, but discovered that unless he led, his employees didn't follow. Warren had hoped that they would initiate some of their own activities, and take responsibility for some programmes. He was disappointed when that didn't happen. So what was the problem? Why didn't more *Retail Marketing* employees take the initiative?

While it's impossible to know the exact reasons for this situation within Warren's company, many of the people questioned in social networking groups say they feel that they don't have 'permission'. One attendee at a *HOASBG* meeting summed up the situation when he said, "As I became more senior in my career, I began to realise that I had more influence and social impact. I always had, and most employees do, they just don't realise it or feel empowered."

It seems that in general, employees do not feel empowered without explicit direction. While many complain that they don't have the freedom to perform socially relevant activities during their working day, as we saw in Chapter 2, it can be done. But it takes a brave intrapreneur to step up to the mark and actually do something within a large business.

For individuals such as Béla, Erika and Warren, who each had the skills, drive and energy to start a business where social values were embedded into the workplace, this approach is one way of putting the soul back into business. But not everyone can tread this path and many employees need encouragement, even within an enlightened organisation. All three of these individuals boldly moved out of the mainstream to create a socially engaged working environment. While they all had a strong vision to create values driven businesses, all of them elected to work in a commercial, 'for profit' environment. Bad experiences of working in other companies inspired their aim to build a company that was a great place to work - a place where employees looked forward to coming to work in the morning and a business that customers liked and trusted.

Chapter 4

BUSINESS SUCCESS – WHAT NEXT?

"What you get by achieving your goals is not as important as what you become by achieving your goals."
Henry David Thoreau

This chapter focuses on a very special breed of socially involved individual - that person who makes lots and lots of money and then experiences a sudden change of purpose and decides to leave the business environment to spend time and money 'giving back' to the world. While not everyone can aspire to this position, it's worth highlighting that it does happen. The thought that traditional business executives can experience a change of heart offers a glimmer of hope to many, and shows that not everyone who starts out in the rough and tumble world of business is devoid of values. Perhaps for some business people the issue is that they cannot see a way of combining these values with working life. Whatever the reason, a discussion of the urge to 'give back' within the corporate environment would not be complete without looking at the philanthropist.

Not everyone who makes a lot of money in business becomes a philanthropist but when it does happen, these people tend to spend their money in a spectacular and unique manner. In doing so, they give back a great deal, and in a way that can only be accomplished by an individual, rather than by an institution or government. Long-term projects can be funded - projects whose needs extend beyond the brief terms of elected officials. These endeavours are often of the type that governments shy away from supporting, because there will be no immediate impact for the 'next election'. For example, aesthetically beautifully buildings cost more than facilities that are merely functional, so their construction usually relies on the generosity of individuals rather than the government.

The 19th century American industrialist Andrew Carnegie, is a good example of a businessman who took a 180 degree turn when he moved from the commercial to the philanthropic world. A Scottish immigrant who arrived in the United States in the late 1840s, he started at the bottom of the employment ladder in various menial roles and worked his way up to building and owning *Carnegie Steel.* He rose to this position at a time when the country was using steel in vast quantities to expand westward and build railways. At one point Carnegie was reputed to be the richest man in the United States.

During the growth of his business, Carnegie would never have been considered 'an enlightened employer'. In fact, at one point when he needed to cut prices, he reduced his workers' already low wages, which drove them to start the Homestead Strike of 1892. This strike is famous in American labour history for the brutality used to break up the picketers and get the factories working again. Whether Carnegie was personally responsible or not, it happened while he was in charge and he did nothing to intervene.

So we have an ambitious, hard-working and callous man (even by contemporary standards) who made millions in the latter part of the 19th century. Then, in 1901, at the age of 65, everything changed. He sold his business and devoted the rest of his life to good works. Many, many libraries in the Eastern United States have Carnegie somewhere in their name. That's because one of his first acts was to donate money for the construction of libraries in various cities. More than 2,000 libraries owe their existence to these initial grants.

He established an institution of higher education - now known as Carnegie Mellon University. In a further effort to support education and the promotion of knowledge, he founded the *Carnegie Foundation for the Advancement of Teaching.* The creation of the *Carnegie Endowment for International Peace* reflected his interest in the wider world. Many of Carnegie's philanthropic establishments were so well-funded that they are still going strong today.

Carnegie believed that individuals with wealth should help the less fortunate, and use their money in a socially responsible way; concepts which were rare at the time, and have a modern resonance. However, Carnegie was certainly <u>not</u> a social entrepreneur as the term is used today. He was an individual who, having made a vast amount of money, came to believe in 'giving back' and did so on a grand scale, but he never tried to integrate philanthropy and business.

A modern example of this type of philanthropy is Bill Gates. Throughout the late 1970s, 80s and 90s, Bill Gates built *Microsoft*'s business from nothing, and by the 1990s he was one of the richest men in the world. Throughout these decades he, and everyone in his company, worked hard and focused on improving and growing the business. Bill Gates seemed to experience a change in focus soon after his marriage and the death of his mother in 1994. He took time off work in 1995 and travelled around the world with his wife and when he returned in 1996, announced that he would begin a planned transition out of his day-to-day management role within the company.

In 1997, he established the *William H Gates Foundation*, which was renamed the *Bill & Melinda Gates Foundation* in 2000 when it merged with the *Gates Learning Foundation*. By this point he had endowed the *Foundation* with approximately $2 billion. By 2008, he had moved out of working at *Microsoft* to spend more time working with the *Foundation*.

The *Foundation's* activities range from work in education and libraries as well as relief for the poor, emergency response in the United States, and the support of various health care initiatives and agricultural development in Asia. It is also involved in translation services and libraries in Europe. Furthermore, the *Foundation* invests in long term research projects using technologies to improve social conditions. Bill Gates is now focusing the same determined effort he used in his business, to select causes, and recruit other wealthy individuals to support the *Foundation*. Perhaps he has discovered what Andrew Carnegie summed up so well, "I resolved to stop accumulating and begin the infinitely more serious and difficult task of wise distribution."

Bill Gate's behaviour has helped to galvanize other wealthy individuals to make an impact. In 2006, Warren Buffet, then the world's richest man, pledged millions of dollars to the *Foundation*. Setting this sort of example to the business leaders of the world creates a precedent and makes it acceptable in the corporate world to focus on giving back to society rather than merely chasing further profit. As Erika Uffindell mentioned in Chapter 3, many executives would like to do this sort of thing, but are worried about how they will be judged by their peers. Bill

Gates' leadership in this area goes some way to making this behaviour acceptable in the traditional corporate world.

But not everyone can climb from their current rung on the corporate ladder and create a business that will make them the richest man or woman in the world. All the same, business people do not need to be 'the richest' in order to follow a similar path. Some individuals follow a traditional business career, become successful and then, like the famous philanthropists, invest their money in one or many social businesses, or set up a charity or foundation. True social businesses, while they might be for-profit, make the profit in order to fund improvements to a selected constituency or cause. These enterprises need profit to fund their work, but the business goal is not to chase a never-ending growth in profits.

It doesn't take millions of dollars, pounds or Euros to start these ventures, just a passion for giving back to society or supporting a cause. The stories in this chapter will focus on individuals who have followed this route, some with substantial funds and others with considerably less. What each of them brought was the experience and know-how to make organisations, for-profit or not-for-profit, a success.

The first example looks at one of the businesses that Béla Hatvany (see Chapter 2) fostered and funded, *JustGiving*. When Béla finally left the corporate world, having created substantial personal wealth, he began to investigate ways to invest his money in social causes and in socially driven businesses, or social enterprises. He set up an organisation to fund startups and tried to ensure that each of them embraced his personal business values. The example that follows shows that these social businesses may start small, but they don't need to remain small, or local. *JustGiving* is now a global enterprise, but it has not strayed from its 'for profit, for good' principles.

JustGiving – A business that embodies Béla's philosophy

How it started

JustGiving was one of the companies that benefitted from Béla's time, focus and investment and the company that today comes closest to the embodiment of his business philosophy. He joined as both an investor and board member but before that, he put in time with the principals to ensure that his business philosophy could be incorporated into the fabric of the organisation.

JustGiving is a for-profit company that provides a platform for collecting donations on behalf of a wide variety of charities and causes. Its eventual goal is to enable a worldwide one-to-one relationship between the 'haves' and the 'have nots' by building an 'engine' to match 'causes' with 'donors'. The business serves:

- Charities
- Fundraisers
- Donors (these are seen as the 'customers')
- Event organisers
- Employees
- Investors

Béla first got involved with *JustGiving* in 2001 when it was just three or four people, the founders, who faced multiple competitors vying for market position in this business area. Business growth was slow during the first years while the company established trust with those it served. By 2014 it collected approximately 30,000 gifts every day, each with an average value of £32. That's a daily amount close to £1m, for distribution to the 'have nots'. In fact, Béla explains that with the current platform he can foresee a time when *JustGiving* would process over £1 billion every week.

Why not a charity?

Looking ahead, Béla envisages a split in the ways charities will work and cites the example of the transformation of the traditional publishing business. In the old days, publishers both published and printed their offerings. Over time, publishers began to divest their printing divisions, and this work was outsourced to separate businesses. Béla sees the same schism in charities with a division between the process of fundraising and what they 'do' for their deserving causes. Furthermore, he believes that *JustGiving* can facilitate this split so that charities cease to be burdened by fundraising activities and can focus instead on their core objectives or target constituents.

When asked about why *JustGiving* was structured as a business and not a charity, Béla responded that profit was not necessarily a bad thing.

Just because businesses were profitable, it did not mean that executives were being paid million pound salaries and that money was squandered. Indeed, some large charities pay their management as much as large businesses pay. Profit is a good thing - it can be used for growth, spreading the service throughout the world and continuing to build infrastructure.

Béla went on to say that if *JustGiving* had been established as a charity, a great deal of effort would have had to have been expended on fundraising in order to provide for future services and growth, and that these activities would have been a distraction from the organisation's main goals. In fact, it was just this effort and 'distraction' from goals that were driving more and more charities to use platforms like *JustGiving* to raise money.

Businesses who 'serve' can fund their activities through profits while, in contrast, charities are constantly at the mercy of donors in order to carry out activities or grow. Today, Béla describes *JustGiving* as a part of the 'fundraising industry'. Events-based activities (e.g. the friends of marathon runners who sponsor the participant) provide the bulk of their donors.

JustGiving's approach has stood up to the competition. Béla explains that its platform worked better because it was more 'useable'. He attributes this design to his original philosophy of setting out to serve all of its constituents. In order to collect money to fuel potential growth, not only does the business need a scalable platform, but the platform's usability and approach must be right. And providing a good service can be a real challenge. Even with today's volume of online traffic, there are days when *JustGiving* has more traffic than *Facebook*.

Béla firmly believes in *JustGiving*'s mission and explains, "Enabling people to open their hearts can bring a safety valve to relieve the differences between the 'haves' and the 'have nots.'"

Currently, *JustGiving* is building a 'recommendation engine' by getting to know about its givers ('givers' support specific charities, while 'sponsors' support friends' efforts such as running the London Marathon). *JustGiving* aims to match potential givers to causes. Stories are key to describing impact and by helping supply statistics and anecdotes, *JustGiving* hopes to be a world changer by encouraging more donations and helping billions to pass from 'haves' to 'have nots'.

Béla attributes the success of the business to a 'service mindset' that prevails within *JustGiving*. He believes that the company's employees treat everyone with respect and that this value does not get in the way of 'good business', rather, it ultimately feeds success.

JustGiving's success has provoked an interesting range of reactions among donors. Some resent the fact that the business is not itself a charity and that it charges for its services. On the other hand, many of the smaller charities that are recipients of the donations are grateful for the collection and administration services. *JustGiving* can carry these out in a more cost effective way than small charities could do for themselves. And, as Béla explains, the whole infrastructure relies on large, sophisticated IT systems and these cost money to build and service. If *JustGiving* had to rely on donations to raise these funds, they might never do so and a disproportionate amount of time would probably be spent chasing donations rather than focusing on the customer. Fundraising activities can be expensive.

Béla's investment has been a success by all his personal measures: impact, values and growth, so it is good news that he is, by no means, the only person who has moved from running a for-profit business to investing in a more social business. Another man who built a company, made money and then, 'retired' only to start a social business is Roy Moëd. Roy is a classic entrepreneur, so it's no surprise he couldn't manage to retire quietly, but his motivation to start a social business came later in life. In his early career he was too busy working to think about much else.

Roy's Story – Helping the Elderly

Finding the right job

Roy began his story by explaining that his academic performance had been weak. A series of family moves at just the wrong ages left him at a disadvantage in his studies. He moved from South Africa to Jersey when he was seven years old and, he explains, "At the time, the school system in South Africa was well behind that of Jersey." Seven is an important age in education and Roy struggled to catch up. He was 'kept down' one year and regularly received a caning from the headmaster. "Every year, I was worst in the class." The family moved to London in

1967, and Roy, now a young teen, found himself enrolled in the local grammar school and, once again, behind the rest of his class because the English schools were far ahead of those in Jersey.

In 1969, the grammar school was converted to a comprehensive and Roy's father, concerned about his youngest son's education, enrolled him in a private school. But it was the same old story. All the classes were 'out of synch' with those in Roy's previous school and Roy struggled. He studied for A-levels in French (which he spoke fluently), Economics and Maths. However, Roy didn't do well in his exams, so he didn't go to university. As a next step, Roy enrolled on a catering course at Westminster College and during the summer, took a job running the first drive-in restaurant in Jersey, which was owned by his father.

This role was a 'baptism of fire.' On the second day, the chef walked out because he didn't want to be bossed around by the young, inexperienced son of the owner. In spite of this and other challenges, Roy persevered throughout the summer and learned a lot - the hard way. One thing he definitely learned was that he did not want to be in the catering business so when the autumn came around, he set out to find a job in London instead of taking his place at college.

Soon, Roy found what would be the first of 29 different jobs, all in rapid succession. "I was very, very good at the interviews," explains Roy, "but the day to day jobs just didn't work out for a variety of reasons."

One position of note was at a restaurant, *Lyons Corner House*. Roy noticed two jobs advertised, one of which was a much better paid supervisor's role, requiring the skill of 'smoked salmon slicing'. When Roy sat waiting for his interview he spoke to a fellow applicant and asked him which job he wanted. The other candidate replied that he was after the lower paid, less skilled role. On that day, both of these applicants were successful and Roy became a smoked salmon carver as well as a supervisor. At the same time, he learned a great lesson "If you don't ask… you don't get." Of course, Roy had to go home and learn how to slice smoked salmon, but he got the job!

More jobs followed in swift succession. One position of note was as Night Manager at *GAD* (Great American Disaster), a famous London nightclub. In the line of duty, Roy had to fire a 'shady employee' who had been pilfering and appeared to be involved in illegal activities. Four days later, Roy himself was fired without explanation. Even now he is unsure what he inadvertently stumbled upon that day. There was no malice on the part of *GAD* because every time Roy went back to ask them for a reference, they gave him an outstanding one. Roy wonders if, perhaps, he had seen something that the bosses didn't want to explain.

Roy's other jobs included running a hotel, working in a kibbutz in Israel and a variety of sales positions. The final job that catapulted Roy into his entrepreneurial career was as a commissioned salesman, making most of his salary by selling non-dairy cream for a firm of butchers. Roy explains what happened. "They thought I would go around and sell a container here and a container there, going from shop to shop. Instead, I went to companies like *British Airways* and sold hundreds of times the amount that was forecast."

The entrepreneur emerges

While selling to *British Airways* and similar businesses involved with airline catering, Roy uncovered the need to supply pineapple juice in small quantities to the caterers who supplied *Iran Air*. The quantities were too small to be of interest to the existing suppliers. Roy mentioned this situation to a friend and together they decided to try to solve it. Roy would supply the money (he was still working as a non-dairy cream salesman) and his friend supplied the labour, and they made a deal to supply pineapple juice for *Iran Air* and mineral water for *Japan Air*. The deal was that Roy would get 50% of the business for his investment.

Together they bought a yoghurt machine and a tea urn, and rented an inexpensive room in a cheap part of London. They bought tins of pineapple and bottled mineral water and every day they made six cases of pineapple juice plus mineral water, in small, airline portions. Gradually, the quantity increased to ten cases per day. The deal was that if this small business successfully filled the orders, they would be given the much larger order for orange juice. Things went well. Roy's partner did the work while Roy supplied the funds, did the books and kept on working his day job. Then, disaster struck.

As a result of this over-performance in selling so much to airline suppliers, the CEO became jealous and Roy's manager was ordered to fire him. However, his manager felt so bad about the way that Roy had been treated that he went out of his way to create opportunities for Roy to find more work and grow his new business. At this point, Roy threw himself into getting sales for his growing airline supply business, which they named *Pourshins*.

In the first year, 1978, *Pourshins* achieved a turnover of £30,000. When Roy got further involved as the company driver, he began to discover additional customer needs and started supplying more and more products to airline catering services. The business began to grow at a tremendous rate. Every year for the next few years *Pourshins* doubled or tripled its annual turnover. At the peak of its performance, it had four factories in three countries and more than 600 staff. And all of this growth was achieved organically. There were <u>no</u> external investors.

"It grew," recalls Roy, "because I listened to my customers and tried to solve their problems. I like solving problems. I'm good at it." And solve problems he did. Their motto was 'it never hurts to ask'. However, Roy's business partner began to suffer from nervous ailments and after three years in the business, he sold out his share in *Pourshins* to Roy.

In the 1980s and early 1990s there was no supply chain for 'chilled' food, so Roy created one. He started a US division and began to manage the airline food supply chain for most of the US carriers. But Roy noticed that he was forever trying to recover from the annual crises that depressed the airline business. Roy called them 'the seven plagues' and they included the avian flu scare, the 9/11 attacks and the global economic downturn - all events that had a dramatic effect on air travel. In addition, the airline catering business became increasingly complex and bureaucratic as governments introduced more stringent regulations. So Roy took a careful look at *Pourshins* to see how he could restructure with the aim of minimising risk.

Roy began to consider outsourcing different operational areas. He also started to sell off non-critical components in order to reduce his exposure to market fluctuations. Finally, he decided to get out of manufacturing altogether, selling some of his companies and keeping only the distribution component. As a result of these changes, his staff numbers dropped from 600 to 140 people. Many of the staff transferred with the businesses, but some did not. When redundancies were necessary Roy was always honest and straightforward and kept everyone informed about what was happening and why the reorganisation was essential.

He kept the US operation and a large warehouse at Heathrow for his distribution business until, having spoken to a customer about coordinating the delivery of knives and forks along with the food, Roy discovered another opportunity and reshaped his business yet again. With the growth of computer technology outsourced logistics, known as 4PL (Fourth Party Logistics) and communications, he realised that his real skill and opportunity was in managing customers' supply chain needs in a timely and cost effective manner. He didn't need to make the products, nor did he even need to supply the warehouses and trucks to distribute them, so he reorganised and sold these businesses while continuing to distribute the products from them.

When Roy outsourced his warehouse and his distribution services, he reduced the headcount again, from 140 to 60 staff. *Pourshins* would now act in a sales and supply chain management capacity, sourcing the customers' needs from the best supplier at the time. This approach cushioned his own business against the wild fluctuations in the airline industry. He threw a party for the 80 staff who were made redundant. "I didn't feel I had to hide the fact that they were going," he explains. "It wasn't their fault. I wanted to treat them well." Most soon found jobs in the same industry and carried on working with Roy and his team, and the ones that stayed behind realised and appreciated the kind of company in which they were working.

Within the new structure, Roy continued to deploy technology in new and interesting ways to advance his business. By this time, the business had a turnover of $100m and employed only 32 people. Over 30 years, Roy had reshaped his business four times, always having just enough vision to keep ahead of the rapidly changing business environment.

What next?

In 2007 Roy finally sold the company because, he says, "I wanted a change. After 33 years of solving problems and driving the business alone, I was tired. My father had always said that if you want a business then find one without staff and without stock, like insurance or estate agency, where one call could be for £100 or £1m. At its peak, *Pourshins* had 600 staff and £2m of stock." Roy took what he described as a "gap year" and others would call a holiday. He and his family spent six weeks in South America doing things like flying over the lakes in Chile in a small plane. He then bought a polo farm and set up a club near Windsor.

Despite enjoying his leisure, Roy couldn't help himself and started another business. This business, called *Meet Me*, focused on airports - Roy's old stomping ground. *Meet Me* was to be a computerised system to link up travellers with the drivers who had been sent to collect them, replacing the old-fashioned system of a sign with the passenger's name on it. After almost two years in development, and having been installed in Heathrow's Terminals 1, 2, 3 and 4, the business details couldn't be worked out satisfactorily with the airport, so Roy went back to playing polo and retirement.

Meanwhile, outside his business life, Roy started to work with the homeless and in 2004 he and his wife were approached to help out with *Crisis At Christmas*, a charity that supplies food and other necessities to homeless people during the Christmas celebrations. Roy was already aware of this organisation because airlines provided some of the food. He went along thinking that he could be a driver and have no responsibility, but within two days found himself in charge of managing a shift in the logistics department. He supervised more than 300 drivers (all volunteers) and 100 vehicles, organising the pick-up and delivery of food, medical supplies, equipment, people and whatever else was needed over a ten day period. From that point on, Roy and his wife took part in this effort every year.

Roy became deeply interested in the issues around homelessness and the reasons behind it. "Many were depressed," he explains, "and I began to wonder: how do you make people care about themselves when they are depressed? How to you get them to engage with life?"

Roy's 'ah ha!' moment

These thoughts whirled around in Roy's head and he began to think about his father - now old, blind and feeling he had little to live for. His father was depressed, and Roy wondered how he could motivate and help him. He decided to get his father to tell his own life story - that of a Dutch-born Jew in South Africa who moved to Jersey and then London, setting up businesses and raising a family of four children along the way. The regular weekly storytelling sessions gave Roy's father something to look forward to and when they came to an end, his father had a book of his family stories, all preserved in one place. The process helped his father and it helped Roy - it was a 'win/win' solution.

Roy thought about the process. He knew that there were many other older people just like his father - perhaps depressed and housebound - with nothing much to look forward to each day. Roy also knew that there were other families like his, who would appreciate the treasure of a family history and capturing memories and moments that would otherwise be lost. This activity could be an opportunity to make a lasting difference and, always the entrepreneur, Roy wondered if there was a way to roll out his idea, to make it a self-sustaining business that could reach more and more older people and help more and more families around the world.

Roy can't help it - he solves problems and thinks 'big' and now his vision became to "move the needle in the way in which elderly adults enjoyed their lives."

In 2010, while advising a friend's daughter, Alise, on social entrepreneurship, he asked for her help in researching his concept as a social business. They tested their ideas on relatives and friends and started the business in a barn at Roy's home. Roy could now enjoy the challenge of applying his entrepreneurial skills to solving a very real social problem.

Together, he and Alise came up with a sustainable format by deconstructing the process. The business could use interviewers who were local to the 'author' and could regularly visit the older person. The interviews would be recorded and uploaded, and then downloaded by a ghost-writer who would turn them into a book which would then be prepared for typesetting and printing by an editor. In this way, geography wasn't a restriction and the business could reach around the world. *LifeBook* was born and was truly scalable.

"I could have just carried on just doing *Crisis at Christmas,*" Roy says, "but I wanted to create something that would make a difference. With *LifeBook* I have created something that can, one day, be independent of me and can impact the lives of hundreds or thousands of elderly people and their families each year. For me, that's hugely exciting and rewarding. I feel like I have made a tiny difference on this earth."

As Roy's story shows, for the majority of his working life, all he thought about was the business. He wasn't a bad boss or employer, but his business aim was to make money and he threw himself into this work with an all-consuming passion. It wasn't until he neared retirement that he had the perspective to consider other motivations. Being first and foremost a business person, it didn't occur to him to set up *LifeBook* as a charity, so the social enterprise model was a perfect way for him to deliver social benefit.

So far in this chapter, both successful businessmen shifted the bulk of their efforts to businesses with a social goal as their vehicle for giving back - 'for profit, for good' as Béla describes it. But is this a realistic aspiration for everyone? Most individuals will be employees in someone else's business. What options can they pursue after a successful but more traditional career? Some may well have made a comfortable amount of money, but nowhere near the amount that Béla or Roy achieved.

There is another route for successful business people who don't own a business and who haven't made millions. There are those who decide to use their business skills to give back, but set up a charity rather than a social enterprise. What's the difference? As Béla's story explains, it really can just boil down to the source of funding. Peter Ryan's story illustrates how a high achieving businessman can shift gear, and give up a successful career to help less fortunate people. Rather than supplying substantial funding, Peter supplied his experience, skills and professional connections to do good.

Peter Ryan's story – Giving his expertise and resources

The businessman

Peter Ryan began his working life as a businessman. With a degree in marketing, he had a flair for setting up new businesses and company divisions. He worked in the UK, Europe, the Middle East and Africa and held many senior positions with companies such as *BP* and *Duracell*. To anyone observing, he would have been the poster boy for hard work, achievement, money and success in the traditional business world.

When employed by *BP* he worked in a division that dealt with mergers and acquisitions and was responsible for overseeing, on average, ten companies scattered around Europe. When something new needed to be set up, Peter did it. For *Duracell*, he worked at establishing new international businesses in Europe, the Middle East and Africa. By this time, he realised that his core skills were in setting up and running new enterprises. From *BP*, he moved to setting up a food business in the UK for a French company, supplying the French company's products to major retailers and caterers in the UK. By any standards, Peter was a successful entrepreneur and businessman.

Alongside his professional achievements, Peter enjoyed a happy family life and good friends. One close friend ran sports clubs. Peter described this friendship as the sort in which they had discussions about philosophy and world affairs, things that interested them both. One day, this friend (then in his 30s) decided to 'pack it up' and travel. Peter kept in touch.

Eventually his friend settled down in the Philippines where he ended up giving out loans to the locals who needed help with their businesses. Peter decided to help his friend and sent him some money to boost his burgeoning small loans enterprise. After a while, Peter decided to go out to the Philippines to see exactly what his friend was doing. This decision represented a key crossroads in Peter's life.

A crossroads

While visiting the Philippines, Peter was moved by both the poverty he found and, more importantly, the impact his friend was making with relatively little money. Peter was hooked. In 1997, he set up the *MicroLoan Foundation* - a charity - to help his friend raise more funds for the work. Peter felt that a good business approach was necessary in their quest to help alleviate poverty and he soon put his many years of experience to good use. He established the UK charity and began fundraising by giving local talks. He even put £25,000 of his own money into the organisation.

At this time, Peter still had a full-time job and he was running *MicroLoan Foundation* all by himself. The situation was frustrating. He knew that he wanted to make a bigger impact, but time and resources were scarce. As a man with business experience in mergers and acquisitions, it's not surprising that his first impulse was to search for a partner organisation. He found a partner charity who wanted his help in Malawi, so Peter flew there to see what could be done and whether

MicroLoan could help. It could, and the rest is history.

Peter returned to the UK where he used every moment of his free time to work on the new charity, which he ran from home. He established a local base in a garage in Malawi, and came up with a mission statement: 'To help poor women in rural areas set up sustainable businesses.'

But Peter's personal vision was bigger still - he wanted to plant a seed and see it grow into a large microloan organisation operating in a diverse range of countries, helping women establish businesses that could feed their families and support their local communities in the process. Peter didn't feel strongly that it had to be <u>his</u> charity doing the work; the important thing was to make a difference. As a result, he spent a great deal of time advising and helping others who wanted to set up similar organisations. With big ambitions, Peter approached another man with a big vision - Bob Geldof - to be a patron of his charity.

Taking the big step

At this point, Peter had a charity, a patron, a makeshift UK office and two locations to service - the Philippines and Malawi. By now, he was in his early 50s and about to take a life-changing new direction. Fortunately, his wife and family were very supportive. As he recalls, "It was like setting up a new business from scratch - all-consuming. I just couldn't leave the office at 6pm and ignore things over the weekend. I felt passionate and this work consumed me 24/7."

Peter treated the activity as he would any new business. He developed a business plan, mapped out funding and business requirements and sought support. And as in any business, things didn't always go to plan. His early partnership with another charity did not work out, but Peter carried on. He explains, "We started this organisation 15 or 16 years ago and we would like to have been further ahead by now. However, because of the setbacks we did overcome, we are now building on a much stronger base. We have good people and robust processes and are in a position to continue growth, one new country at a time."

Peter is justifiably proud of his organisation which to date employs around ten UK staff (most full-time) plus some volunteers, and another 140 or so in Malawi and 25 in Zambia. In the UK, half of the staff are fundraisers. Peter wants to continue to expand the organisation and consolidate what he has learned. He explains why his business background is so useful, "Today, most microfinance operations are good with running numbers, but not always quite so good with the people element. In our organisation we have tried hard to do both."

Peter described a methodology that *MicroLoan Foundation* developed to train both their own employees in target countries and then in turn to train and support the women who came to them for a loan. In fact, Peter took training so seriously that he convinced a professional services company to volunteer its help in developing the course and techniques.

Peter says, "We took great care in developing our training and it works well - especially when you consider that we have to deal with individuals who may not be able to read. We make extensive use of role-play and pictures to get our messages across... and it works!"

He described how the organisation puts the women into groups and how they are trained to help and support each other - personally and in each business when, for example, one of the women falls ill. The employees at the local branches of the charity work with these groups, help the women to get bank accounts, discuss the whole situation with husbands to gain support and also include the village head man so that the entire community becomes involved and supports the women. This process was developed over time until Peter found a winning formula.

When asked 'Why women?' and 'Why Africa?' Peter replies, "In Africa, a little goes a long way so it's easier to make a big impact. I considered the need in the UK, but the bureaucracy would stop us in our tracks. In Africa, the local government doesn't really get involved except for a little regulation around banking and loans. Regarding our focus on females - we asked everyone, even the local men, and all agreed that the women were the best bet and a secure group to finance. They had children to feed and would be more reliable."

"Our next step has been to add another country and we are now setting up in Zambia," Peter adds. "Why Zambia? Its proximity to Malawi, and the fact that English is spoken, plus they have a need; all these factors combine to make it a logical next step."

Peter's long-term ambition is to set up operations in many countries and turn each into a sustainable operation. In Zambia, the costs are nearly covered and in Malawi, which is a much bigger operation, Peter expects costs to be covered within the next two years. The 'business objective' of the organisation is to ensure that all operations become self-sustaining. In the very long term, Peter is building the charity so that it can carry on long after he is not around. At the moment it's his vision and driving force that sustains it, but he is actively working toward building a capable management team to carry on his work.

Peter admitted that he had tried to volunteer at earlier points in his life and things just never worked out. However, later in life, after a few years setting up a French food company, he was becoming bored. The timing was just right and his foray into charity became his destiny. In fact, shortly after he founded *MicroLoan Foundation*, he took a job helping a computer software startup in the UK but admits, "it just didn't move me anymore." He returned to working full-time at the *MicroLoan Foundation* and confesses, "I couldn't go back to corporate life. It just didn't excite me enough. It was no longer fulfilling and it's been the best decision of my life."

When asked by others how to start a charity he replies, "If you really want to do something, don't think too much, just take small steps. My first small step was to give money to my friend in the Philippines, my second was to go out to the Philippines to observe, first hand, what he was doing. By then, I was hooked. Life looked after the rest and things just fell into place."

In a charity one is only able to provide help in relation to the funds raised, and within the prescribed guidelines. Such work is laudable, but charities sometimes lack access to the specialised skills and experience that could help them to have a greater impact. As head of a charity, fundraising alone can monopolise a top executive's time. This is what makes Peter's use of good business skills in the establishment and running of his charity so powerful. Microloans - if handled well - can make some money which helps to sustain and even grow the charitable efforts.

Peter has aspired to establish self-sustaining organisations and thus reduce the focus on fundraising for existing set-ups, and any extra money funds new organisations in new locations. In fact, the separate country organisations could be regarded as social enterprises that have been funded and supported by Peter's charity, *MicroLoan Foundation*.

In this chapter all three stories demonstrate different ways that successful business people can 'give back' after they retire from a mainstream corporate career. None of these individuals merely gave money. All three of them, to a greater or lesser extent, gave their business expertise to the organisations they supported as well as funds. And all of them worked to ensure that their personal values played a significant role in the organisations they fostered.

So there are many paths that highly successful business people can take, from giving away their money to redeploying their skills in the service of others. Most successful and driven individuals find it difficult not to get personally involved and those who have held senior roles find it difficult not to be 'in charge'. That's ok; social enterprises and charities both need the skills of good business people in order to maximise their impact and efficiently deliver their goods or services. Money is vital to both. The only difference with these socially driven organisations is that money is the grease to oil the wheels, it's not the end in itself.

Chapter 5

BUSINESS – "THINKING OUTSIDE THE BOX"

> "Man can alter his life by altering his thinking"
> **William James**

Not everyone aspires to, or is able to, go out and start his or her own business or charity. And sadly, not everyone works for an organisation that supports its employees' efforts in socially beneficial projects. So what can someone do who wants to continue working in their profession while adding more meaning to their day-to-day work environment? What happens if this person finds him or herself in an unsympathetic work environment? Many, many professionals struggle with this challenge and many move from company to company, and role to role, until they find something that fulfils them. The way forward is not always easy or obvious. This chapter will explore what others have done when faced with these challenges.

One young professional summed it up very well by explaining, "Many large companies express values that don't reflect their corporate behaviours. You have only to look at the retention rate of new graduates. Most of these young, idealistic individuals believe what they are told at the job interviews, accept a job and then discover that the company didn't practice what it preaches."

This interviewee asked to remain anonymous and she was not alone in her desire to hide these views from her employer. There are many more stories that might have been included in this chapter, but in the end, most of those interviewed did not feel safe giving their personal details or the name of their employer. The general feeling was that to do so would put their job, if not their entire career, at risk.

Even individuals who carried out only small initiatives that didn't impact on their job performance felt at risk, and made a great effort to ensure that their manager or boss did not learn about their charitable work. Despite this fear, another anonymous contributor encouraged everyone to do what they could. Her view is, "At its most basic, the world depends on people just living their lives, going to work, doing their jobs. But these same people can affect many, many small changes, just by being conscious of their own impact on everything - at work, at home and in between. And it's important that they give themselves credit for this consciousness and the behavioural changes that it elicits. These smaller, individual impacts are also important."

Another quoted from Gautama Buddha who sums up the ultimate extension of this belief, "What we think, we become."

One example of a personal activity, which might be considered to be 'small', took place in a large - again, anonymous - corporation. This activity involved an individual who worked as front desk security for a professional services business. He knew most of the employees and engaged in friendly banter with them, so he knew who was going on business trips and who was not. When he had developed a sufficiently comfortable relationship with someone, he would ask them if they could bring in the unused toiletries from the hotels where they stayed while travelling for work. He then collected these items and regularly took them to the local homeless shelter. He related how one woman cried when she was given a small shampoo and she told him that she hadn't had shampoo for her hair in years. A small act, the gift of what's literally a small item, made a big difference for this woman.

Sadly, this individual's activity remained 'under the radar', undetected by senior management for many years when, in fact, management should have celebrated the initiative. It cost them nothing and everyone who took part felt good about their personal involvement.

Today, there are many of these guerrilla acts of 'giving back' going undetected in unsympathetic organisations, each person doing their regular job while quietly doing 'a bit more'. As one individual explains, "It's about awareness and defining potential social impact within any role." So, while it has been a challenge to get stories of how people find a way to work around, manage or 'convert' the organisational culture, there are some brave professionals who have spoken up. Most of the attributed examples were successful because the individuals 'took on' the top management and produced a business case to support their activities.

Business sectors, particularly those concerned with money itself, seem slower to amend working practices to accommodate social programmes. It wouldn't take much. As one young professional suggested to me, "A big organisation? A small one? Banking? Technology? Retail? It doesn't matter. What matters is how you behave within that role and the impact you as an individual can make on the company culture. For example, perhaps a banker could decide to focus some efforts and money on people rather than just profits. But it really doesn't matter where a person works, a person can do what he loves as a profession and still make a positive personal impact on improving the world and society."

In fact, there are some social initiatives that have become acceptable within banks. One of these, microfinance, is becoming more and more mainstream in these traditional institutions. What is microfinance? Well, definitions vary, depending on who is asked. At its most general, it is the provision of finance (loans) and often, advice, for groups or individuals who want to set up a business and who do not qualify for standard bank loans. To others, microfinance is a movement that aims to create, "a world in which as many poor and near-poor households as possible have permanent access to an appropriate range of high quality financial services, including not just credit but also savings, insurance and fund transfers". (see References).

Peter Ryan, whose story was told in the last chapter, created a microfinance organisation, which alongside loans, offers training and other services to poor women wanting to start a small business.

It should come as no surprise to learn that many microfinance initiatives are actually profitable. They may not generate big profits, but they can make money. Additionally, for some businesses, microfinance also provides an entry into emerging markets. In the end, such initiatives can actually do more good than harm for the financial institutions that adopt them.

The chapter that follows contains the stories of individuals who did manage to engage the institutions in which they worked, sometimes temporarily and sometimes permanently. In all instances, they created compelling business cases to support their efforts and to gain support from senior management, investors or the senior partners. This approach is very courageous - it can feel like putting a career on the line, but in all these cases, the efforts succeeded and some cases, succeeded more than once.

The first story in this chapter illustrates exactly how an individual, Maya Mehta, helped shift the consciousness of two big organisations. Both were challenging institutions - a law firm and a bank - and yet she found a way to gain support.

Maya's great commitment to causes has led her to tackle injustice wherever she can. For her it is impossible to turn a blind eye. Her passion and tenacity have enabled her to devote her time and energy with maximum effect, to both her profession and her chosen causes. Maya has not yet totally transformed the organisations in which she currently works, but she has made inroads and gradually enticed fellow workers and friends to join her, where possible, in her efforts.

Maya's story – "I Just Can't Turn a Blind Eye"

The early years

Maya exemplifies the new breed of young professionals, who try to balance a career with social causes and, where possible, encourage work colleagues to do the same. Having studied law at Oxford from 1996 to 1999, she joined *Clifford Chance* in 2001 to begin her training and her legal career and eventually qualified in the Capital Markets department of the firm. However, despite the pressure of her role, even during her training years Maya developed a parallel interest in helping others.

Her first opportunity occurred soon after joining *Clifford Chance* when Maya spent six months in Hong Kong. Going about her daily routine, Maya noticed the same groups of Filipino domestic helpers gathering together to talk and share a meal on the pavement during their free time on Sundays. After some investigation, Maya learned that many of these workers suffered from physical abuse from their employers and, sometimes, lack of payment and that a volunteer service, *Helpers for Domestic Helpers* (*HDH*), had been established in a local church to help them. Maya went to the church one Sunday to join the helpers. She discovered many Filipinos who were held in virtual slavery, being beaten and receiving little money, despite the promises that had been made to lure them to Hong Kong.

Maya explains, "I learned that by applying basic legal skills and even just by listening, I could help these people and point them in the direction of the appropriate specialists to resolve their difficulties. The high point for me was when I accompanied a domestic worker to a tribunal in order to give her moral support to fight for her right to payment. She was elated when she won."

Maya continued volunteering her services until she left Hong Kong to return to London in 2003. At that point, her employer *Clifford Chance* moved to Canary Wharf. When Maya took the DLR (Docklands Light Railway) to work, she couldn't help but notice the poverty that surrounded the shiny new high-rise Canary Wharf development. This view was reinforced when she volunteered to teach reading at a local school during her lunchtimes.

It came to Maya's attention that young girls, mainly from Bangladeshi and Pakistani backgrounds, and some as young as 15, were being tricked or forced into marriage. The 'honour killings' that appeared in the news at this time reflected an extreme version of this activity. Appalled by what she found, Maya decided to use her position in the law firm to try to mobilise forces to help protect these girls from abuse. It was during this time that Maya had attended (as an observer) the trial of Zoora Shah, a young woman who was being accused of killing her husband by poisoning.

The story that unfolded was of a woman who was driven to this action after years of abuse and further anguish when her husband began to abuse her daughter (his step-daughter). Zoora Shah was culturally disadvantaged, didn't speak English and didn't know of any other way to escape her situation. The day in court made a huge impression on Maya and at the trial, she picked up a leaflet from *Southall Black Sisters*, a women's group in West London. Maya's experience that day at the trail, combined with her exposure to similar girls during her volunteer teaching efforts, helped to firm her resolve. She couldn't turn a blind eye any longer and wanted to be part of a movement to help these girls and women.

Gathering followers

As a first step, Maya began to ask her peers - other young, professional, Asian women - if they would also like to help. She approached a sympathetic partner at *Clifford Chance*, one who understood the cultural issues, and proposed the idea of a Wednesday lunchtime legal advice surgery, in partnership with a local charity called the *Newham Asian Women's Project*, the patron of which was the actress and comedian, Meera Syal. Maya developed a working model based on 20 legal volunteers who would work on a rota. In 2004, the new surgery was launched, and as word spread around the community, women would queue up, often with their children, to talk about their problems and get help. Men were not allowed in the centre as it was felt that their presence could intimidate the women.

When asked what this group did each Wednesday, Maya replies, "We listened - and that was a big thing - and gave them emotional support. We also interviewed them to understand their problems. Then we gave them basic advice and, where more was needed, pointed them in the direction of other professionals or agencies. None of us was trained in the typical legal issues involved, but we could identify the issues and apply common sense, and our knowledge and understanding of UK systems, to refer them to the right professional. We could also help interpret for them and help save local support organisations time by completing basic tasks such as form filling. Above all, we gave women the self-confidence to take action when appropriate."

Maya adds, "There were some specific instances that really touched me. One such case was a teenage girl who came into the centre after having been beaten up by her boyfriend. She told me that she wanted to learn how to write so she could tell her story, so I gave her guidance as to where to find courses in journalism so that she could express herself and tell her story in her own words. It was very satisfying."

When *Citigroup* got involved as a partner, this increased the number of volunteers and helped to provide a stable foundation for the new surgery. These large organisations were able to help in additional ways. For example, when the government cut its funding for the mental health programme that had become part of the group's activities it looked likely that this service would be terminated. Instead, Maya, together with her counterpart at *Citigroup*, did a 'whip round' and *Clifford Chance* and *Citigroup* managed together to raise the £25,000 that was needed for the programme to continue.

Maya's activities continued until 2007 when she relocated to *Clifford Chance* in New York City for two years. By that time, the *Newham Asian Women's Project* was stable enough so it could carry on without her, and she left it in safe hands. However, her interest in supporting worthy causes did not abate. While in a New York café one Sunday she saw a poster advertising a talk by Muhamed Yunus, the founder of modern day microfinance. Yunus was known to be an inspirational speaker, so Maya went along to listen. She was moved.

Microfinance

Yunus explained how microfinance had enabled millions of people in the developing world to lift themselves out of poverty by providing them with much-needed access to finance (loans) in order to start their own businesses. Traditionally, these people had been completely ignored by the mainstream banks and so for want of small amounts of money - often just £100 - they could not better themselves and therefore remained in poverty.

After the event, Maya spoke with a group of ex-bankers who had left their conventional jobs to create their own microfinance fund. She and a *Clifford Chance* partner arranged to provide them with legal advice. It soon became apparent that there were growing pockets of microfinance expertise around the world within *Clifford Chance*, so Maya saw the opportunity to pull together these various groups to form a single global group.

Thus, when Maya returned to London in 2009, she immediately set up a meeting with the second in command at *Clifford Chance*, Stuart Popham, and proposed a five-point business plan to formalise a global microfinance group. He readily agreed to support her. Maya then sent out an email to the whole firm and was deluged with responses by lawyers who were passionate about microfinance and wanted to be a part of it. The response was particularly gratifying as it included lawyers from all practice areas. This spread of expertise meant that the group could offer a more complete microfinance advisory service.

Despite the time and commitment that was needed to establish the microfinance group within *Clifford Chance*, Maya managed to do it alongside the 8-plus daily hours required by her 'real job.' Even with this pressure, Maya stayed involved with her new initiative and the experience convinced her of the importance of legal involvement in commercial ventures. With legal involvement, lawyers can help to formulate appropriate regulations and consumer protection principles to help manage the more exploitative lenders.

As a growing business trend that can hugely benefit developing countries, many people debate whether microfinance businesses should be commercial entities. Maya feels that the fact that some players in the microfinance arena are now being criticised, more and more, for overly commercial and sometimes, abusive behaviours means that there is an even greater imperative for lawyers to be involved.

Maya left *Clifford Chance* in 2011. *BNP Paribas* offered her a new position that focused on emerging markets, particularly in Africa - an interest that was sparked by her microfinance work and her family roots. It was a hard move in some ways because she found it difficult to leave her two initiatives: her advice surgery at the *Newham Asian Women's Project* and the *Clifford Chance* microfinance group. Looking back, she had found it profoundly satisfying to create something from nothing, with both groups serving real social needs.

When she joined *BNP Paribas*, Maya immediately launched a microfinance group with colleagues in the London office. Again, she runs this group 'on the side' in addition to her everyday work supporting emerging markets. Her current focus is to encourage other professionals to lend their skills to microfinance businesses in the emerging markets. So far this initiative has culminated in a pilot microfinance trip to Kenya (for which Maya used her holiday and volunteer day allowance). In Kenya, Maya examined things like potential new legislation and developed a business plan to make this idea work.

There is real excitement in Maya's voice as she explains, "In a bank, we have even more of the relevant skills to help than in a law firm. For example, we have experts in compliance, IT and a huge variety of business skills. We should also consider if we should widen the remit to include 'social businesses' and try to use microfinance to help them too."

Supporting this idea, Maya is now taking small steps to help social businesses in the UK. In February 2013, Maya held an event at *BNP Paribas* that showcased five UK social businesses to about 100 of the bank's staff. Maya is working on other ideas designed to help small businesses and social businesses around the world from within her job and trying to do so without impacting her company's bottom line. She is also the co-founder of the *Harvard Oxford Alumni Social Business Group* whose inaugural event was in May 2013. This group connects alumni as well as other interested individuals, and offers inspirational panellists and discussions around the theme 'Putting the Soul Back into Business'.

Maya's story illustrates the way in which individuals within big corporate organisations can make a difference. She has learned along the way that it requires individual initiative, a lot of effort and excellent performance in the role for which she was employed. Most importantly, any idea must be 'sold' to the employer organisation. However, Maya's experience also illustrates how, once she took a risk and led the way, many others in the organisation were keen to be involved too. Maya may have shown the leadership and provided the energy to get her projects off the starting block, but, once started, the combined efforts of others gave the initiatives a life of their own.

Maya's efforts also demonstrate how it is possible to engage directly with businesses in some of the most challenging, even 'resistant', sectors - finance and legal partnerships - and, because she didn't allow her urge to 'do good' to impact upon her job performance, she was able to engage others in the business to put in extra hours in order to provide socially beneficial services.

Businesses and professional organisations set up as partnerships tend to offer a greater challenge to changes in working practices. Why? Because, typically, profits are split according to a formula and divided among the organisation's partners and the financial performance of the organisation will probably impact the salary or bonus of all the partners. Therefore, in extreme situations all partners must have a vote on such changes and it can be a challenge to convince everyone. As a result any change is very slow or non-existent - unless it brings profits! It's probably no surprise that many of the individuals whose stories are told in this book have spent time working in law firms or large consultancies. What that means is that to make a major change in working practice many, many partners must be won over, and even someone who has attained partnership status will struggle without the support of peers.

However, many of these organisations now permit their employees to take part in social initiatives. Much of this change has come about through the open and honest efforts of individuals who 'sold' their ideas within the organisational hierarchy. Progress was slow but significant and successful, and these individual efforts have inspired and galvanized others to act. As yet another anonymous contributor explains, "I realised that if something needed to happen, I couldn't wait for someone else to do it."

As we have seen, it can be challenging to get large, professional partnerships to donate significant time, resources and money to a cause, but it can be done. All such expense comes off the personal bottom line of each partner and each is motivated by different causes and personal philosophies - so how is it possible to reach agreement on which causes to support? That is why Paul Lomas and his story provides such inspiration to socially conscious solicitors, accountants and other professionals hoping to work in a traditional firm while still managing to make a social contribution.

Paul Lomas is a partner at *Freshfields Bruckhaus Deringer LLP (Freshfields),* one of the largest and most prestigious international law firms. He has managed to combine traditional legal work with making a social contribution and has successfully balanced the commercial and social aspirations of his employer. His contribution has been both significant and lasting.

Paul Lomas' story – Weaving *pro bono* activities into the fabric of a partnership

The 'ah ha!' moment

Paul began his narrative by saying that many, many others played a role in creating a *pro bono* practice at *Freshfields.* However, because this section focuses on Paul's personal journey, many significant names will of necessity be omitted. Paul was closely involved in the changes and played an important role in encouraging others to follow.

When asked why he became responsible for setting up the *pro bono* practice, Paul said that an incident about 15 years ago was the turning point at which he first began to look at his legal efforts in a different light. Paul explains, "My 'Damascene moment' came when I ran into Clive Stafford Smith. Clive's brother was best man at my wedding so I knew him and encountered him socially. It was 1997 or '98 when I bumped into Clive and he asked me what I was doing with regard to *pro bono* work. He kept pushing me."

Paul explained that Clive Stafford Smith was then well known for *pro bono* death row defence and campaigning in the USA (although he has now returned to the UK, and has set up a charity, *Reprieve*, to offer free legal support for selected death row cases, and campaigned on other human rights questions including war on terror and drone issues.) "Clive told me about a case in the USA, in Florida, involving a UK citizen in prison for a murder and sentenced to death and, eventually, I became involved."

Until this point, Paul's experience of *pro bono* legal work had been limited to evening volunteering at Legal Aid centres supported by the firm, as part of a scheme set up by a senior partner about 40 years earlier. This activity had been when he was a trainee in 1982 - at the time, and now, many trainees did such a rotation. He then went on to develop his career and carry out fee paying activities. So, when he agreed to help out the Florida death row client, it was a shift for Paul. His work in the late 1990s for this death row case involved a great deal more time, effort and commitment - on his part and others in the firm, than his earlier rotation through the law centres. Among other initiatives he took to assist the UK prisoner in Florida, he assembled more than 300 members of the Houses of Lords and Commons and, with the presence of the BBC, presented briefs to the effect that the original conviction was 'unsafe' and should be overturned.

Eventually, Paul and his colleagues wrote an appeal to the Supreme Court of Florida and were part of the team that ultimately had the death penalty overturned. Later, Paul began to get involved in other death penalty cases and in the treatment of prisoners at the US Guantanamo Bay facility. As a result of his very public success he was asked to set up a global *pro bono* practice for *Freshfields*.

Paul remembers, "Before this point, people in the firm did do *pro bono* work, but the choice of activities was haphazard. There was no policy governing what type of work was done, or who should do it. There was no structure for ensuring that it was done the right way or for making our work strategic and giving it impact. There was certainly no way to ensure that people's contributions were recognised." So, from within the litigation department, Paul set about structuring and formalising all *pro bono* activities at *Freshfields*.

Gaining support from the Partners

When asked about the challenges of gaining the support of partners, Paul explained that with some 450 partners of differing views, it was tricky. The majority of partners thought that *pro bono* was 'a good thing', although some regarded such activities as a private matter and not something for the firm and there were differing views as to how much should be done and how. People were concerned about risk - raising questions such as, "Would the firm be doing things outside its area of expertise, or contrary to the interests of its clients?" and, "What are the brand implications?" Of course, the other issues that arose were around recognition and compensation. How should the contributions of the lawyers in the firm be recognised and did *pro bono* work sit comfortably with those processes? From the outset, the support of the leadership of the firm had been critical to the success of any proposition, and that support was still necessary in order to convince partners.

Paul explained that different reasons for doing *pro bono* work appealed to different partners. To gain support it was necessary to deploy the best argument in each instance - so long as partners agreed for one or another good reason, it did not matter if they had differing reasons or priorities. He went on to list eight key reasons that helped him to gain support from different partners:

1. *Pro bono* is a professional obligation Although not a legal requirement in the UK, it is in some of the other countries in which *Freshfields* operates
2. *Pro bono* is an ethical obligation Many partners feel that, having benefited from the practice of law, they have a duty to use those skills for the benefit of the community and should give something back to society
3. It is great training When carrying out *pro bono* work, lawyers often gain an opportunity to work in new areas of law or expand their area of expertise. In addition, *pro bono* work often deals directly with the person who has the problem whereas most of *Freshfields'* work involves people in departments in businesses who have no personal

stake in the outcome

4. It is motivational Doing *pro bono* work makes people feel good about themselves, their profession and their firm
5. *Pro bono* work enhances the firm's culture Encouraging individuals in *pro bono* activities helps to create a positive culture in the firm
6. It helps to attract the best new recruits Most of the newly graduated law recruits are interested in doing *pro bono* work. Having a top *pro bono* department helps attract and retain 'the best' in a competitive environment
7. It rebounds to the brand *Freshfields'* image is, in part, formed by its reputation around *pro bono* initiatives and what these initiatives say about the firm's values and culture.
8. Client pressures Clients are increasingly interested in working with people and firms who do *pro bono* and use this activity as a measure of the firm's ethics and culture

After selling the idea of a *pro bono* group to the partners, there were still many challenges to resolve:

- How to balance *pro bono* work with any political impact "There are some risks around this," Paul explains. "Some *pro bono* work has political implications: but the firm is politically neutral and does not support specific political views."

- How to 'value' *pro bono* activities against fee paying work and contribution Paul elaborates, "Some partners say that we are in this business to be outstanding at the law, and build a really successful and profitable firm, and that charitable acts and *pro bono* activities should be individual choices (and personal financial sacrifices) and not a collective effort."

- What's the 'tax' a firm should pay for these efforts? Is it 2%, 5%, 10% of effort? Some scale had to be agreed.

Institutionalising the *pro bono* work

Paul and the team took a radical and innovative approach. *Freshfields* organised itself, in part, along business sector lines, so it was decided to set up *pro bono* as another sector. This automatically embedded *pro bono* in the firm's operational systems and 'normalised' it. The *pro bono* sector produced data that fed into and engaged with the firm's control processes and organisational structures. This approach meant that *pro bono* work was treated and accounted for as any other work when it came to resource allocation and booking time. Conflicts and client acceptance issues worked within normal systems. Indeed, even the partner selection process took into account the amount of *pro bono* work the candidate had completed. However, *pro bono* work always remained optional and a personal choice for the individual (outside those jurisdictions where bar rules required it).

Another unique approach was for the *pro bono* work to be strategic and to have a 'business plan' for the growth and type of work - for example, to target clients with whom *Freshfields* wished to work. For proactive efforts, there was a focus on serious intermediaries, large organisations such as *The Global Fund, Save the Children, Oxfam* and *Shelter.*

While work still continued in the law centres, helping individuals who needed support, the firm was also interested in mandates that changed the law or altered a charity or created a new situation. Paul explains, "We wanted to take 'catalyst mandates' - where by doing them, we could have a multiplier effect, helping other situations as well. In our other legal work, we like to do the innovative cases which have a big impact on what is happening; it was consistent with our brand to try to replicate the same effect, where possible, with our *pro bono* work."

Another activity was to support commercial clients in their charitable efforts. For example when an insurance company set up a 'free fund' for charitable works, *Freshfields* set up the legal structure for the fund as part of its *pro bono* efforts - in essence, joining with and supporting the insurance client in its efforts. And when *Deutsche Bank* set up a microfinance fund, *Freshfields* offered similar *pro bono* support.

Another unusual feature of *Freshfields pro bono* sector was that these activities were progressively plugged into the firm's work allocation, evaluation and remuneration systems which were, in effect, 'fee blind' when selecting available individuals to work on cases. Staff were judged on 'number of hours worked' but it had no impact on their careers whether the work was for fees or *pro bono.* Furthermore, individuals were given recognition for the *pro bono* work they performed just as they would have been for fee paying work.

Of course, there had to be a balance between the overall needs of the firm, the wishes of individual lawyers and the goals of the *pro bono* sector. So, while *pro bono* work was voluntary and the wishes and personal motivations of the individuals were always important, the team did try to ensure that no lawyers became too committed to *pro bono*. They ensured that the work was fairly divided and that it supported (rather than hindered) the professional development of their lawyers. In other words, Paul set up and ran the sector with the same business disciplines and professionalism that he would have applied to any sector, and integrated it into the structure of the overall business.

As part of institutionalising *pro bono* at *Freshfields*, a global structure was created with partners in different offices with practice groups taking responsibility for developing a varied programme, based around certain firm-wide *pro bono* goals. Some of the focus areas included education, homelessness and access to justice. This disciplined approach helped to ensure quality and to encourage and support the commitment. The strategy set high level targets which varied from location to location. In London (in 2014) the firm aspired to spend 2.3% of its time on *pro bono* activities. Like any business, it doesn't always achieve its targets, but the systems are set up to support this aspiration. In the USA, levels of *pro bono* work tend to be higher, while in continental Europe, they are a little lower. This variation reflects the expectations, opportunities and tradition of *pro bono* in the various countries involved.

Paul believes that *Freshfields* was one of the first large firms in the UK to formalise and actively promote *pro bono* work. "In the UK, other firms have followed and many have done some valuable and creative things in their firms to make *pro bono* an effective force." But he adds a note of caution, "Personally, I am concerned that in some cases the drive behind the *pro bono* activity is more a marketing effort that misses the point and could undermine the role of *pro bono* itself."

Paul ran the *pro bono* sector for four years and passed on the job a couple of years ago. The strong foundation he created ensures that *pro bono* activities continue to grow and that *Freshfields* remains committed to the sector.

In addition, Paul's personal efforts continue. Paul mentioned that one of his best moments was the result of his *pro bono* work on behalf of detainees at the US Guantanamo Bay facility when it was agreed that they were entitled to the protection of the Geneva Conventions and were not, "in a legal black hole". His team had submitted some of the briefs on that issue to the US Supreme Court, which had determined that detainees were entitled to such rights as a fair trial without delay. Paul remembers with pleasure the day, "when President George W Bush came out in front of the White House and told reporters that the US Supreme Court had told him he was wrong and that the Geneva Convention did apply to Guantanamo Bay detainees. I felt like I really had been part of something that had made a difference. It was a great moment!"

He confessed that what really drove him was to be able to use the power of the law to good effect. In 2010, Paul was instrumental in setting up the *Bingham Centre for the Rule of Law*, under the auspices of the *British Institute of International and Comparative Law* (*BIICL*), an organisation which dedicates itself to preserving and promoting the 'rule of law' worldwide. Paul is also a Trustee of *BIICL*. "Lord Bingham used to say that the rule of law is a secular religion for him," explains Paul. "I go along with that. It is not a panacea for the world's problems but better integration of the rule of law into life makes for a fairer and better society. Then the weak are less vulnerable to the strong and society becomes the kind of place that most of us would want to live in. Most people would call me a rational type - the first part of my degree was in Natural Sciences before reading Law - but the rule of law is a subject about which I can get very emotional!"

Having said that, Paul's charitable efforts do extend beyond the legal realm. He has recently become a director of a web-based company called *Localgiving.com.* This not-for-profit provides charities, particularly small local charities, with a place online where they can raise funds, make appeals and ask for help.

Paul's efforts and those of his team have not only helped to change laws and improve outcomes for the individuals they represented, they have also eased the way for other lawyers to make a significant contribution - by using their specialised skills rather than just giving cash. These individuals can now find deeper satisfaction within their chosen career, feeling that they not only earn money, but also give something back. Many others share Paul's personal view that, having been fortunate in life and prospered in society, it is only fair that they return something to that society which supports them.

From reading Paul's story it will be clear that, although *pro bono* activities had clear benefits for the firm, it was no trivial task to get the organisation to accept this work. A great many people were involved in establishing the department, and they made extraordinary efforts not only to perform *pro bono* work, but to design and integrate these activities into the infrastructure of the firm. Their efforts succeeded and *Freshfields* was changed. Individuals within the firm now have the opportunity to carry out socially beneficial work within the context of their job.

The next story has a different twist. Sometimes the issue involved isn't about engaging the management, it's about engaging the staff and building an appropriate company culture. Andrew's story illustrates how, from the top down, he built a cohesive culture, maintaining an awareness of his investors and the pressures to attain his bottom line profits. As usual, a bit of background is helpful in understanding the man in order to appreciate the path he took.

Andrew Warren lost his father at the age of 12, and he and his brother were raised by their mother, who managed to keep the family together. He attended the Royal Military Academy Sandhurst and became an army officer. In this capacity he served in many of the 'hot spots' of the 1980s, including Northern Ireland and the Falklands War. When he eventually left the army, he entered the commercial world of large corporates. At this point his motivation was solely to develop a second career and earn a living.

Perhaps the army left an indelible mark on him or perhaps the skill was intrinsic to his nature, but Andrew excelled at building and motivating effective and engaged teams. The size of the team depended on the number of people under his 'command' but the result was the same - most employees enjoyed working for him and his approach added something extra to their daily job. Andrew's story demonstrates this impact when he ran a business division that included thousands of staff. He understood the power of a motivated employee community, and understood the value both to employees and to the company bottom line.

Andrew's story – Mobilising staff around supporting a cause

The challenge

Andrew began by saying, "For me, corporate social responsibility has always seemed to be about pictures of the CEO dispensing largesse and companies patting themselves on the back. I'm sure it's useful, but I'm not sure about the motives."

So, when questioned about how to engage a large organisation to 'put the soul back into business', Andrew answers, "...that depends. In large professional organisations, like law or a consultancy, there is one type of challenge. Basically, the people at the top and people at the bottom are similar. Typically, the only things that separate them are age and experience. I wasn't in this situation."

When Andrew addressed this challenge it was in a very different type of organisation - one that had many differences in culture and aspiration between the top and bottom of the corporate hierarchy. The people near the bottom of the organisation - the vast majority in terms of numbers - worked to live. Much of their life took place outside of work and typically they were all involved in the local community. The company Andrew worked for, and which forms the centre of his story, must remain anonymous.

Often these staff wanted to raise money for children or families in the community and would use work premises, but their own time, to do so. When asked what they wanted to do, they were all keen to support local causes, so Andrew, managing director (MD) of an autonomous division in a large company, let the employees run their own initiatives. He felt good about supporting these efforts, which fell outside the auspices of Corporate Social Responsibility which he describes as, "... like 'filling pages for a company brochure, not authentic.'

"I just let them get on with it and do it," he says simply. "I didn't let them use company time, but I did let them use the premises." Andrew's belief was:

1. Don't stop people from doing something that's important to them
2. Trust the local managers to ensure that the activities were appropriate
3. Make certain that the activities were about 'doing something' rather than just giving money
4. Let the activities be local and meaningful, but designed so that they stand outside of the business while enriching the nature of the workplace.

Creating a win/win/win situation

These activities were all local - but there was no reason that they couldn't be 'franchised'. "We supported charities," explains Andrew. "But there was no reason that this support couldn't achieve multiple aims. For example, our customers were the Government and we knew that one of their initiatives was helping the aged, so we elected to support *AgeUK* as one of our charities." Andrew tells how, in doing so, he came up with a plan for employees to take part in these efforts so that the business contributed both money and 'warm bodies'. "If you believe that there is any merit in having a sense of purpose that's about more than just the job, then people must take part. We demonstrated that you don't have to be a public servant to provide service to the public."

"We also reported back on the results of the efforts," he adds, "and described the results in ways that the staff could appreciate. For example, post a result on a common bulletin board that states 'Last month we took 10,000 children out of poverty' or whatever the cause that has been supported."

In carrying out these types of activities, Andrew searched for something that would give the company a common purpose, and would transcend the corporate hierarchy and the geographical spread of the organisation. He sought to find an activity exciting enough to make employees go home with 'stories' that made them feel good as they related the tales to family and friends. He wanted to find something that would make the staff feel good about what they did at work, as well as feeling proud of where they worked. He wanted to give his staff a sense of purpose and belonging and do so in terms that meant something to them. "We needed to find something that would bring our people together and that would have a long life…well, more than a year," Andrew recalls. "It needed to be something relevant and interesting to give people a sense of purpose and belonging."

As an added 'plus' he sought activities that appealed and/or supported his customers - the UK Government. His timing was good and he selected the forthcoming Olympic Games which were to be hosted in a few years' time in London. The Olympics was an activity that everyone followed, but unless you could buy tickets, one in which few people could participate.

It doesn't need to cost a lot of money

Given the business circumstances, Andrew knew that he could not compete with the international corporations who gave millions and millions of dollars and pounds in support of the popular sports. Fortunately, there were people in UK sports organisations who needed support for other Olympic disciplines. Andrew could not give money, but as luck would have it, the *British Olympic Association* realised that it needed other types of support.

Andrew looked for a sport that everyone could identify with, had general appeal and would allow the employees to become involved in without having to give money. In the end, he was given a list of four teams:

- Boxing
- Weightlifting
- Handball
- Volleyball

His first choice was boxing, but he found that the general interest in this sport was low. Then Andrew met the Chairman of the *British Volleyball Federation* who pointed out that everyone, male or female, had played volleyball at some point during their school days. He also asked Andrew, "Do you know what the two most watched events were at the Beijing Olympics?" The answer, unsurprisingly, was that the opening ceremony was the first, but second was the Women's Beach Volleyball finals. Volleyball had great general appeal, with both men's and women's teams as well as a Paralympic team, so it gave the employees an opportunity to work with a wide range of athletes.

Being an IT services business, Andrew agreed that the first way in which they could help the teams was to rebuild the *Volleyball Federation's* database and revamp their technology centre. In this instance, he gave the appropriately skilled individuals within the business the time off to do this work. In return, the athletes came to the various work locations to practice, play games with employee teams and give talks on general health and fitness. Andrew even put someone from his senior team onto the *Federation's* Board. His people wrote scripts, helped them with campaigns and used the call centre staff to help with 'cold calling'. In effect, during a period of about two and a half years, Andrew's staff 'enabled' the *Volleyball Federation* by providing business resources and know-how.

When the teams played matches, Andrew's division would lay on coaches and food so that employees and their families could have an enjoyable day out. This activity had a positive knock-on effect for the business. In their excitement, employees would tell customers about the activities. There was even a staff competition to design the team mascot, and staff could volunteer to dress up as the mascot and attend a match. The company sites displayed boards on the walls announcing matches and results. As the Olympics drew closer, there were more activities involving both staff and customers.

The activities certainly involved everyone and made work a more interesting and engaging place to come to each day, but how did these activities affect the business? For a start, the division lost fewer staff. Attrition rates in call centres are very high - about 25% a year - and this company already had one of the lowest in the UK. Andrew's division showed the lowest attrition rate of the entire business - just 4-5%. In a people-intensive business, this drop in attrition rate represented a substantial cost savings.

Savings on recruitment costs were estimated at £250,000 per year and there were consequential improvements. Fewer staff leaving meant that those remaining were more experienced, and this profile was reflected in improved productivity. Many call centre contracts contain productivity targets and Andrew's division met these targets. Productivity rose by 5% and there were fewer errors in the work carried out. Management used far less time in recruiting and training new staff. Overall, Andrew estimated that the business gained £350-400,000 per year in reduced costs, improved productivity and payments for meeting customer targets.

"And there were other secondary benefits we hadn't considered," Andrew explains. "With a more consistent workforce we were able to monitor performance better and, as a result, could select individuals for promotion."

"Our activities may <u>not</u> have made the world a better place, but we did make the work environment more engaging. We made people feel that they were truly part of something bigger than their job, so they stayed."

Andrew's approach illustrates the importance of treating employees like people. He clearly understood that people like to feel involved in their workplace and that they wanted to focus on something more than merely their desk jobs. His Olympic project created a common local focus which was 'bigger' than the daily activities and yet, his results show that when such activities are skilfully executed, it need not damage a business's profits and can, in fact, increase them. This story is of critical importance because it illustrates the benefits that all companies could achieve - whether or not the leadership team is committed to social benefit - when employees are engaged in socially meaningful activities at work.

All three stories in this chapter focus on change from the top of the organisation, and although not all of the individuals occupied the top position, they all had to provide a compelling business case for their causes. In every example, this approach succeeded. The activities met both business and social targets and enriched the lives of all the employees involved.

Of course, some companies take this approach to the extreme and make a social mission their key business strategy. Such businesses honestly consider social causes, people and/or the environment as equal to achieving profits. In fact for some, profits may be a means by which to further a particular social cause. The next chapter explores this trend toward social enterprises in more detail.

Chapter 6

SOCIAL ENTERPRISES

"Big businesses risk losing out to social enterprises unless they adapt"
Headline from The Guardian Professional Network, 15th May, 2012

This chapter focuses on yet another business option available to individuals who wish to incorporate social values into their daily working life. These workers do not need to leave the business world, instead they can set up, or move to, a social enterprise whose business values they support. While there have always been a few companies who were committed to ploughing their profits into supporting a selected social cause, this movement has grown in size and intensity over recent years and is now a viable option for those who seek a meaningful job within the business arena.

Before telling the stories of individuals who have chosen this path, it's worth taking a moment to understand this relatively new phenomenon.

*"A **social enterprise** is an organization that applies commercial strategies to maximize improvements in human and environmental well-being, rather than maximizing profits for external shareholders."*

"Social enterprises can be structured as for-profit or non-profit, and may take the form of a co-operative, mutual organisation, social business or a charity organisation." (see References).

Social enterprises should...

- have a clear social and/or environmental mission set out in their governing documents
- generate the majority of their income through trade

- reinvest the majority of their profits
- be autonomous of state
- be majority controlled in the interests of the social mission
- be accountable and transparent

(Socialenterprise.org.uk – August 2015)

In essence, this definition encompasses the majority of the personal stories in this book. For clarity, in this chapter a social enterprise will refer to a 'for profit' business expressly set up to address social betterment as well as profit. This narrow definition is crucial because social entrepreneurship has become a popular concept and for now, there is little regulation around the use of this label. Lots of businesses have jumped onto this bandwagon and call themselves 'a social business' in order to exploit the popularity of the concept.

Why?

Because today, the label 'social enterprise' appeals to many potential customers and thereby, improves sales and sources of funding. In fact, the headline of an article in *The Guardian* newspaper (9 July, 2013) shouted, "New survey suggests social enterprises out-performing mainstream businesses." Similar editorials have appeared in recent years on the TV and radio news as well as in print media. As a result, both the genuine popularity of this trend combined with the news coverage, has led many businesses to call themselves 'green' or 'a social business' not because of their fundamental or corporate values, rather because they believe that such a label will improve their bottom line.

So how can a consumer tell if a social enterprise is a genuine, conviction-driven business?

The first social enterprise in this chapter focuses on trying to solve this problem and it straddles two chapters in this book - it's both a social business and a business that helps other social businesses. In its capacity as a genuine business, with employees and the need to sustain itself by generating revenue, it deserves a position alongside the other social businesses. Lucy Findlay travelled many paths before settling on her current role as managing director of *Social Business Mark*. Her story illustrates the circuitous route she took as she struggled to find, and eventually create, a business that encapsulated her values.

Lucy's story – Making social businesses her mission

Getting started

Lucy's story begins at university. She attended what is now Kingston University and studied Geography because she wasn't sure what she wanted to do and it gave her the broadest education. She particularly liked the human aspects of geography although, in the early 1990s, it was difficult to find many classes with this focus. Perhaps this interest stemmed from her childhood; her father was a farmer in rural Bedfordshire and her mother was very involved in local community work. Whatever the reason, Lucy's preference was to do tangible things and work with people.

Lucy graduated in the midst of a recession, jobs were difficult to find and she still didn't know what career she wanted to pursue so she decided to take a post-graduate degree in Town Planning.

"I thought of Town Planning as applied geography," Lucy explains, "but it was still difficult to find classes that focused on people - most of the course focused on land use. About that time I developed an interest in regeneration - although one couldn't do a degree in the subject back in 1993-4." Lucy carried out research on a variety of regeneration models, both urban and rural and, when writing up case studies for a book, made contact with a development trust in Ystalyfera, Wales, which ran a successful model.

In 1995, with the help of a government grant, a trust was set up in the town of Ystalyfera in an effort to reverse the decline in social and economic conditions in the community. The work began by restoring a few old buildings and using them for social enterprises entirely run by the local community. The aim was to make the trust self-sustaining so that the regeneration work could spread.

From this experience, Lucy discovered the existence of a *Development Trusts Association* (renamed *Locality* in 2011) whose mission was to support rural and urban community-led regeneration. Lucy started working as the South West regional manager for the *Development Trusts Association* and learned how regeneration projects could be self-sustaining. "This position gave me my first taste of community enterprises and I discovered that the idea of local communities taking control of their own community and changing things for the long term excited me," Lucy confesses. She worked in this position from 1998 until 2003.

During these years Lucy also had the opportunity to do a secondment in the *Government Office for the South East* working on Neighbourhood Renewal (a big Government programme). "It was eye opening," she says. "I saw millions of pounds being overseen by civil servants lacking training or experience in what community-based regeneration was really about. That's when I learned that most government employees are 'generalists', so they are able to move within the civil service, but few have the specialist knowledge that's also needed. I also saw how each department is really just a very small cog in a very big machine and it's easy to become swallowed up by the system."

The Social Enterprise Mark

In 2003, Lucy applied for the position of CEO of the South West Region for an organisation called *RISE* (*Regional Infrastructure for Social Enterprise*). *RISE* was set up by an initial grant from the Government with a mission to spread the word about social enterprises and provide advocacy in the South West. "We became the voice of social enterprises for South West England," explains Lucy. In addition to this, Lucy helped with other initiatives including acting as an advisor to the first Social Enterprise Strategy led by Ed Miliband.

It was while she was at *RISE* that Lucy came up with the idea of a 'Mark' for social enterprises. "It had become clear that there was a need to help social enterprises distinguish and market themselves differently than charities and off-shoots of Corporate CSR projects," declares Lucy.

"In fact, the term 'social enterprise' is only a decade or two old and has really only risen to prominence during the last few years. In the USA, the emphasis is on the individual - the social entrepreneur - rather than on the particular business he or she may run. In the UK, a social enterprise is more concerned with the business and how it sustains itself," Lucy clarifies. "The emphasis for me is that it makes profits (hopefully) but the majority of those profits are ploughed back into the community, the environment or a particular focus group."

While at *RISE*, Lucy set up *Social Enterprise Mark* - itself a social enterprise - as a business which would publicise the concept of social enterprises and help establish this approach as 'the' alternative business model. *Social Enterprise Mark* has a single shareholder - *RISE Legacy Trust* - and the majority of the profits, when generated, are distributed for the benefit of social enterprises in South West England.

Social Enterprise Mark (*SEM*) spent a great deal of time and effort setting up standards and criteria to clarify what constitutes a social enterprise. Some of the standards were straightforward: the business needed to get the majority of income from trading, not grants, and it could not be owned by a local authority or a large corporate body. *SEM* gathered together 'best practice' from existing business and applied these practices to the model. Finally, *SEM* created a comprehensive, online certification process to ensure the integrity of the Mark that is awarded. Should an applicant not fulfil the requirements, they are told what to do in order to complete the process successfully.

An extract from the *SEM* website gives a clear and concise description of the organisation's vision and values:

Our vision
A world in which there is commitment to social enterprise as a means to achieve positive social and environmental change.

Our values
Working with representatives right across the social enterprise sector, the Social Enterprise Mark's values were agreed as: creative, distinctive, driven, clear, inclusive.

The organisation itself is funded by an annual licence fee from the organisations which have acquired the Mark. Lucy is the managing director and spends much of her time campaigning on behalf of the Mark holders - for example, for their inclusion into corporate supply chains. Although initial funding was provided by a government grant, the Mark alone has no official status. Use and adherence to the Mark is totally voluntary and, in a way, this is a measure of the dedication of many of its members to the aims of the sector.

One of the challenges that Lucy faces is that, as the founder, she supplies the emotional energy as well as the drive and direction for

SEM. It's a small business (employing only five people) just like those of her customers, and she faces similar challenges. She genuinely understands what her customers face and she works hard to overcome similar challenges. Whatever the hardship, Lucy has finally found what she wanted, a career working with people in a social enterprise that helps in two ways: *SEM* helps other social enterprises plus its profits go toward financing social enterprises in the South West.

Lucy started her career by working closely with government-backed schemes. But it is a good thing that not all social enterprises take this route. Government funding and policies change frequently, and small businesses find it difficult to grow big enough to gain a foothold before the funding dries up and the policy changes yet again. Lucy's attempts to help regional social enterprises funded via a commercial route offers hope of more reliable and better qualified support. Her activities satisfy her person quest to both help other social businesses and continue to work in a job which supports a social cause.

Not all social enterprises are founded by individuals with a public sector background. Others are established by people with a business pedigree. In earlier chapters you will have read how Béla Hatvany set up a fund to support technology businesses that embraced, in some way, his holistic business beliefs. Others too, have emerged from traditional business careers and, like Béla, aspire to initiate an enterprise that embodies strong social and/or environmental beliefs. Many of these derive their funding not from government, but from more traditional commercial sources - investors and bank loans. Mark Brunton's story about his business, *College Green,* illustrates this alternative approach.

Once again, to understand Mark's personal journey, it's necessary to start at the beginning of his business career.

Mark's story – Capturing the spirit of organisations

Business life

Mark left university with a Political Sciences degree and then went straight to work as a graduate trainee for a large telecoms business, newly set up by a national utility company. "When I started employment, perhaps I naively had a view that large businesses were paternalistic," Mark explains. "I envisioned behaviours that included investment in the future development of the employee within a long term framework. The world changed very quickly in the 90s - attitudes and behaviours changed fast."

Mark stayed with the company for nine years, working in a variety of roles as the business grew and expanded. "In hindsight," Mark confesses, "I stayed too long. I was advised by a colleague that I was doing my career no good by staying with one company so long and that if I wanted to progress faster I should change companies often."

The advice Mark received was common during this era and in this market sector, where great career progress could be achieved by changing companies every three to five years. Interestingly Mark also sought the advice of older business mentors who suggested that he should stay put and be loyal to the company. This advice from earlier generations seemed sound, but sadly was no longer relevant. When Mark finally left, he joined a prestigious global consulting company. After only a year Mark left the business, discouraged and without a clear path forward. Why? He explains, "Having spent many years in the large corporate world as an employee I noticed some things that disturbed me greatly:

1. Lots of people did not derive enough pleasure from their work
2. Many of my colleagues felt they were 'losing five days a week' by going to work yet happy to sit in flat atmospheres of quiet desperation
3. Few people felt that work was personally fulfilling in any way
4. There was often an unnecessary tension between employer and employee
5. Too much energy was directed internally and channelled into corporate politics and political manoeuvring."

Mark remembers many people 'abusing the system' as a way of expressing these negative feelings. When they didn't believe they were being treated well, they took advantage of the company and when they felt the company didn't really care about their interests, they in turn didn't care about the company. It became a dysfunctional relationship.

"One problem was the short-termism in the business world," Mark explains, "and this behaviour was driven from the top. The business - rather naively - followed the market messages and the game. For example during the late 1990s, executives were encouraged to grow inorganically and borrow heavily to acquire other technology businesses, even if it made little strategic sense; yet it pleased the banks. As a result they were basically working for two arms of the banks, the brokers were fuelling the rush and generating unrealistic sale valuations and the investment banking arms were facilitating the means of acquisition and issuing the bonds or cash loans."

Mark describes management behaviour at that time as being on a short-term treadmill. All actions became 'reactions' in an attempt to just make the numbers that had been promised when they reported every 90 days. This 90 day cycle drove everything. Everyone was under pressure, and this pressure was passed down the organisation. No one seemed to be taking a longer view, or was able to put all this frenetic activity into perspective. The business world in this era became a more and more uncomfortable place to work.

"I witnessed a proportion of the human cost as a result of this pressure, and a new culture emerged," explains Mark. "The HR department had become a less influential part of the organisation so there was less input from the specialists who should have helped balance the human issues. Although the company did make some worthy attempts to work on cultural integration, it came too late. The IT bubble had burst by then and more specifically the business went to the wall, after an admission that they had submitted questionable numbers to the markets."

Mark's response

Mark went into the company looking for a career in a business that cared about its customers and its employees. He didn't find it. Instead he found a business focused solely on revenue and maximising short-term shareholder value. Hoping that he could find a better fit with his own work philosophy, he moved to in 2003 to an IT services company. Sadly, that didn't fulfil his expectations either. While working at the consulting group he immediately found himself in a challenging and complex political situation resulting in coming to work and being paid to do almost nothing. He could see that this situation might go on forever and he was intensely frustrated, so he began to develop plans for a business of his own.

Mark played with ideas and drafted plans for an innovative business that would be creative and a stimulating place to work and, above all, an organisation with values and respect for people. He wanted to build a product that he couldn't find elsewhere. Starting a company was a big risk, but so was working for a large corporate. He had worked in big business for over a decade and felt as though the companies had little to offer in terms of future security.

"From the beginning, I always wanted to believe in what I did as I spent a large part of my life working," Mark says, "and maybe I lost this belief in corporate jobs too easily, was too idealist or impatient, but I wanted work to be about more than personal gain and status. I want to be involved in a business that was producing something tangible, something that adds values such as joy and meaning to people's lives and I could feel that connection in the everyday."

Having watched his friends in high powered finance jobs in 'the City', Mark concluded that those types of career included a large element of gambling, with people betting that certain numbers (share values, for example) would increase or decrease, but not producing anything truly tangible. Mark was more determined than ever to do creative work he could be proud of and work with people, not compete against them. He wanted to work with people he liked, who liked coming into work. In short, he wanted to work in a balanced way, so that customers, employees and even the local environment was a better and happier place for his efforts.

Up until this point, Mark's experience was that the relationship of customers to large corporates was not always based on mutual respect or benefit for all parties. He decided to formulate a business in which he could work honestly with his customers, offering transparency and a good deal without trying to squeeze as much profit as possible out of every opportunity.

"I wanted my ideal company to be, not only about what we produced, but also, how we did business," Mark explains. "I wanted anyone who worked with us to thoroughly enjoy the process and I wanted the whole experience to be innovative and fun - why should work not be enjoyable?"

When Mark left his job at the global consulting company, he had the kernel of an idea and some plans, but no income. He decided to take an undemanding job so that he would have time to develop his business ideas during his own time.

College Green is born

By this time, Mark had decided to focus on publishing for the academic sector. But not just 'publishing'; Mark envisioned creating a visual documentary that artistically captured the spirit and culture of educational institutions, in particular, universities. His initial investigations suggested that there was, indeed, a gap in this market. The typical books produced for alumni and prospective students were slim picture books - usually produced by the campus photographer or a mass market company that used an inexpensive, formulaic approach. No university seemed to offer a beautiful book of the type proposed by Mark.

The next questions were: where to focus and how to start? Mark considered investing in a small UK business that aspired to produce something similar but, upon closer inspection, found a number of issues with their approach. The company had a different creative vision and was already well funded by venture capitalists (VC) who wished to drive the business to make profits. This approach was not consistent with Mark's philosophy.

As he continued his research, Mark also discovered that the UK was <u>not</u> the best market for the high quality heirloom publications that he had in mind. In the UK, alumni tend to feel a less responsible for the financial health of their educational institutions, believing it to be a government duty to provide the majority of funding. As a result, until recently, universities have done little to foster close relations with their graduates, so the bonds and loyalties that might induce an alumnus to purchase a book costing around £150 did not exist.

However, in the USA, there was a long history of alumni loyalty to educational institutions, with graduates returning regularly for reunions and donating often substantial funds to support their alma mater. These alums have a personal identity invested in their alma mater. Furthermore, there was a greater number of universities in the USA and many of them had very large alumni followings. Mark's ideas began to gel. He visualised creating, in cooperation with universities, a beautiful documentary in book form which he would market and sell to that university's alumni.

However, Mark didn't have the money to start. He was now married and his first child was on the way, so he put his idea on ice and worked in a number of freelance, consulting jobs to provide for his family. Finally, at the end of 2010, encouraged by friends and family to follow his dream, Mark set up his publishing company to create his Fine Art alumni memorabilia. Throughout 2011 he worked from scratch to develop contacts with publishers, distributors and anyone with an academic connection in the United States.

Mark's initial plan was to bear the production costs himself. The product, which he designed, involved months and months of work with an academic institution, involving photography, editorials and use of the university archives. Alumni were the target market and Mark hoped that they would buy enough copies of his beautiful books to recover costs and make a small profit. Therefore, he needed the university to provide their alumni list and support his marketing and sales efforts. He also proposed to donate 10% of all profits to the participating university's scholarship fund and loan the newly commissioned photography back to the archives. It was a win/win proposition.

Determined to create something different from, and better than, the typical flimsy university yearbooks, Mark insisted on editorial independence so he could offer an outsider's perspective. Of course he would offer the participating university final approval, but he wanted to produce something rich and timeless - not just university propaganda overtly aimed at encouraging more donations or securing more student applications. This work would do both, but would do so because it reflected the unique spirit of the institution and made alumni proud to be associated with it.

Two backers bought into Mark's vision and provided him with funds to start. In his discussions with them he was adamant about his values and approach. Everyone that *College Green* touched was to be treated with respect and consideration. Of course, the business needed to make some money, but it was not going to be a huge profit engine. The product and the quality of the process were of paramount importance. Mark was determined that he would enjoy his business - it would be hard work, but he would enjoy it. He also took a long term view, hoping to create a business that his children might one day want to work in, and eventually take over.

In 2012, after a lot of hard work, Mark finally secured his first customer, Oberlin College in Ohio, USA. Oberlin is a unique and radical institution and proud of its forward thinking and liberal tradition. While working with Oberlin, Mark strove to ensure that his principles didn't falter. It was a challenge. He had many issues with his own, mainly freelance, personnel as he negotiated a steep learning curve in people and business management. When there were difficulties, he didn't try to hide them, but informed Oberlin and let them know how he planned to fix things. He tried to 'give back' to the local community by hiring an Oberlin student for some of the on-campus work and used an Oberlin-based printer for some of the marketing work.

The final product was outstanding. It won accolades and Oberlin were very pleased. Mark's vision was proven; his next task was to repeat the process over and over again. Today, he is out on the road, flying from university to university, trying to interest them in the *College Green* approach and product. Will the business ultimately succeed? Mark has no idea. His belief is so strong that he now personally funds the business. He and his staff enjoy the work, Oberlin enjoyed the process, the book produced was unique and widely appreciated. It would certainly be shame if other universities didn't see the benefit.

Today, Mark works harder than ever before, and spends most of his time involved in the business. He employs people on a single project basis, so he does everything else as well as providing all the energy and drive for *College Green*. If he doesn't do it, it doesn't get done so he is a very, very busy man but he enjoys the work. It is creative and the whole effort embodies his philosophical beliefs. The end product, a publication which is a work of art, enables him to exercise his aesthetic approach in a commercially viable way. However, he has little 'down time' because the business depends on him.

Many social entrepreneurs find themselves in this situation. Their enterprises are small, often comprised of just one or two people, and driven by a passion for a cause. For this reason, it is notoriously difficult to meet with the founders or get them to give interviews or meetings because they have so little free time. One such example is Ayesha Mustafa and her business, *Fashion ComPassion*. As with most of our examples, Ayesha's motivations can be found in her early years.

Ayesha's story – Helping women around the world to help themselves

Inspired by early experiences

Ayesha Mustafa's story begins a little earlier than many of the others. She was born in Pakistan and lived there until she was 10 or 11 years old. After that, her family moved every few years and she lived in Egypt, New York and Dubai, finishing her high school education in Dubai. It was during her high school years that she had her 'ah ha!' moment.

When she was 16 years old, Ayesha did a summer internship for the *Grameen Foundation*, an organisation founded in 1997 to help the world's poor improve their lives. The foundation was started by Nobel Laureate Professor Muhammad Yunus, known for his early work in microfinance (work that was based on helping people reach their full potential by giving them access to finance, funding and training).

Fascinated by the model of *Grameen*, Ayesha wanted to learn more. After many months of perseverance, she finally obtained an internship at the *Grameen Foundation*. Ayesha did a rotational program in the *Foundation* but the project that was closest to her heart was one that aimed to revive the handloom industry in Bangladesh - a skill that was disappearing as a result of the growth of mass production mills.

Ayesha's first introduction to a blend of fashion, social development and business resulted from this internship. She worked with teams that developed business plans and market strategies and gradually, introduced new fabric patterns that could be marketed globally. More importantly, she observed the impact of this work on the people involved. Previously disheartened weavers became more optimistic and confident and began to make entrepreneurial efforts, once more taking charge of their own lives. Inspired, but still young, Ayesha needed to finish her own education before she could do more.

Having travelled the world, Ayesha elected to return to the USA to study Politics and Economics at Mount Holyoke College in Massachusetts, one of the original 'Seven Sisters' US Colleges dedicated to providing high calibre education for women. Driven by her experience in Pakistan and what she saw in Bangladesh, Ayesha planned to study law in college so she could become a women's rights lawyer. Her initial intention was to return to Pakistan to support women there.

In the US, law school forms part of a graduate education. To test one's appetite for law, individuals often do a few years work as a paralegal in a top tier law firm. Ayesha followed this path and took a position at the prestigious law firm of *Hughes, Hubbard & Reed* on Wall Street in New York City. After the first year, Ayesha realised that a legal career might not be the answer for her, so she did not follow up by applying to law schools. She also realised that her family had been out of Pakistan for so long, that she no longer had the infrastructure to support her efforts in that country. Still keen to help women in these countries but unsure how to do it, she quit her job and returned to her parents' home in Dubai to figure out her next steps.

Searching for the right path

While at home, Ayesha started writing and even published a small newspaper. Her writing covered many topics, but often focused on political and women's issues. She wrote about the poor treatment of many of the foreign women workers who came to Dubai to do domestic jobs, and she continued to focus on women's rights in Pakistan. Occasionally she wrote about her other interest - fashion. Ayesha's writing talent landed her a job in a Dubai PR agency and she stayed there for a few years.

Still trying to figure out how to pursue her passion, in 2005 Ayesha decided to apply to graduate school in the UK. Not entirely dismissing her earlier ambitions, she applied to law school too, but she also applied for a programme that conferred a master's in Media and Communications. She was accepted in the law programme but, in the end, decided to study Transnational Media and Communications at City University in London.

While working on her master's, Ayesha continued doing PR work for an IT company and after achieving her degree, became a retail marketing manager with *Pepsi UK* where she remained for the next three and a half years.

However, Ayesha still felt passionate about women's issues, and knew she didn't want a future practicing law. Her challenge was to find something that combined her business experience with helping disadvantaged women to improve their lives. She never forgot her experience with the *Grameen Foundation* and how good she had felt helping Bangladeshi women lift themselves out of poverty by setting up their own handloom businesses.

Although she had business and marketing know-how, Ayesha lacked experience of the fashion industry. However, she did remember what she learned in Bangladesh and decided to focus on creating a business selling hand-crafted products made by women in 'third world' countries. So, Ayesha decided to create a sales vehicle for marginalised communities all over the world. Her vision was to inject modern design to create fashionable goods that used traditional craft skills. She hoped that in the process of creating this business and working with suppliers as she had done when she was 16, she could revive and support dying skills, create jobs and businesses and enrich local communities.

Fashion ComPassion is born

Gathering her courage, Ayesha decided to set up her own business combining her interests in helping other women and fashion - and so, in 2011, *Fashion ComPassion* was born. Ayesha's goal was that everyone in her supply chain should be treated fairly and have a right to make money. Her socially responsible and sustainable fashion products - mostly accessories - are now sold both online and in selected boutiques. Ayesha's path has not always been easy and she has learned the hard way. Originally she sold a wide range of products from jewellery to clothing and everything in between - but Ayesha quickly discovered that such a broad approach was too much for a young business. So, in April 2014, Ayesha restructured and rebranded.

Since 2011, Ayesha has been selling products and travelling to meet with her suppliers in order to understand how best to help these women to do business. Ayesha has been flexible in response to the diverse situations she encountered. Some suppliers held inventory and she helped them work out the best way to pack and ship product. For these suppliers she acts only as a 'shop front.' For those who could not hold inventory or couldn't manage to pack and ship, Ayesha holds inventory and does the shipping. She does whatever she can to help the producers to be involved and sell successfully.

Ayesha now sources items from about 20 different countries,

including India, Pakistan, Malawi, Nigeria, the Philippines, Vietnam, Cambodia, Lebanon, Jordan and Palestine. Where possible she tries to understand the specific help that her producers require - can they hold stock? do they need payment quickly? - and strives to satisfy their requirements alongside running a self-sustaining company. "This business has definitely changed me and my priorities in life," Ayesha confesses. "At the moment it's very challenging to find a work/life balance because my passion for the business and helping these women takes all my time. It's very fulfilling, but it's certainly not easy. Its hard work and it takes over my life!"

Ayesha now partners with more than 15 socially responsible brands from all over the world, working closely with their founders to create new and exciting products. These products have received acclaim from leading fashion publications, such as *Vogue*, *Marie Claire*, *The Observer*, *Financial Times*, *How To Spend It*, *Grazia* and many more.

As the business expands and prospers, Ayesha intends to increase her reach and social impact. She hopes to grow her company and thereby help more women, and is now actively searching for financial backing and/or partners to support these plans. Ayesha may not achieve a good work/life balance anytime soon, but she aims to increase her social reach, helping more women and communities in more countries around the world.

Ayesha is not alone in her motivation to start a socially conscious business. The list of social enterprises grows longer each day and these businesses take many forms. Not everyone is in a position to fly around the world to source items, or to sell. Many individuals have families they want to be near or prefer to work closer to home. Vari McLuskie exemplifies a completely different approach to establishing a business that capitalises on her professional skills while addressing the needs of the not-for-profit, or charity sector. While slightly older than many of the new social entrepreneurs, Vari is no less sincere in her aspirations and it took time to gain the knowledge and experience to offer a broad range of skills to her selected market.

Vari's story – Helping charities to be more effective

The early years

In many ways Vari was ahead of the trend, a trailblazer who pursued what is now a growing trend in trying to combine personal values and 'giving back' into a professional career.

When Vari started out, she followed the path dictated by her traditional family and educational institutions. After graduating from Oxford in 1982, she took a job at what was then considered to be one of the most outstanding businesses in the world, *IBM*. At the time, *IBM* was cited as one of the top organisations in terms of business excellence and a place to learn best practices, so Vari was doing exactly what was expected of a bright, young professional in the early 1980s.

In 1988, she continued on a predictable business trajectory, attending Cranfield Business School, and being awarded her MBA. At this point she hopped right back on the career ladder and joined *Capgemini* (then *Hoskyns*), an up and coming IT professional services company. But things were changing in Vari's personal life.

At this time, Vari discovered meditation. She was introduced to the practice by a friend with whom she went on a meditation course, and then attended a meditation retreat with a well-respected Zen Master. From that point she was hooked and took up a daily practice of mindfulness and meditation. "It was simple and straightforward," Vari recalls, "and it made sense to me as a way to live my life in the real world."

Within the meditation community, practitioners strive to work mindfully in their jobs as well as their private lives and they try to select jobs that contribute positively in some way to the rest of the world. During this time, Vari continued to work at *Capgemini*. She performed various customer-oriented roles and used her focus and skills to look at ways that *Capgemini*'s customers could improve their profits while she continued to build her career along a traditional path.

Dissatisfaction grows

"As time went by, I could see my whole future mapped out ahead of me," explained Vari. "Climbing the career ladder and continuing to work for large corporations who, in turn, helped other large corporations improve their profits. I had no choice about the customers I worked with, regardless of their values, and no choice about the type of work I undertook. Gradually, I became more and more dissatisfied."

Vari explained that her dissatisfaction was not about career progression or salary, rather, it was that she wanted to carry out work that gave a positive contribution to society. There were very few business projects within *Capgemini* that fulfilled these criteria.

"I did stay 14 years," explains Vari. "Longer than I wanted and, this timing was, in part, due to my pregnancies and maternity leave." Finally in 2002, when Vari's youngest child was three years old, she left. She had no job, two young children, a mortgage and a husband whose career in the performing arts brought in an irregular income. It was a brave move, but Vari was determined to follow her convictions.

Vari's starting point was a week long course called Working for a Charity. The course included a placement in a charity and Vari's placement was in a (now defunct) organisation called *Family Service Units*. Upon completion of the placement, the managing director asked her to stay on and do some change management consulting. It was this project that made her realise, for the first time, that she could pursue a consulting career in this sector.

After completing her initial project, Vari began to chase up old friends and colleagues, to find anyone associated with the sector who could help her to get more work. Eventually she did uncover some opportunities, but they were few and far between. Not many of her friends from university ended up in charities and those that did were the exception rather than the rule. In fact, many of her old university and business school acquaintances couldn't understand what she was doing and why she wanted to work in the charity sector.

Her meditation practice kept her centred and helped her as she tried to establish a viable business in this sector. At the same time, Vari became more and more involved with meditation, becoming a trustee of a meditation charity and a regular teacher of meditation and mindfulness. Doing this activity helped her to align her life philosophy with her working practices, and Vari was able to use her knowledge of organisational best practice and her consulting skills, for organisations who 'did good' and contributed to the community.

"One thing I found was that I enjoyed doing things I felt were more worthwhile and that offered a greater challenge," she remembers.

She learned a lot from her time working in large corporations. From *IBM* Vari observed a business whose culture and processes, at that time, focused on excellence. At *Capgemini* she worked as the company experienced rapid growth and multiple changes of organisational structure and focus. From this experience she understood that change involved both processes and culture, with culture often presenting the greater challenge.

Discovering her niche

Vari soon discovered that there was a significant demand for change management in the charity sector. She learned how rapidly advancing technologies, changes in government policies and funding, and other market forces drove change in the charity sector just as much as they impacted the commercial sector - sometimes more. Such change was also being driven by an increasing use of charities' services by government and local authorities, to take on work formerly carried out by the public sector. In addition, the recession that started in 2008 meant that all organisations, including charities, needed to streamline and organise to ensure that they were both getting and giving value for money. But the challenges driving change in charities were far greater due to the culture in that sector.

"In some ways," Vari says, "the charity sector is more challenging. For example, measurements and motivation are straightforward in corporations, but in charities, it is usually much more difficult to define the benefits being delivered and to keep everyone focused on them."

"You have to recognise how people in charities are motivated. Mostly they are very committed to both the organisation and its cause - which is very positive," Vari continues. "On the other hand there can be the feeling that because they believe that they are doing their best, they don't want or need to change. The thinking tends to be along the lines of: 'Everyone is doing his or her best - so why do we need to change anything?'"

"Of course," Vari concludes, "a change programme can work to better align all these hard working individuals and better coordinate their efforts - thereby delivering far more to the charitable cause."

Vari went on to emphasise how in charities, measuring the benefits of any change programme had to be qualitative as well as quantitative in order to ensure its success. The nature of what some of these organisations are trying to do is complex, and measuring the impact can be costly and more complicated than in a commercial enterprise. Yet, overall, Vari has found working with this sector very rewarding, partly because she feels she is working with organisations whose aims are to benefit people or society, but also because the work itself is challenging.

To provide this work, Vari co-founded a small, specialist consulting business, *Verve Consulting Ltd. Verve* offers services at a far lower fee rate to charitable organisations, which now constitute 70-80% of its work. The other work she does for interest or to enable her to provide for her family and she continues to devote the majority of her effort to the charitable sector at a much reduced fee. "If I did it all *pro bono* - and *Verve Consulting Ltd* has done some *pro bono* work - we couldn't afford to do as much work in charities as we currently do," Vari explains. "And there is a high demand in this sector for good quality, experienced consultants. The challenge is: how do you integrate socially involved working? Either you do it on the side, after work, or do it for money so that you can do more of it."

Another key reason for charging a fee is that key individuals in an organisation must be involved in any change programme and these individuals always struggle to find enough time. When something is 'free' it tends to drop to the bottom of the priority list and is, in fact, valued less by the client. When clients pay, they usually participate more fully. Finally, *pro bono* work is, of necessity, short term because some fee paying work must fund the effort or *Verve Consulting Ltd* and any other consultancies like it, would go out of business. A short term commitment is just not enough to ensure the successful design and implementation of a major change programme.

Over time, Vari's professional work and interest in meditation are merging together. To enable the organisations that she works with to both survive <u>and</u> thrive as they progress through their organisational changes, Vari has begun to introduce meditation and mindfulness training into her work. This support gives the teams an increased awareness of the emotional impact of changes on them and their colleagues and offers them the choice to react in effective and low stress ways.

Now that mindfulness has become a buzzword, Vari is in a privileged position where she can integrate her decades of mindfulness practice with her organisational change experience so she can offer a uniquely tailored approach to culture change.

"I am happy with my career path now," Vari concludes. "I'm doing the kind of work I want to do and integrating my personal philosophy and values with my daily work."

Vari is another example of someone who 'dropped out' of the typical career trajectory to look for a more personally fulfilling career. She didn't jettison her education and experience, rather, she built on it to create a new career. In doing so, she took a significant financial risk and has settled for a less financially rewarding job. However, she now leads a balanced life, doing a job she loves, spending time with her family and actively pursuing her interest in meditation and mindfulness.

In fact, all the stories in this chapter show individuals driven by conviction who have sacrificed the opportunity to gain greater personal wealth in order to fund and work in a business that gives something back to society, and gives them personal satisfaction. The work isn't always easy nor is it always a success - many lessons are learned along the way. But in all cases the process of 'work' is more fulfilling. In fact, this trend has become so prevalent that social enterprises now attract young people who are just starting out in their work life. These millennials are skipping the step of working in corporations and heading straight for the values driven jobs in social enterprises and charities.

Chapter 7

CHARITIES

> "A career in the charity sector?
> You can't make a career out of rattling a tin can and collecting spare change!"
>
> **Advice given by an Oxford University careers counsellor in the 1980s**

Why 'put the soul back into business?' If people want to 'give back', why fool around in business at all? Why not just start, or join, a charity and make 'giving back' a full time profession? The simple answer is that, until only a few years ago, working in the charity sector wasn't viewed as a profession. Traditionally, in the UK, becoming head of a charity tended to be a 'retirement post', taken up by individuals who had left the armed services. It was an end-of-career move rather than a career in itself, often a final step toward obtaining an 'honour' for service to the country. In the main, a charity's staff tended to be volunteers, typically married women without paid jobs. But things have changed.

Over the last few decades, more and more married women have moved into paid employment, so this source of volunteer labour has diminished. Other things have changed too. Many services once provided by government - national or local - are now being outsourced to not-for-profit and social enterprises. These changes, plus other shifts in society, mean that the charity sector is now seen as a viable career path. Furthermore, many of its managers transfer across from the private sector and have brought more rigorous business practices to the delivery of their services. In fact, some charities now help their constituents to set up businesses, and some of the examples in this chapter illustrate this new approach.

Typically, throughout most of the 20th century, young people who were well-educated and pursuing post-graduate degrees simply didn't 'waste' this education by working for a charity, and certainly not at the start of their career. The quote at the beginning of this chapter exemplifies the challenge that once faced individuals considering working in this sector. In the 1980s, bright, qualified individuals were encouraged to seek careers in the business world, government service, academia, law, accountancy or medicine. High-powered young people with a social conscience tended to opt for a public sector career.

In Britain, up until the 1980s, the public expected government to take a leading role in balancing the inequalities in society and to support those who needed help. Healthcare, pensions and education were a universal 'right', paid for by the state. Young people who had grown up in the 1980s with these assumptions tended to feel less inclined to take personal responsibility. In that decade, a new government came to power that espoused a less socialist approach and 'The Big Society' philosophy of post-war Britain began to be dismantled. These changes led to an evolution in the charity and not-for-profit sector as the government slowly devolved many of its activities to this sector.

So, despite what the Oxford careers counsellor said in the 1980s, something did change in UK society that made working for a charity a viable career option. Statistics compiled since 1993 indicate that the number of paid employees in the charity sector doubled between 1993 and 2009, moving from a little over 1% to 2.6% of the total UK workforce. This growth occurred despite a significant recession that saw a contraction of jobs in the private sector. Some of this shift was fuelled by a change in government policy, which led to the outsourcing of services and transfer of staff from local authorities and government departments to charitable organisations. But outsourcing alone does not account for all the growth. While the number of individuals working in this sector has increased, so has the percentage with higher degrees and professional qualifications. (see References).

Despite this shift in the job market and an increasing number of people electing to work in this sector, it takes a very special and very determined individual to turn away from a more traditional and lucrative profession to follow such a career path. In this chapter you will read the stories of individuals who made this choice because they very much wanted to make a difference. In one case, public service was a first step, then jettisoned because the slow pace of change and the politics of the job proved to be too frustrating. Others started out in a traditional career - the law - that, in the end, did not provide enough personal satisfaction. Finally, another used his professional training in law and finance to establish a new type of charity. All of these individuals were spurred on by ideals that led them to select lower paid positions in order to do more personally fulfilling work.

Adam Sampson's story provides an excellent example of a highly educated person trying to carve out a meaningful career in this sector when there was no obvious path. The quote at the beginning of this chapter has remained in his consciousness for more than 30 years. Against the prevailing current of the times, he did end up pioneering a career in and around the charity sector. He built his career initially in the public sector, later moving into charity work in order to contribute significant social benefit. Adam's own words express the attitude and determination that were necessary to build his career. As always, we will start in his youth to understand the circumstances that shaped his attitudes and approach.

Adam's story – Pioneering a career in the not-for-profit sector

Early life and education

"I have a deep suspicion of people who speak in visionary language," Adam stated as the interview began. "If there is any single, driving force in selecting my jobs, it's been to avoid taking jobs where people tell me how to do something."

Adam grew up in a house that his father bought with a small amount of money left over after bankruptcy. His family valued knowledge, 'thinking' and the Arts; Adam describes his childhood home life as "culturally rich but financially poor." His father, though very intelligent, would have been diagnosed today as suffering from Bipolar disorder and spent much of his life at the depressive end of the spectrum. When Adam eventually obtained his place at Oxford, he would be the first in his family to attend university.

Starting at the beginning of his career, Adam explained how his work in the third sector began during his 'seventh term', the period after A-levels (the end of school exams in the UK), when some students spent time doing extra study for the Oxford University entrance exam. As he had no money, he couldn't use this time to travel. He needed a job. Checking the advertisements in the back of *Private Eye* magazine he saw that the Petrus Community Hostel for homeless people in Liverpool was recruiting. The pay was low - the equivalent of 'the dole' (unemployment welfare payment in the UK) - but it was a job and it offered accommodation.

Adam ended up running a homeless shelter, which was located next door to a brothel. It wasn't in the most salubrious neighbourhood in Liverpool. When asked what he took away from this experience, Adam replies, "lice and a couple of scars!" He then went on to say that this short, eye-opening period cemented his views about some of the social issues present in British society. Nonetheless, he continued on his path to attend university. He passed the Oxford entrance exams and was offered a place to study Classics.

After graduation, Adam knew only what he <u>didn't</u> want. "I didn't want to do 'the milk round' (the nickname for the process by which blue chip companies compete to recruit new graduates). When my career counsellor at Oxford heard about my interest in the third sector he told me 'you can't make a career out of rattling collection tins!'" Indeed, Adam's experience highlights the point that in the 1970s and early 1980s, in England, there was no such thing as a 'career' in the charitable sector. Rich individuals did 'good works' or 'founded charities', and socially-minded people volunteered to run them. Even so, it was the third sector where Adam focused his job searches.

Finding his way

After finishing university, Adam briefly managed a pub before he finally got a position working in the Probation Service in West London. After doing this job for a while, he went back to Oxford to complete a master's degree in order to return to the service as a probation officer. This work was based in Tottenham, an inner London district, and Adam stayed until he became embroiled in a very public, political situation.

Standing by his principles, Adam left the Probation Service and found a job in a charity, the *Prison Reform Trust*. In his five years working at the *Trust*, Adam started as the policy officer and later became deputy director. In the early 1990s he played a key role in drafting the government agenda for prison reforms. As a result he found himself setting up the Prison Ombudsman where he took on the role of assistant Ombudsman.

Adam explains, "I like solving problems, finding solutions to challenging issues. I bore easily and these situations provide a challenge. When I have done as much as I can do in a given organisation, I need to move on." And Adam did move on - to *Rapt*, a charity set up to help ex-offenders to overcome alcohol and drug dependence. He remained there for six years and then moved on to become the CEO of *Shelter*, a charity for the homeless. Adam spent seven years at *Shelter*, making changes to adapt the organisation to the challenges of homelessness within the confines of shifting government policies and support. When he finally left *Shelter* it was to establish a new Legal Ombudsman and take up the role of Chief Ombudsman.

Despite the cynicism of the Oxford careers counsellor about finding a career in the third sector, Adam has moved from role to role and strength to strength. He credits his interest in this sector to two things:

1. A desire to believe in what he's doing
2. A desire to experiment and solve problems in new and different ways

Expanding on the first point, Adam explains, "I'm not interested much in management, but I'm a good leader and if I have to lead and sell an idea, then I absolutely have to believe in it. I would never survive working in a bureaucracy - so that rules out more traditional businesses and the public sector."

"I could have set up my own business and I have considered it a number of times, but I'm just not that interested in money. I like having it, but it doesn't motivate me the way ideas do."

Adam then talked about his personality, and why the desire to experiment and solve problems is so important to him. "My personal challenge is that I like ideas and I like to 'do'. I would rather be in a 'do tank' than a 'think tank'. That's why I like the volunteer sector. I believe it's a crucible for experimentation in novel ways to solve problems. There is no harm in trying something new. Sometimes things fail, but sometimes they succeed. There is nothing wrong with hoping for the best while expecting the worst. That's why I believe it does little good to campaign against something. What people should do is campaign <u>for</u> some positive alternative."

So, while Adam didn't exactly choose a career in the charitable sector - after all, at that time it was not really an option - he accepted jobs that chimed with his principles and motivation. Then it was with his eyes wide open that he began working in the Probation Service. Even at the time he was aware the he was taking a career path that was leading him away from the traditional trajectory. He saw this direction as a fertile ground for experimentation and the implementation of new ideas and social solutions.

Adam describes UK society at the time in which he entered the job market. "I was brought up in the 1960s and 70s - a product of 'The Big State,'" Adam explains. "When I left Oxford and was ready to look for work, Thatcher was in place and 'The Big State' began to shrink. There was then a lot more work for charities to do."

Taking a leadership role

Adam continued to be involved in charitable institutions. In 2010, he joined the charity *FareShare* as chairman. *FareShare* takes food from retailers who would have thrown it away and redistributes and provides it at a low cost to charities around the UK. Adam remembers very well his days working in hostels, and how he had to purchase food at full price from retailers. Today, these types of charities can apply to *FareShare* and purchase food at a lower price, making their funds go further.

The *FareShare* website describes its objectives as "tacking the twin issues of food waste and food poverty". In this role, Adam interacted with large corporations through the food supplier chain in an effort to sustain a steady and reliable source of goods fit for consumption. Contributions from major retailers are not a 'done deal'. Every quarter *FareShare* must deal with shifts in corporate trends which could steer the waste food to a different source, such as composting. Having invested in a substantial infrastructure - warehouses around the UK to store the food and vans to distribute it, these unpredictable changes in policies by food retailers or wholesalers can wreak havoc on *FareShare's* own 'customers' and decimate its supply chain.

Having now moved on, and left the Ombudsman role, Adam

continues to be involved in other creative initiatives with the private sector - initiatives which strive to alleviate social problems. Having been CEO of *Shelter* for many years, Adam is very aware of the shortage of social housing. Even after Gordon Brown (when in Government) made housing a top priority and announced an increase in funding, this action was not nearly enough. Adam calculated that the UK needs at least four times as much funding in order to provide adequate social housing and was determined to find a way to tackle the housing shortage.

"So, I figured that there was going to have to be a private sector model for social housing," explains Adam. "There is always money to be made out of housing so all I needed to do was to figure out a business model that supported some social housing as well as regular rental properties." Having determined that any successful model meant 'long term' payback, Adam considered which investors took a long term view and came up with… pension funds. "This thinking is unique," Adam believes. "But when I left *Shelter* I was approached by a couple of guys with the right mix of skills and contacts and I thought we could make it work!"

Adam spent two years trying to identify 'killer flaws' in his plan and when he found none he became convinced that his model could work as an alternative to state funded housing. The current challenge has to do with how fund management is organised in the pension companies. Currently, this kind of funding falls between two different departments, making it everyone's, and yet no one's, focus area within fund management departments. Adam and his partners continue to pursue this vision and regularly speak to the pension funds to further their idea.

Adam enjoys working on creative solutions to social problems. In fact, Adam just plain enjoys solving problems. His 'accidental' career in the third sector provided an ideal crucible for this activity. But things are changing in this sector. Adam explains, "Today, the charity sector is crowded. Now, people <u>do</u> move into this sector as a career and there are lots and lots of charities. Why? Because charities come into being very easily… and it's much more difficult to get rid of them." Adam goes on to explain that the increasing number of charities means that there is a 'white noise' of campaigning and fundraising that can deafen the contributing public.

"When I went into this sector, it was really an alternative to a career. Today it is a career and as a result, many of the charitable organisations are moving farther and farther from the end-user. This means that the charity moves farther from understanding the problems of its constituents and becomes divorced from them," Adam continues. "There are also issues with the effectiveness of many of the organisations themselves. Unlike businesses, charities don't 'fail' in the face of competition. Hostile takeovers are unknown. And, although both these situations are unpleasant, in a commercial business, they serve a Darwinian function - improve, adapt or disappear."

Fundamentally, Adam believes that charitable status should be subject to review and renewal and at that point, the following questions should be asked:

- Is the charity still giving social worth?
- Is it still necessary for the charity to exist?

In fact, in the end, despite the dire predictions of his university careers advisor, Adam did create a successful and fulfilling career in the charity and not-for-profit services sector. He continues to seek out challenging problems to fix - as much to satisfy his own need for mental stimulation and to be close to real issues. His creative approach blurs the lines between private and third sectors when designing long term solutions for social issues and his professionalism has introduced some of the effective and efficient organisational principles often missing from charitable organisations. His work continues and his actions, although ahead of his time, illustrate universal truths about how others stumbled onto this career path.

One important point that Adam makes is that it is important for him to 'do' something and feel like he is solving a problem. Interestingly, many individuals in the traditional professions, particularly those mid-way up the corporate ladder, complain that their work doesn't 'do' anything significant - except perhaps, make money for their employers. And it is this sense of personal effectiveness, whether making a big or a small impact, that is important. It is the 'ability to act' that's critical. Large corporations and governments have a role to play, but the way they are run today, things happen very, very slowly. Good social solutions may be sacrificed to the pace of bureaucracy. And, as Adam noted, even large charities can suffer from bureaucracy and poor management.

So, today the not-for-profit sector is recognised as a career option. However, while those who opt for such careers are admired by their peers, they are still the exception rather than the rule. Most individuals who take this route won't realise the same financial rewards as their peers employed in a business. However, many are driven by a passion that they feel balances any remunerative shortcomings, and most strongly value the sense of 'doing something meaningful' and seeing the impact of their actions. Like Adam, the people chronicled in this chapter are all very intelligent and all of them enjoy the challenge of solving problems and getting results.

While Adam started working before there was really such a thing as a career in the charity sector, Baillie has only recently graduated from university. She has not only worked in partnership with the public sector - the prison service, just like Adam - but worked as a volunteer before starting not one but two charities herself. In many ways she exemplifies the theme of this book. Baillie's charities help to teach people who have been in prison the entrepreneurial and practical skills necessary to start their own businesses as a route to economic self-sufficiency and desistance from crime.

Baillie's story – Teaching entrepreneurial skills to people in prison

Family culture and education

Baillie Aaron began by talking about her youth, explaining that her parents were always involved in community affairs and charitable activities when she grew up. Both were professionals - her father was a family lawyer who often took *pro bono* cases and her mother trained as an architect. "Even as a child I took part in a lot of volunteer activities, both with my family and by myself," Baillie explains. "It was just a part of the family culture."

Baillie's childhood and teenage years were busy and she took part in many academic programmes in addition to her volunteer work. One such programme was Junior Achievement, an entrepreneurship programme for high school students. "Today," Baillie observes, "most of the students in a similar programme in the UK create social businesses.

These are typically for-profit businesses with an ethical focus and/or ethical sourcing policies; but this approach was not the norm in Canada when I was in high school. There seems to have been a shift in outlook amongst this generation of students."

After high school, Baillie went to the United States to attend Harvard University where she studied Economics and Psychology because she assumed, with her entrepreneurial tendencies, that she would pursue a career in the business world. Baillie did well in her studies and, at the same time, continued to volunteer wherever she could. For example, she was a mentor for younger Harvard students during her Sophomore, Junior and Senior years.

As her graduation approached, Baillie began to consider her next steps. She looked at consulting, a favourite first step on the career ladder for business-oriented graduates. However, after careful examination, she rejected that path because it didn't feel right. She wanted some balance in her life and consultants typically worked extremely long hours. In the end, she applied for two jobs, one at Harvard and another at Stanford University, but ultimately, turned those down as well. Finally, without an obvious 'next step', Baillie returned home to her parents in Calgary, Canada where she explored her options and applied for jobs.

After three months she took a risk and moved back to Boston, ultimately securing a research position at the Program in Criminal Justice Policy and Management at the Kennedy School of Government (Harvard University). While undertaking this job Baillie thought to herself, "You know, I have never been in prison. I haven't ever had troubles with the police. How can I research this policy without a better understanding of how it feels to be on the receiving end of policing policy?"

The catalyst

With this objective in mind, Baillie approached *Phillips Brooks House Association* (*PBHA*), a volunteer organisation at Harvard that, among other things, focuses on matching undergraduates with volunteering opportunities. *PBHA* found Baillie a position tutoring individuals in prison who wanted to get a GED (General Educational Development, a high school equivalency test) qualification. Baillie describes this tutoring experience as 'the catalyst' that set her on her current career trajectory.

She explains, "One guy who was in his late 20s had the equivalent of a third grade education and I had the task of bringing him up through nine more years of schooling so he could get his GED."

"My first 'ah ha!' moment came when I understood that the traditional educational format wasn't relevant to him and got in the way of his learning. He couldn't 'do' or 'understand' the homework problems the way they were presented in the traditional course. However, if I 'translated' the questions into things he understood - the type of business transactions he had learned on the street, he suddenly could solve all the problems. I got excited."

Baillie went on to relate how her excitement turned to frustration when she realised just how poor this young man's job prospects would be once he was released from prison. Few employers hire people with a criminal record, GED or no GED. As she pondered the predicament, she remembered her experience in high school with Junior Achievement and entrepreneurial business skills. Then, she thought about her prisoner student.

He had told Baillie about a business he was running within the prison - creating and selling greetings cards. In addition to designing and making a product, and finding supplies within the prison, her student successfully sold his wares to other people in prison and invented a currency that could be exchanged within the prison community. All of these activities were, of course, against prison policy, but they did illustrate a good business mind and entrepreneurial skills. So Baillie was inspired to consider a different option. Perhaps she could help him to take a different approach when he was released, and guide him to start his own business.

As a first step, Baillie began to investigate the entrepreneurial options for people with criminal records. They were far from ideal - for example, in the US it is very difficult for people with a prison record to get a business loan or obtain certain types of business licenses - but after due consideration it seemed like the best option for securing work for appropriately skilled people with criminal records. Many of these individuals had worked for illegal enterprises or run under-the-table businesses prior to incarceration so they had basic (and in some cases, advanced) business skills. Hooked by this idea, Baillie started to design and organise an entrepreneurial business skills course for a select group of people in prison.

Though Baillie was still employed full-time as a researcher at Harvard Kennedy School, she filled all her spare time with organising and preparing this first educational course. She went back to *PBHA* to find more volunteers to help her to deliver it. In the evenings after work, they went to the Harvard Business School (HBS) library to teach themselves the necessary business skills. Her next step was to approach a prison in which to trial her course and here, she had a lucky break, as the prison where she had been tutoring offered to let her give it a go.

The pilot course was offered to about a dozen people in prison, all of whom were adult men who expressed an interested in starting their own businesses post-release. Baillie learned a lot of lessons in these early attempts to build and deliver training. After she expanded the course, she went to Harvard Business School in search of volunteers to help her teach. And here she learned her first lesson. Her learnings?

"Many business school students have a very theoretical approach and my students needed pragmatic, action-oriented instruction with far less analysis," Baillie explains. "Furthermore, the backgrounds of most of the HBS students were vastly different from my students. Most of them came from good homes with lots of family support. And those who had run businesses tended to work in large, multinational organisations not small, low-cost enterprises. Therefore, it was difficult for them to put themselves the position of the students in prison when they taught. Furthermore, the HBS students rarely had to rely only on themselves to do everything when they were working in a business. After engaging with these volunteers for one course, I looked elsewhere for volunteers who really understood the challenges that entrepreneurs in Boston trying to start low-cost businesses with minimal resources would face."

What she did learn from this experience was that the Harvard name really did open doors, both within Harvard University itself and in the community at large. She set out to expand her program, getting more trainers through the Boston entrepreneurial community. Through Baillie's boss at Harvard Kennedy School and her interactions with various prisons, she was introduced to the Commissioner of the Massachusetts State Department of Correction as well as the Commissioner of the Massachusetts Department of Youth Services, who were both women. Baillie found that within the criminal justice system, where women were a visible minority, there was a tight-knit network of women supporting other women, which proved invaluable to Baillie in developing the course. The (now former) Commissioner of the Massachusetts Department of Correction continues to support Baillie as her mentor to this day.

With the support of these women, the volunteer teachers, and other stakeholders in the criminal justice system, Baillie set up courses in other prisons in Massachusetts and soon, she developed another course aimed at 11-18 year olds. Baillie also piloted a community-based course for people with criminal records who were also going through drug and alcohol rehabilitation - yet another obstacle that often blocks the future progress of individuals leaving prison.

Baillie was very, very busy. It's ironic that she had turned down traditional graduate jobs because she wanted more of a work/life balance, only to find herself working flat out - weekends, all day and late into the night. "It was taking over my life," says Baillie. "But I loved it and I loved it more than my traditional research job."

Starting again

By 2009, all this extra work on top of a full-time job became too much so Baillie quit her job and threw herself wholeheartedly into running her prison courses. Eventually, one of the trainers, Laura Winig, became more involved and together they set up an organisation which, in 2010, became a non-profit called *Venturing Out*. The training carried out by this entity included a three-month education course, Entrepreneurship 101, aimed at people about to be released from prison.

Although enjoying herself, Baillie did not see *Venturing Out* as her life's work. She still struggled with the idea that she should go back to university to earn a graduate degree. Furthermore, she was a Canadian citizen in the USA, now without a job, and the US would not issue her with a visa to do charity work.

So, once again, Baillie was on the move - despite doing good work in the Boston area. She took a couple of internships, one of which helped set up an entrepreneurship programme at an 'at risk' high school in Cambridge, Massachusetts, USA and another in Israel doing research on sentencing policy for a Law Professor. It was at this point that she realised that she really didn't want to do research anymore and that she preferred to 'do' things and work with people. However, by this time she had applied and been accepted at Cambridge University in the UK to do a master's degree in Criminological Research.

While working on her master's in the UK, Baillie continued to do local volunteer work in Cambridge and began to work on her business plan for another charitable organisation, which she called *Spark Inside*. As she worked on the business plan she was still undecided about her future. Baillie enjoyed working with people in prison and those with criminal records but knew that Canada was not the place to find serious issues of crime and reoffending - especially when compared to the USA or the UK. She already knew she could not get back to the USA on the basis of starting a charity due to visa restrictions, no matter how great the need for the charitable services. *Spark Inside* was devised for the UK. She entered her business plan in a contest and promised herself that if she won, she would stay in the UK and implement it. If she lost, she would return to Canada.

In 2011, Baillie's plan won the Cambridge University Entrepreneurs Social Enterprise Award, so she moved to London and set up *Spark Inside* in January 2012. Once she started the work, Baillie loved it and decided that running this charity, which offered life coaching to young people in prison, was exactly what she wanted to do. She also remarked upon how much easier it was to do this work in the UK than it was in Massachusetts and how she could make progress more quickly. "The Government here is much more progressive and more supportive of this sort of effort than they are in the USA," Baillie explains. "Here there are more foundations and philanthropists who will give money and support for charities operating in the criminal justice system. It makes it so much easier to have an impact."

Happy for now and the foreseeable future, Baillie does <u>not</u> see *Spark Inside* as her lifelong career. "Social Entrepreneurship, yes," she says, "but there are so many causes that I'm passionate about and to which I could make a difference and I may not always focus on the criminal justice system. From the work I have done I know that I am much better at setting things up than running established organisations. When *Spark Inside* is fully established I will probably hand it over and start something else."

"Where will I go?" she asks rhetorically. "Canada just does not have as many problems as the US and the UK and I would rather be challenged and tackle a big problem. So I will probably <u>not</u> return to Canada in the short term."

"My interest? Well, I'm not really interested in criminal justice research - or not as interested as I was when I was in university. I just want to do practical things, fix problems."

"My biggest struggle still, is finding that work/life balance. I am happy and I love my job so I haven't resented the time I spent on it, but I need to figure out how to make time in my life for relationships with friends and family as well."

"I still struggle with some 'big questions', like how do you achieve broad change in society - the sort of change that's needed to help fully integrate people with criminal records back into wider society? It will take a shift in thinking. Well, while I struggle with this question, I can still do practical things to help."

Although her experience of this situation is a few decades later than Adam's, Baillie's personal drivers are the same: she wants to 'do' rather than theorise and she wants to solve problems. In Baillie's case, she started her own charity - twice, once in the USA and again in the UK - in order to create a vehicle for her efforts. She has made an impact and she has helped people. Still only in its fourth year of existence, *Spark Inside* has already garnered support from a huge range of corporate sponsors, charitable trusts and government bodies. In fact, *Spark Inside* won the 2014 Charity Staff and Volunteer Award.

So, Baillie did not start the traditional climb up the professional career ladder expected of a Harvard graduate with a master's from Cambridge. Instead she has elected to follow her passion and her desire to solve problems, to do 'something meaningful' for society and to help people. Although she didn't follow a well-defined route, none of her peers or mentors criticised her choice. Times have moved on, and unlike Adam, Baillie is not alone. Baillie, like the others, takes a more 'business-like' approach - not only in the services she provides but in the infrastructure and measurements of her own charity.

This move to create new practices and measures in charitable organisations is also growing. No longer is it good enough to be 'doing good' - it's also important to make a significant impact and to measure effects. With the influx of professionals into this sector, many new charities have a different culture, something closer to that of a social enterprise rather than a traditional charity. How does one define these cultures and what are the differences? In fact, the lines are blurring. The impulse behind Paul Cheng's charity, *SharedImpact*, is very similar to that of *JustGiving* (a 'for profit, for good' enterprise mentioned in an earlier chapter). However, there were good legal reasons for Paul to take the route he did, and having studied the law, Paul was well positioned to select the best legal structure for his work.

Paul C's story – Strategic philanthropy

Starting out

Paul was born in London to parents who were both doctors. They came to the UK from Hong Kong to pursue their education, met, married and settled in London. Paul's upbringing was 'typically' English. He went to boarding school when he was 12 years old and he describes it as a very privileged education. "I didn't realise it at the time, of course," Paul explains. "I thought it was normal that everyone studied to enter Oxford or Cambridge. I didn't question the future, I just followed the well-worn path that was laid out for me." So follow it he did, and very successfully too.

He left boarding school to attend Oxford University where he read Law. From there Paul moved to a top London law firm where his work focused on corporate finance. In most ways Paul fitted the model of a burgeoning successful professional. Yet, after about five years working in law, he began to realise that 'something' wasn't right - he wasn't happy. This realisation has led him to where he is today, the founder and chairman of *SharedImpact*, a charity - a new kind of charity, but a charity nonetheless. Why? What happened?

Well, Paul didn't exactly turn away from his education and his experience working in a traditional law firm. Rather, he has built on his background and his knowledge to create something new and unique. While Paul hated the work in the traditional firm, he loves what he is doing now and he makes use of his legal education. So, what's the difference? The answer is similar to that of our other stories: the meaning and objectives of his work have changed and Paul's personal journey illustrates why.

Having followed the traditional path and found it unsatisfying, Paul quit the law and went to the Kellogg School of Management in Illinois, USA, to study for an MBA. He still didn't know what he wanted to do, but he studied business management, keeping his eyes open for interesting opportunities. It was in business school that he first heard the term social enterprise and he began to explore it for himself. Unfortunately, when he returned to the UK with his MBA in 2003, no one had heard of it, so he was faced with a blank slate.

As a 'first step', Paul spoke to someone who ran an investment fund that loaned money to charities. Such activity was a 'big deal' in 2003 because, at that time, most charities raised money from donations or they didn't survive. Taking out loans, even low cost loans, was just not done. Charities ran on a 'shoestring' and tended not to set up their organisations with the same disciplines as 'for profit' businesses. In 2003-4, Paul decided to work for *Venturesome*, part of the *Charities Aid Foundation*, and became one of the pioneers in developing new ways to finance charities and social purpose organisations

The idea crystallises

While he ran a fund that supported charities, Paul kept asking himself how he could make more of a social impact. In analysing his personal 'wants' as well as the market, he realised that the critical issue wasn't to scale up his current organisation, or a charity modelled along the same lines. Rather, it was about acting as a catalyst in the market to enable others to adopt and carry out his ideas and build a greater force for good.

"It's counterintuitive, but unlike traditional businesses which fear copycat activity as competitive," explains Paul, "I wanted others to offer the same services so that more charities could benefit." Paul went on to explain his belief that it's time to rethink how we finance charities and engage in effective charitable giving. "The traditional image of a rich person giving money to a poor one is no longer accurate. It doesn't work that way anymore."

Paul continues, "A rich man does not give to a poor man anymore. Instead, a rich man gives to an intermediary (the charity sector), which ultimately deploys the money to help the poor man. But as a society we expect the intermediary (i.e. charities) to be as poor as the poor man. This is not only irrational, but also results in a highly dysfunctional and ineffective charity sector."

"The debate around charity overheads is a vivid example of how wrong much of our society thinking about charity is," Paul elaborates. "A charity with low overheads does not mean that it is an effective charity. In fact, quite the contrary - low overheads are often a sign that the charity has not invested sufficiently in its infrastructure, and as a result offers a poor service to its beneficiaries. People who obsess about low overheads in charities completely miss the point. We should be obsessed about good outcomes, not low overheads. If you are an ineffective charity, I really don't care how low your overheads are!"

Paul explains his theory about the evolution of these attitudes. "There are some irrational ideas about charities that pervade the community at large and the charity sector in particular. Many of these stem from the days when puritans worked hard to make money, but felt guilty for doing so. Therefore, they set up charities to alleviate their guilt - but they made certain that the charities did not resemble businesses in any way. In fact, these charities resembled their beneficiaries - poor, makeshift and unbusinesslike." Paul believes that this attitude persists in many charities to this day and does no good for the communities that they purport to help. Instead, he believes that we should focus on the effective outcomes that we want charities to achieve, rather than become obsessed by process and procedural niceties that may no longer serve the purpose for which they were originally intended.

At the other end of the spectrum, many charities resent paying a commercial rate for products or services and end up wasting money by paying money for inferior goods just because they feel they shouldn't have to pay the same as everyone else. Paul mentions Dan Pallotta, whom he praises as one of the greatest fundraisers of our time. Dan Pallotta raised millions of dollars for charity - but eventually his charity had to close because of a media backlash against his apparently high overhead costs.

Much of charitable giving today is 'expressive giving' which often has more to do with the good feelings of the donor rather than the help given to the recipient. However, there is a new movement afoot, 'strategic philanthropy' which is geared towards solving social problems - especially the root causes of such problems (rather than simply putting a *Band-Aid* on problems). Paul supports and promotes strategic philanthropy.

Taking the plunge

So, although Paul continued to work for *Venturesome*, running a fund and helping charities, he felt that he was not making a big enough impact. He was also becoming frustrated by the company, which he felt had become very political and bureaucratic. So in 2012 he left and set up *SharedImpact*. His experience up to this point had taught him many things. Among them was the fact that although we now live in a global world where donors think globally, the services currently provided to donors have not kept pace and seem more suited to the 19th century than to the 21st.

SharedImpact offers a platform that helps to overcome some of these limitations and is a real example of a philanthropic engine that enables people to solve social problems. The business model is one that combines fund management with charitable giving. Donors can view a range of options presented (and vetted) by *SharedImpact*. Their money is deployed and any profits can be distributed as the donor dictates. If the fund continues to do well, then the investment continues to 'pay out' and these funds will then be distributed as selected by donors, on an ongoing basis. Donors cannot recover any profits for themselves personally, but they can continue to designate recipients. In this way, charitable money can be recycled over and over again.

Paul describes his organisation as a cross between a private bank and a law firm. He now uses his knowledge of the law in earnest as he works with tax officials in Hong Kong, the United Kingdom and the United States to create this new type of philanthropic fund management service.

Global tax systems often inhibit international giving. One of the things that Paul has accomplished with *SharedImpact* is that taxpayers in multiple jurisdictions can now claim, via *SharedImpact,* all the charitable tax benefits that they are legally entitled to (and which until now have been very complicated to claim). Paul describes *SharedImpact* as a "one-stop shop" for effective, charitable giving and he is trying to set the standard for how this service can be delivered around the world.

At the moment, *SharedImpact's* target donors are high net worth individuals and families. Many of them wish to make anonymous donations and *SharedImpact* can cater for that wish too. Most of these people are cash rich and time poor, so *SharedImpact* does much of the laborious administrative work for them, carefully vetting both donors and recipients - not just anyone can sign up to be a charitable recipient or investee via *SharedImpact*.

Paul explains how he measures the success of his organisation. "Most donor-advised funds are just tax planning vehicles. This is great for the donors who get tax benefit and good for the fund managers getting their fees, but not so good for charities. For example, donor-advised funds tend to measure their success by how much money they have under management. But funds should not be judged by how much money they are sitting on, rather, by how much money they are actually deploying to charities - after all, that is the whole purpose of the tax break for donations to charities!"

Paul finds his work very satisfying - intellectually challenging and meaningful. He admits that he feels very privileged to be chairman of the organisation. "Fifteen years ago this industry didn't exist! It's very satisfying to be part of the beginning and to create something that others can follow. Young people starting out in the job market today, people in their 20s, want to have work that's meaningful and I believe that we are providing an avenue for them to follow."

Paul had a big vision and has already gone some way to achieving it. He wants to create a global institution and, he declares, "I want to raise the standards in this sector and help to foster a new breed, next-generation charity which is 'businesslike' in its efficiency and impact-oriented."

So what kind of an organisation is *SharedImpact*? Is it a social enterprise or a charity? "Oh, definitely a charity," Paul replies. "And we are proud of our charitable status. Charities can be as strategic and as professionally run as the best businesses. I hope to lead the way by example."

Paul's comments about the old values and ideas surrounding charities reflect the ideas of many people today. Merely 'wanting to do good' should not justify a charity's existence and simply being a charity does not mean that 'good business practices' should be ignored. This attitude can waste donors' money and diminish the potential impact of the organisation. And just because a charity might, for example, help the poor, it doesn't mean that the charity itself should be poor. However, as Adam mentioned in his story, a charity shouldn't become too large, or so complex and distant, that it gets cut off from its beneficiaries or, in the case of traditional charity fund managers, it shouldn't serve itself and its donors before its beneficiaries. After all, every charity is set up to serve the beneficiaries.

SharedImpact is a 21st century organisation in that it uses current technology and addresses 21st century issues. Paul's investment in and use of technology enables him to run his organisation with very few staff, keeping personnel costs to a minimum so that he can invest in technology and new product development. He strives to make his service, both the donors and recipients, truly international. However, to do so is extremely complex and requires his legal expertise and negotiations with various tax authorities that can inhibit charitable giving. Unfortunately, many of the world's governments and tax regimes have not evolved with the times.

People travel around the world more freely now than ever before and international businesses move their employees from country to country. However, the tax laws of most countries still assume that everyone lives in their native country. For example, a US citizen who lives (and is tax domiciled) in the UK must file and possibly pay taxes to both countries. If he or she donates to a UK recognised charity, he can gain relief for this donation on his UK tax form, but not the US form. The US recognises only charities registered in the USA. For dual nationality citizens or expats not living in their own country, these tax restrictions often hinder charitable giving and prevent individuals from obtaining any tax benefits when they make charitable contributions.

SharedImpact has overcome this obstacle and donations through this channel are recognised by the tax regimes in both the UK and the US. Paul continues to work with other tax authorities on similar issues in order to broaden the reach and effectiveness of his charity.

Paul's journey offers another illustration of the growing trend in the charity sector: a well-educated professional trying to find a career that is meaningful, intellectually challenging and emotionally fulfilling. Paul, like others, wants to see the result of his work. In all these stories, the individuals wanted to solve problems - big and little - and have a direct impact on the world. The question remains, do you have to start a charity or run one to make this impact? Can individuals who want to make a difference do so by taking employment within an existing charity? The answer, of course, depends on the organisation, but Laura Malone's example illustrates how one woman managed to do just that.

Laura 's story – Finding a satisfying role

Starting out

"Finding meaning in work can even be a challenge for someone working for a charity," Laura explains. "Personal expectations are higher. And charities have some of the same tasks as any organisation - accounts, administration - unrewarding, but essential activities that somebody must do."

Laura Malone is a senior manager in business development for *Save the Children*. Her background and upbringing trained her for a more commercial and professional position, so she understands both worlds. Born in Edinburgh, her father worked for *BP* and when she was nine years old (in the 1980s), the family moved to Buffalo, New York when her father's job changed. Living in the US opened her eyes to the bigger world as she adjusted to the changes in culture and schooling between Scotland and the United States.

By the time Laura reached high school age, the family moved yet again, this time to Surrey in England. When her father was transferred once more, to Pittsburgh, Pennsylvania, it was 1995 and Laura was near the end of her studies, so she elected to stay in the UK to finish her education after which she went to the University of Edinburgh to read Law. By now she had begun the professional career expected of someone of her upbringing. She finished her Law studies after five years, and went on to do a two year traineeship in a top Edinburgh law firm.

Laura became a corporate lawyer and was successfully launched on the career ladder. She remained with the firm for three more years. She was well respected and seen to be 'going places'. "At the same time,"

Laura admits, "Something kept pulling at me. I was doing what was expected and the kinds of things my friends were also doing, but I felt guilty about being relatively affluent and successful when I knew that there were major problems in the world. I worked as a lawyer to help make rich people richer."

The 'ah ha!' moment

"One day, I saw things from a slightly different perspective. I saw my boss working hard, very long hours and chasing these rich people in order to help them become richer. I thought to myself, if that's how I will end up, it's not worth it."

Perhaps some of Laura's activities outside work led her to these insights. In 2005, she and her father did a charity trek in Peru to raise money for a cancer charity. The father and daughter team were celebrating the 10th anniversary of Laura's mum's 'all clear' after suffering from cancer. Two years later she did another sponsored trek for charity, this time to India.

"I met lots and lots of different and interesting people on my treks, people leading different kinds of lives I hadn't even known were possible," Laura said. "This perspective made me realise that I sort of 'fell into law'. I did well and just kept on going. My horizons were too narrow, certainly not wide enough to understand all the options available to me."

Soon after her India trek, Laura decided to leave law and in 2008 she resigned from her job. She intended to take some time out do some serious thinking. After first taking a holiday, she returned home and began to ponder. She realised that, though she had a good job and a house and mortgage - the whole professional set-up - she had no personal life, no partner, and she had been working so hard that she was often ill.

"I was lucky," she recalls, "My parents helped me by supporting me while I tried to figure out what I wanted to do. At the time, all I knew was that I couldn't keep on doing what I had been doing. I knew whatever I chose to do next I would take a pay cut."

Laura started applying for jobs in the charity sector. She took a temporary job in business development at a local branch of a charity called *Maggie's Centres*, a cancer support charity. It soon became clear that Laura would need to move to London to pursue a career in this sector and *Maggie's Centres* put her on a short-term contract and allowed her to transfer to a London office. Inspired by her treks abroad, Laura's ambition was to obtain a business development role in an international charity. In fact, she stayed on at *Maggie's Centres* in London for four more years before she finally achieved this goal.

A new career

While speaking at a conference for charities, she was approached by an attendee from *Merlin*, an international health charity that delivers medical care to disaster and war torn areas. *Merlin* offered her a job in business development and in 2012 Laura finally achieved her ambition to gain an international role. From this position, she moved to that of Senior Business Development Manager for *Save the Children* in September 2013, where she feels happy, intellectually challenged and, to a significant extent, fulfilled. "I'm still working long hours," she says, "but, at least I know why I'm doing it."

Laura continues to expand her horizons and her formal education has not entirely ceased. She has begun a master's course at University of London School of Oriental and Asian Studies. Unfortunately, the demands of work have forced her to put these studies on hold for a while, but she has enjoyed them nonetheless.

Laura explains that *Save the Children* is a very professional organisation, on a par with commercial enterprises. Her colleagues are very bright and intellectually stimulating. The work is fulfilling and, while she may not remain in the same job for the rest of her working life, it satisfies her now and she knows that there are many other interesting options within the charity. Of course, the money is less than she made as a lawyer, but she is happier in her work.

When she speaks to her friends who took up more traditional professions or business roles, she compares her position with theirs. Many of them tell her they are jealous of her and her job, but they are all more affluent, taking regular holidays each year and indulging in luxuries that Laura can't afford. Would she go back? "I've had opportunities," she admits, "but in the end, I decided I really didn't want to go back to that world even if I could 'do good' from that position."

"In fact, I recently spoke to someone from Corporate Social Responsibility (CSR) at a major bank - this woman too, told me she envied me my job. But I had to tell her," Laura declares, "that in her position and with the money the bank allocated to the department, in many ways she could do far more good than I could in my role - all she had to do was to think a bit more laterally about her activities if she wanted to add more impact."

In her business development role, Laura works with quite a few businesses and has learned and seen a great deal. She says, "Businesses should always do things in an open and honest way with the people they are trying to help - we should be able to have a grown up conversation about the reasons a commercial organisation gets involved in supporting development work. And businesses should seek to work with organisations who understand how to implement solutions, not create their own solutions."

"I've almost come full circle," Laura explains. "From my position in 'the third sector' (i.e. charity or not-for-profit) I am now a strong advocate for the role of private sector in driving change and improvements. In fact, overall, the third sector has not yet seized the opportunity as effectively as it could." Laura believes that by developing closer, longer term, more committed ties with businesses, both businesses and charities could benefit.

"I'm in a unique position. There are not many like me who 'sit between' these two sectors and can see the potential and failings of each. The reason I now sit where I sit in the charity sector is because it makes me feel good to use my skills to do something worthwhile. I'm incredibly passionate about the cause."

Laura continues, "I believe that business will have to get even more involved in the challenges faced in international development because many of the problems that we face are, to some degree, made worse by commercial and/or government activity. And conversely, the impact of these problems is felt on a global scale by businesses as much as by the rest of society. At some point, we are all going to have to re-frame our social contract, what it means to be a global citizen. The current situation, with climate change, population increase and urbanisation, could be a ticking time bomb."

Laura has summed up very eloquently what many others feel. With globalisation and a better awareness of what's happening around the world, there is a sense that the situation is getting worse and that no one agency can fix everything. Coming at the same point from a different perspective, another young professional summarises the situation as follows,

"I am no more cynical about the public sector than I am about the private sector. In fact the issues with both are the same. They are both slow and they sometimes get things wrong, but they cannot be ignored as a force for change, so we have to figure out how to make them work."

All the stories in this chapter share a common theme. All these individuals have given up the potential for more lucrative careers for a personally satisfying job where they could put their intelligence to use in an attempt to solve social problems. Their backgrounds and ages are varied, but all of them share an excellent educational foundation and most watched their peers move up a corporate ladder to attain wealth and professional status. Although now less affluent than their peers, none of these individuals expressed regret about their choices.

Whatever the reason, today 'the business' of running a non-profit organisation is a viable career choice for both those entering the job market and for people disillusioned with the more mainstream professional careers. While the financial rewards are typically lower, the personal satisfaction with the work is typically high. For those with a social agenda, this sector now offers a viable career option.

Does job satisfaction - the satisfaction of feeling one's own actions have made a difference - balance the job equation when the financial remuneration is low? What is the job satisfaction equation? Does working with a 'purpose' provide the motivation that money alone cannot? Purpose certainly seems to make the difference for more and more people, of all ages. But, perhaps the motivation is more than merely personal satisfaction. Perhaps there's a genuine fear among these individuals that "if I don't do something, at least take a small step, then the world situation will become worse, perhaps irrevocably."

Chapter 8

MANY PATHS

"The long and winding road..."
The Beatles

In the stories so far, many individuals describe how they experienced an 'ah ha!' or 'lightbulb' moment, and after that point, their way forward seemed clearer. In most cases, though, even those with a profound sense of purpose continued to struggle to balance career and financial aims with their sense of mission. Some were 'lucky' and found what they needed immediately while others lived through a series of failed attempts or challenging detours. This chapter focuses on stories from social pioneers who have successfully headed into an uncharted wilderness and built organisations that satisfied their personal aims, and helped others.

Just as having a degree from Harvard or Oxford does not guarantee a successful or socially conscious career, challenging circumstances and a disrupted education has not prevented others from developing meaningful roles that contribute to society. Even if the journeys travelled took a long and winding road, the desire to give back remained strong. These individuals kept trying and kept looking to create a new role in which they could combine a career with providing social benefit.

And not all opportunities to 'give back' are blindingly obvious. Sometimes, it takes a convoluted route to find or create the right situation. Some attempts fail, but ultimately, these failures provide the foundation for future success. These days, a role is often a job or a service that has never been done before, so it takes some time for an individual to build up the nerve and the resources to begin. The stories in this chapter will follow more unusual or complex journeys and illustrate less traditional or more tortuous routes.

Alex Cole's life to date exemplifies that of many social entrepreneurs, with a series of challenges that he had to face and overcome before he could move into a job that combined his business experience with his desire to give back to the community.

Alex's story - Helping job seekers

Background

Alex was born in Doncaster in the north of England where his father was stationed in the Royal Air Force (RAF). Alex was in such a rush to be born that his mother didn't make it to the hospital, and he was born at home on Christmas Eve. However, as a child of an armed forces family, he didn't stay anywhere for very long and by the time he was three years old, he moved to Singapore where he started school, returning to Oxfordshire and the English school system when he was five.

Life remained fixed in Abingdon for a few years until Alex was nine years old, when his father left the RAF. At this point, his parents decided to return to Jamaica, the country where they were both born. Alex quickly adapted to his new school but, unfortunately, he didn't have long to get settled before his family once again moved back to the UK. His father had been working for *Air Jamaica*, but decided that he wanted to return to England to find another job. So, it was back in England that Alex finished his schooling after taking O-levels (Ordinary levels, an 'achievement' exam that used to be employed in the English School system providing a first level of qualifications. Many students then left formal education at 15 or 16). At 16, Alex was ready to go out in the world - all he needed was a job.

At first, Alex thought he might want to study the law, so he worked as an articled clerk at a solicitors firm. Soon, however, at the prompting of his father, he joined the RAF at 17, as a junior technician with a specialty in telecommunications. He received good training, but didn't really enjoy the RAF. Despite these feelings he waited until he was almost 21 years old before managing to leave by utilising a process of paying back the RAF for the costs of training - costs they attempt to recover if someone leaves the service before their contracted time.

Starting out in the commercial world

"When I got out, all my friends were at uni," Alex explains. "It felt like the world had passed me by. I was now out of the military and needed to hit the streets to look for a job." And that's exactly what Alex did. He passed a recruitment agency and went inside to enquire about a job that was posted in the window. While the agency interviewed him, the tone of the interview began to change. In the end, he was offered a job at the recruitment agency itself! It was in this job that Alex received his first sales training education and he was so successful that, after a time, another agency headhunted him for a sales role.

Finally, at the age of 24, Alex decided he wanted to continue his education. He went to Luton University (now the University of Bedfordshire) to do an HND (Higher National Diploma) course in computer studies and then did an MSc in digital systems at Edinburgh Napier University. By the time he finished, Alex was 27 and although he tried hard, he couldn't get his preferred job as a programmer or systems analyst. "Fortunately," Alex recalls, "I could fall back on my sales experience. You can always find a job in sales. So I went to work in sales at *Rank Screen Advertising*. You know, the ads you see in the cinema before the feature films."

While it put food on the table, the *Rank Screen Advertising* job only served until Alex could find something he liked better and within a year, he discovered that an electronics distribution company called *MicroWarehouse* was recruiting in the UK for a sales job in the USA. He applied, got the job and moved to Connecticut. His job was to sell the *MicroWarehouse* offering to Europeans while based in the main office in the USA.

In the midst of all this change, Alex also decided to get married and his wife accompanied him to America. Unfortunately, after about two years, both became so homesick for the UK that they decided to move back. "When I was in the USA, I got some perspective on my life. I realised that, along the way, my sense of self was changing," Alex reflects. "When I was in the RAF, I felt like a fish out of water. I only joined to make my father happy, rather than something I really wanted to do."

"And then, while I was in the USA, I realised that I enjoyed having conversations with C-level executives (the most senior people in a company) about things like brand, marketing and business. It just felt more natural to me."

Starting over again

Back in England, Alex took another sales job with *AIG-Conferences* (part of the *Daily Mail* group) and soon moved to take a role with their *Ideal Home Roadshow*, selling exhibitor space. Alex rose to become marketing director for this division and very much enjoyed it. "I liked the story they weaved around their offering and I liked what they were trying to achieve," he explains. But nothing goes on forever and a 'management buy-out' disrupted Alex's job. He was asked to stay on to be a part of the management team in the new company, but decided against it.

This employment decision coincided with changes in Alex's personal life where divorce loomed. "1995 was a difficult year for me," Alex confesses. In order to 'take stock' and regroup, Alex decided to go back into education. Using the redundancy payment he got from his job, he took a variety of courses, in things like management studies and programming, achieving diplomas and certificates from Northampton College. "In my mind," Alex says, "I was on a trajectory toward getting an MBA." However, an unexpected job opportunity disrupted his progress.

Alex was asked to be a director at *Francis Williams*, a design agency in Brixton, London. This agency had no C-level sales capability, so Alex took on this role. He soon created business for the company and worked there for about 18 months, focusing on brand management. He used his connections from a previous role to move *Francis Williams* to Islington in North London in 1998, into more prestigious premises at the Design Centre. Alex explained how this work in a small creative business sent his ambitions in a new direction. "My entrepreneurial flame had been fanned!" he recalls. "The embers were always there, faintly glowing. When I was much younger, I read Richard Branson's autobiography and I thought 'I can do that!'"

Again, there was disruption in Alex's private life - his parents decided to divorce. He took a trip to visit his mother, now living in Jamaica, and wrote the bulk of a business plan for a new company while on the outbound flight. His father decided to stay in the UK, but had nowhere to call his own, so Alex bought a house and they lived together.

With his business plan now complete, Alex went with his father to see the bank manager to ask for startup funding. It was a successful meeting and the bank matched the funds that both Alex and his father had raised to launch the company - *Voyage Brand Management*.

Throughout his experience of marketing, Alex had noticed that ethnic faces were typically 'blurred'. He was certain that many retailers wanted to reach these sectors, but just didn't know how, so this was where he focused his efforts. "I saw a market that needed help," he explains. "Of course there were other people in the community who could have helped, but they didn't seem to have my depth of experience in the business world. They couldn't speak to the senior level at corporates in a strategic context; I could, and this approach resulted in a significant pipeline of sales revenue. I felt I was the right person with the motivation and skill, who was around at the right time to make a difference and fulfil this role."

In 1999, he created a campaign called *Black Lifestyle 2000*, capitalising on the approaching millennium. He used this campaign as a vehicle for other companies who wanted to sell to the black community. Working with modelling agencies, musicians and lots of creative young people, he developed *Black Face 2000*, a show that toured the UK, showcasing many of his clients' products.

Alex's friends and family were supportive of his efforts. Being sensible, he decided to give the business a year to succeed or fail and set about trying to find customers. Although his show was a success, he worked so hard that he developed pneumonia. He realised that he couldn't carry on - he just didn't have the physical strength - so he closed down his business.

While recovering his health, he did a bit of volunteering at *Knights*, a London organisation which helps young people, providing housing and various activity programmes based around sports. He worked at *Knights* in Crystal Palace, in South East London for a year, living in a bedsit provided by the organisation and receiving only nominal payments for food and other necessities. He also used his business skills to help write a grant application to the *National Lottery* fund, successfully securing £2 million in funding.

Starting over... yet again

To get back into business life, Alex took a short course in computer skills and then, in 2001, found a job at the *BBC* as a help desk analyst. As a first step back into regular working life, the job was perfect. It was a 'nine to five' type role and he could switch off each evening when the job was over. He liked his work colleagues and there were plenty of opportunities to socialise. Alex stayed at the *BBC* for three and a half years, moving from his role at the help desk to that of a project manager and finally, a programme manager.

He planned to marry again and already had a daughter. He needed more money and he was already at the top of his pay scale at the *BBC*. If he wanted more money, he would have to leave. So in 2004, just before his wedding, he found employment at *Kent County Council*. He became the programme manager for the inter-authority partnership unit, an innovative new business unit designed to enable high performing councils, such as Kent, to provide consultancy services to support lower performing councils.

One of Alex's first projects was to lead some work at *Swindon Borough Council*, which at the time, was rated as a poor performer in the areas of health and social care. "My first attempt at engaging the people at Swindon was a failure," says Alex. "As a group we very much tried to 'tell them' what we did successfully in Kent and they got defensive and were not open to our recommended approach. So I went to Dr. Bell, a senior lecturer at the time in systemic practice at The Open University, who was already working with *Kent County Council* to improve services".

Together, Dr. Bell and Alex created a programme called The Reflective Practitioner Programme. "It worked amazingly well!" recalls Alex. "We used Dr. Bell as well as five occupational psychologists and 40 people attended. And from this experience I became a 'reflective practitioner' - an attitude and approach which helped me to build high performance teams at the previously resistant *Swindon Borough Council*."

In 2006, Alex left *Kent County Council* and not long afterwards created a company of his own called *Cardio*, which specialised in culture change consultancy. Alex applied all his experience from the previous years into creating an effective approach and methodology. The business began to grow until 2009, when the banking crisis and recession hit and, once again, circumstances forced him to close his businesses. It had been a good idea, it had worked, but the timing was wrong. Alex needed now to find work.

Eventually, Alex found another job at *Capgemini*, an IT services provider, as a senior transition manager. This role helps to move from the proposal and sale of a large IT services contract to the implementation. "This was the first time I was actually on the inside of a global IT company. It was exactly what I wanted to do, and really stretched my stakeholder and technology skills in new directions," Alex says.

For a number of years, Alex worked hard and kept his entrepreneurial instincts under wraps. But eventually, he was given a programme to run that gave him the chance to exercise these skills once more. He set up a team to run a global facilities IT implementation project and did the whole thing very successfully. Soon afterwards, Alex was asked to run an 'innovation centre', which was a business unit responsible for creating new services and finding new market opportunities.

For most employees, finding happiness in large firms depends a great deal on having a similar approach as one's manager and, in the innovation centre, Alex and his boss did not share the same vision in terms of approach or what could be accomplished. By the end of 2013, when Alex was thinking of looking for another job, an email appeared in his inbox. A charity called *Business in the Community*, of which *Capgemini* was a member, had sent around an advertisement seeking a *Capgemini* employee willing to volunteer for a year-long secondment as business connector in South London.

Helping in the community

"When I saw the email I got very excited," Alex reminisces. "Lambeth was the area under the spotlight and I had significant personal links in the area. My grandmother lived there for many years and I saw it as a great opportunity to 'do good' with my skill set in a locale I knew well. I wanted to go into the community to show what a business could do and how it could help make a real impact."

Alex also explained that, looking back over his previous jobs, he began to understand how his experiences led him to take on this role. "When I did *Blackface 2000*, the whole thing led me to understand how quickly circumstances can change if you provide people with the right information. For example, the companies who struggled to sell to the black segment began to understand that people - their customers - are basically all the same. Although sometimes the approach needed to be altered slightly."

Alex threw everything into being recruited for this post and his efforts were rewarded. He got the secondment to be a 'business connector'. Broadly speaking, his role was to help promote or support or create an organisation or initiative to help with:

- Community cohesion
- Employment
- Enterprise
- Education

To start things off, Alex began by wandering around Lambeth, looking at what was working and not working there and talking to the local people. He was invited to take part in a pilot mentoring initiative in Brixton and a three-day workshop, which was the most successful when compared with the nine other organisations' results. He brought some like-minded colleagues with him to help out at the 'mentoring circle' that they held at the local Job Centre. When he was shown some extra space by the manager at the centre, he asked if he could use it.

Having run an innovation team at *Capgemini*, Alex used many of the same techniques, such as using 'rich pictures' as well as business skills within interactive group session, to help job seekers develop their skills and self-confidence. "While many of the job centres have employability bridging programmes," explains Alex, "they tend to focus on things like CV and assessment clinics. However, I quickly realised that the fundamental problems were emotional and mental blocks and revolved around difficulties with actualising a positive self-image and self-confidence."

Alex began working with another *Capgemini* colleague to develop a training curriculum that he named *Digisheds*. He divided up the area in the Job Centre that he had arranged to borrow to enable different activities to take place. There was the:

- Learning space
- Think space

- Build space
- Show space

Alex collaborated with many people to help him deliver the training, including individuals from the local council, other businesses, and members of the community, while he acted as the facilitator for the whole process.

"The work felt like a breath of fresh air - doing something whose relevance and impact I could immediately perceive," Alex says. "I was energised by the thought of being able to spend a year immersed in something I wanted to do that was doing good for so many people."

As the year progressed, one of the colleagues who helped Alex develop the training left his job with *Capgemini* and they collaborated to set up their own social enterprise delivering impactful social innovation. He formalised the work he had been doing and set up a self-supporting business model by obtaining funding from a number of sources.

As Alex himself states in his blog, "*Digisheds* is a unique and innovative employability programme that provides job opportunities and employability training for individuals at a disadvantage in the job market, such as young NEETs (Not in Employment, Education or Training), and long-term unemployed adults. It currently runs three days a week for 20 people at a time. Participants complete a four-week intensive curriculum with the support of volunteer mentors from local businesses."

Alex now stands at a crossroads. His year on secondment is over and he has accomplished a great deal. He doesn't want to leave *Digisheds* and believes that he could expand it to help unemployed people all over London and the UK. He explains that he is not unusual in wanting to stay with his work, "A number of companies who put forward employees to be business connectors discover that they don't return to the job, rather, they stay working with the community." It looks like Alex will join this group and stay with *Digisheds* rather than returning to his job at *Capgemini*.

Alex's history illustrates many of the challenges that arise in life: family problems, divorce, physical illness, the need to make a living and a growing desire to do something 'meaningful' at work. Alex's pathway expresses his entrepreneurial spirit: making many attempts and trying out lots of ideas before finally finding a situation in which everything 'clicked'. Alex didn't experience one 'ah ha!' moment, rather a series of events all combined to lead him and equip him to move out into the community to try to 'do good'. No single job could have given him all the skills he would need. Rather, he collected the necessary experience and perspective as he travelled from role to role.

Asma Shah, too, has not taken a direct path - although she carried her mission with her from a very young age. Her family circumstances and her personal experiences in school stayed with her when she went out into the business world, collecting skills, connections and the experience to begin to act on her sense of personal mission. Again, no single job could have equipped her to set out on her current path, but as she travelled a convoluted route, she developed the skills and ability to create her charity.

Asma's Story – Helping socially disadvantaged women

Childhood spawned her life's mission

Asma begins, "If I were to try to pinpoint the things that influenced my life so far, I need to go back to when I was one and a half when my mother, a well-educated woman from Pakistan living in the UK, left my father and took me and my three older sisters with her. We stayed in a refuge before being moved to a council flat." Asma points out that, rather than do the obvious thing, like taking in sewing or doing a menial job, her mother took a long term view and trained to be a teacher, and then worked to support her four little girls. Asma's mother eventually divorced her husband, and continued to live without any help or support from her family back in Pakistan.

From this shaky start, Asma attended a school in Bermondsey, London. It had been a good school when her two eldest sisters attended, but after numerous changes in the way the school was run, the education it provided took a turn for the worse. In addition to the poor academic environment, Asma was one of the few Asian students and became the victim of severe bullying and racism from both the black and the white students; she used to hide in the girls' toilet every lunchtime to avoid encounters with her classmates.

Asma hated school - a problem made worse because her mother was a teacher and felt strongly about education. As she got older, Asma played truant more and more often. As a result, when she took her GCSEs (national qualification school exams, taken at 15 or 16), the only subjects she did very well in were English Language and English Literature. Asma loved to read and did so without any input from school. Despite her overall poor exam performance, she went on to study for A-levels (a pre-University examination the results of which are used for university admission) at Westminster Kingsway College. Asma was much happier at Kingsway, and doing well when domestic issues developed which interfered with her studies. Once again, she didn't do as well as she should have done in her A-levels.

Despite this outcome, Asma somehow managed to scrape into Queen Mary University of London, with a place to study Literature and History. Finally, her academic life took off. She achieved a good degree and went on to obtain a master's degree in Contemporary British History and Politics. After finishing her MA, she took a number of temporary positions while she searched for more permanent employment. Finally, she found a contract job as a press assistant/policy advisor in a government department. "I took the job because I thought it would please my mother," Asma admits. "I really didn't fit in, so I hated the job."

Searching for the 'right' job

Asma then applied for a job at a UK-wide grant distributor, taking a position as a policy advisor. She was 23, and the work was exciting. Initially, she loved it and she stayed for more than three years. She left because although she was given plenty of work to do - which she did well, and was given credit for in annual appraisals - she was consistently passed over for promotion. Her next position was as manager at one of the *Sector Skills Councils (SSC)*. Asma very much enjoyed the work at the *SSC*, particularly the office in which she worked which was set up by two hard working and highly motivated women. She stayed for more than three years but then, when she turned 30, she resigned in order to travel around South East Asia for four and a half months. On her return, Asma set about looking for yet another new job.

A contact at a major broadcasting company told Asma about a temporary maternity cover position in the human resources (HR) department as a Training and Development Co-ordinator. Asma got the job and worked hard, so that by the time the woman on maternity leave returned, she had created an additional and more senior role for herself. Asma now had a year-long placement at the channel, co-ordinating and streamlining how the channel developed and celebrated talent. She was also given the task of reducing the budget through any efficiencies she could implement. After a successful year, her role was incorporated into a larger, new position and she applied for the job.

Unfortunately, Asma was told that she wasn't favoured by the HR director and so was unlikely to get the position. At the same time, her mentor at the channel left. So, feeling undervalued and without any internal champion, Asma left and got a year-long role delivering the second half of a programme to encourage young people to make and perform music at one of London's leading music venues. She thrived in this job, but knew that the funding was going to disappear at the end of the year so she looked around and decided to apply to be a fellow of *The Clore Leadership Programme*.

This programme, as described by its website, "... came from an inspirational idea of Dame Vivien Duffield, and was set up in order to help develop a generation of exceptional cultural leaders." It is extremely selective, taking only around 25 individuals at a time. Asma made it through the admissions process and spent her time gaining leadership expertise and making valuable friendships and professional connections. "Getting accepted did a lot for my confidence," Asma says. "It was a tough interview process and I felt proud to have made it through."

Sadly, this time in her life wasn't all happy. Her mother, who had been diagnosed with cancer six years earlier, finally lost her fight against the disease and died. Her death hit Asma very hard and the grieving process led her to think about her mother's life and what she was doing with her own. So, in the midst of *The Clore Leadership Programme*, she came to a branch point in her career path. Asma remembers asking herself, "Do I want to do something cultural and creative, the natural outcome of this programme, or do I want to do something which more directly supports and changes the life chances of women from similar backgrounds to myself? I think my response was all part of the grieving process, which is why I decided I needed to do something that made a difference. It didn't have to be 'big' but it had to make a difference to the women I helped."

The turning point

It was at this point that Asma concluded definitively that she wanted to help women who came from a background similar to her own. Contemplating her past jobs, Asma thought about what she had liked and the areas in which she had excelled. "As part of working at the music venue," she explains, "I learned I enjoyed working with young people, late teens and young adults, so I thought I would focus on that age group in whatever I ended up doing. I looked around and realised that one of the key problems for these young women was that they lacked confidence - they might also lack money and/or education, but it was primarily their lack of self-belief that stopped them from taking courses or applying for training schemes or jobs."

So, in 2011, Asma set up *Ladies Who L-EARN*. With very little money to start, Asma funded the work herself, working as a part-time partnerships and promotions consultant for a commercial theatre company. She was able to work with a coach from *The Clore Programme* who helped her develop a project plan for *Ladies Who L-EARN*. "The more I talked to people, the more I realised that I could get started with very little money," Asma recalls. "I managed to obtain free space and found volunteers to help with various aspects of the programme."

"I recruited the women using guerrilla marketing - flyers posted all over the area." Asma elaborates, "I personally handed out the leaflets to likely candidates, went to Job Centres and other places where these women might be. I also went to other organisations in the area and asked for referrals which I chased up." Her first group was 21 Bangladeshi women ranging in age from 18 to 24.

The pilot programme ran for three months and consisted of weekly workshops that focused on helping the women to think positively about themselves focusing on confidence-building, and interview and CV skills.

Asma described the specific issues affecting the women whom she was seeking to empower, "The Bangladeshi women in the main have come from patriarchal households. Although they are expected to work to bring in some money for the family, very high ambitions are not encouraged. Often, women were expected to help out around the house and take care of siblings, walking them to school and collecting them in the afternoon. Such activities severely restricted job opportunities and as a result, when these women work, it is often in menial and low paid jobs."

"On the other hand, the women I've come across from black African and Afro-Caribbean households have tended to be strongly matriarchal, with no men at all in the house. These women appeared confident and energetic, but sometimes complicated relationships with their mothers had gotten in the way of them reaching their full potential."

In terms of providing interesting work activities, Asma found other groups to help.

"We collaborated with an organisation called *Cockpit Arts* which worked with the women, introducing them to various designers. A couple of weekend events were set up at a local market and the women were encouraged to select and sell some of these designers' works at the market."

The women earned a small amount of money for each item they sold. The activity was mainly focused on developing skills, aiming to create an appetite for what it feels like to earn money. The women loved it! Many of them hadn't spent much time out and about in their own neighbourhood, and although the market where they sold these items was nearby to the estates where they lived, many had never visited it. The women also gained the desire and confidence to go out and about in their own neighbourhood.

The outcome of the pilot was incredible. Eighteen of the women graduated and for those who dropped out, the reason was typically a family or boyfriend problem that required immediate attention. Of the 18 graduates, all but one either found employment or accessed full time education. Since this pilot, two more groups of women have gone through the programme, with 19 graduating from each intake and a similar level of success for each.

Following this success, *the Ladies Who L-EARN* catchment area for recruitment was extended.. It now covers Tower Hamlets and Hackney, both very poor areas within Greater London. The programme has been enhanced and is now six months in duration, with three months of weekly workshops followed by three months of mentoring. Other features include work placements and something called the *Ladies'Den* (something akin to the UK TV show *Dragon's Den*) where women could pitch their business ideas to a panel of experts.

"Seventy-eight percent of the graduates are now in paid employment or full-time education," asserts Asma. "And I hope it can continue. I had hoped to set up as a social enterprise, but there wasn't anything in the activities that could generate enough earned income. So, in the end, I have set up as a charity and, as a result, I am now in the throes of fundraising." Asma's organisation has done measurable good in the community. As she herself states, she didn't start it to make a big splash, rather to make a lasting, significant and positive impact on those women she does help.

Asma's motivation cannot be questioned, but it took many years for her to develop the skills and contacts so she could take the chance to try to fashion an organisation that would help young women. Although still a new organisation, *Ladies who L-EARN* is very much dependent on Asma. While her success rate to date has been spectacular - far higher than any of the usual programmes provided by social services, her 'reach' is small. In the grand scheme of things, she may only have helped just under 100 women, but these are 100 women who might otherwise have not moved out into the world.

Who knows what these women, in turn, may accomplish? If each of them were to help 100 more women, or even just one or two, the impact would soon multiply. And if others were to follow Asma's example, then perhaps additional, equally effective programmes could emerge. Their impact does not have to be enormous, or have global reach. Asma makes the world a little better a few people at a time while she works very hard in a job that fulfils her personal social mission.

The next personal journey is another that was fraught with early difficulties - difficulties that might have led others down a completely different path with a less positive outcome. Jamie Ward-Smith's story starts when he was very young and he has travelled a long and challenging path to arrive where he is today. The way forward was never obvious and he had very little help as he built a life and career that suited his values. Despite these obstacles, he has succeeded spectacularly.

Jamie's Story – Making volunteering easy

Starting at the beginning

Jamie's story starts when he was a baby and he has used his myriad of experiences - both good and bad - to achieve what he has to date. The son of a mother who unexpectedly found herself pregnant at 17, Jamie spent the first three and a half years of his life in foster care. He returned to live with his mother when he was nearly four, but sadly, it was too late to form the strong bonds that naturally develop between mother and child. So, although he was back with his mother, things never felt normal.

Despite this challenging start, Jamie was very bright and won a grant to attend a boarding school when he was seven years old. "It was a great relief," he explains. "Things were never good at home and I was actually much happier at school." Unfortunately, the schooling finished at 16, so Jamie returned home to live and what had been uncomfortable before now became unbearable. During his teenage years, Jamie realised he was gay and began to explore his sexuality. When his mother and stepfather found out what was happening, they became terrified that they would catch AIDS and made him move out.

"When I left home, still barely a teenager, I had to figure out how to get my own sixth form education," Jamie says. "I had no stable place to live, so I 'sofa surfed' among my friends for a while and, for a short period of time, actually found myself with no place to live. It was pretty awful." However, despite these obstacles, Jamie succeeded and won a place at a local polytechnic where he obtained a degree in Social and Economic History. Just getting himself through the course and surviving was a challenge; he faced life one obstacle at a time with his sole aim being to obtain his degree, so when he finally graduated, he had no specific plan for a career.

The voluntary sector

"I took a first job as a credit control assistant," Jamie relates. "And then, I fell into a job in the not-for-profit sector when a friend told me about a temporary position open at a housing charity. The charity focused on tenant welfare, rent control and housing and I really resonated with its aims, having experienced homelessness myself." However, it was a large organisation with a rigid structure and eventually, Jamie felt he wanted to exercise his entrepreneurial skills. So, after three years he decided to look for a new challenge.

He applied for and was successful in being appointed as director at a volunteer bureau (now known as volunteer centres) in Notting Hill, West London. While the charity itself was relatively small, it was part of a much larger network of volunteer bureaux and, at the age of just 25, Jamie was one of the youngest CEOs in the group.

By now, it was the mid-1990s and technology was beginning to play an increasing role in charitable organisations. At this time, Martyn Lewis, the former news broadcaster at the BBC, set up a charity called *YouthNet*. As its website today describes it, its mission was and still is to be "...the online guide to life for 16 to 25 year-olds. It provides safe, trusted and non-judgmental information and advice on everything from sex and relationships to exam stress or drugs." In 1996, *YouthNet* was visionary; it was the first virtual charity. In 1999 its CEO approached Jamie to suggest that he become the charity's first marketing director, to help drive up the charity's online presence and to support the launch of the UK's first national volunteering website, known as *Do-it*.

Like a lot of other people at the time, Jamie was aware of government initiatives to promote volunteering, but he could not help but think that things could be done better. In 2003, an opportunity within the Home Office enabled him to put some of his thoughts into action when he got to lead the *Russell Commission* review on youth social action. This project resulted in a report which was published in 2005 and on the back of this work, the government committed £45m to increase the scope and range of youth volunteering - at that time the largest investment in a volunteering programme. With the commission complete, Jamie left the Home Office and began to consider his next step.

During this time, Jamie's health faced a setback and this situation was compounded by other personal issues. As a consequence, he decided to set up his own business so that he could work with more flexibility to accommodate his illness. So, in the very early days of the social enterprise, Jamie established *Red Foundation* - a development agency aimed at helping charities, public services and businesses to engage with communities and to develop volunteering initiatives. Jamie instilled a strong ethos driven by a genuine desire to place positive social change above profit, which guided the organisation's work. At the same time, he set up the *Red Trust*, a charity into which he planned to put some of the profits from the *Red Foundation*.

In addition to the consultancy services, Jamie launched a pilot social networking platform, called *i-volunteer*, to help bring together volunteers and charities. After five years of working in the business, Jamie decided he wanted to return to the technology side of things, so he found someone else to run the services part of the business and merged his technology into the *Red Trust* charity. And it was in the *Red Trust* that these technology assets sat until Jamie could find the funds to grow and develop them further.

Jamie then spent the next 18 months as a part-time, freelance consultant in order to get the money to re-launch *i-volunteer* as an independent venture. He needed the funds to pay himself for a year as well as to upgrade and enhance his technology platform and in 2012, *Red Trust* and *i-volunteer* became *ivo*, one of the UK's first social network platforms for volunteerism. In the meantime, in 2013 *YouthNet* decided it no longer wanted to run the *Do-it* website it launched in 2000. Jamie, familiar with the service he'd helped to set up, tendered for the opportunity to take over this asset, which now contained more than a million volunteers and volunteering opportunities.

Do-it.org

Jamie won the tender which came with government funding to help with financing the redevelopment of the service, and in 2014, the new *do-it.org* went live as part of the now renamed *Do-it Trust*, a digital social action charity whose stated mission is, "To bring people together to help solve society's problems through voluntary and civic action. Whether it's through volunteering or choosing a career for community benefit, we want to make it easy for people to connect, share, learn and grow and in doing so provide a world class service that is able to extend the capacity of civil society."

By using the *Do-it.org* website, individuals can find volunteering opportunities and jobs in the not-for-profit sector, while businesses can use the site to find opportunities for employees to volunteer as well as opportunities and systems for charitable donations. As its website states, "*Do-it.org* lists over 1.3 million volunteering opportunities that are posted by volunteer centres, national/local charities and voluntary groups across the United Kingdom. Enabling 250,000 people every month to donate their time and build their skills, *Do-it.org* ensures that over 40,000 organisations find the help they need to provide vital services to the community."

"Whilst *Do-it* is a charity, I prefer to think of it as a social business," Jamie explains, "What was important is that we have the right legal entity to enable us to raise our own funds rather than having to survive exclusively on donations and government grants." He now hopes the charity will pay its way by through advertising and sponsorship and by licensing the technology platform to other organisations. Jamie is optimistic, saying, "I want *Do-it Trust* to be a sustainable charity".

Whatever his commercial requirements, Jamie has not forgotten his key customers - the charities who need volunteers, and individuals who want to give their services. This obligation means ensuring that *Do-it Trust* is able to deliver the range of skills that charities need, with media partnerships such as those with *The Guardian* and more recently, *LinkedIn*, where *Do-it.org* is a key partner for the launch of their new UK *Volunteer Marketplace*. In 2015, *Do-it.org* won a People's Voice Webby Award, (considered the 'Oscar's of the Internet') and Jamie felt honoured when he went to collect the prize at a ceremony in New York.

"*Do-it.org* is the UK's number one volunteering website, both in terms of its age and the numbers of people signed up," Jamie states. "It's my aim to make volunteering an everyday thing in public life and I aspire to provide the best platform to enable this social transformation."

Jamie's goals are now clear and he looks well positioned to succeed by providing an enabling platform that can reach out to businesses, charities and volunteers alike. Perhaps it's this integration of different communities and constituencies that will be key to leading social change. It's notable that Jamie's organisation focuses not only on charities and volunteers, but provides consultancy to businesses about how they can best help charities. Jamie's business focus in this expanding sector is a sign of the times, and other organisations are also facilitating the relationship between the commercial and the voluntary sectors.

Jamie's approach works well, but it is not the only way to engage businesses. In the narrative that follows, Deap Khambay decided to take a more direct approach to challenging business cultures and helping individuals within companies to find meaning in their work. Deap, like the other people whose stories are told in this chapter, struggled through many positions, collecting the necessary experience and motivation that would eventually enable her to set up her own business.

Deap's story – Ethical values and employee well-being

Following her parents advice

Deap grew up in Lincoln where she lived until she was eight years old. Because her father in was in the Royal Air Force (RAF), they had the benefit of private education and so, although the family are Sikh, Deap started her education at a private Catholic school run by nuns. She even boarded for a year while her parents were abroad. "This start in life was unique," explains Deap. "No one ever told me I was Indian, or treated me differently. Then, I moved to multicultural London when my father retired and received a big shock!"

So, with her education no longer paid for by the RAF, Deap entered the state school system in London at the age of eight. Thanks to her accent, she was treated as 'the posh kid' and was badly teased. "In terms of my education," continues Deap, "my parents were very traditional Indian. They wanted me to study sciences in preparation for entering a profession, such as medicine. My sister, who was much older, became an accountant, a career that was of no interest to me."

Not wanting to fight her parents, Deap carried on taking classes she hated. When, in 1998, the time came to study for A-levels, again, she acted according to her parents' wishes and chose Biology, Chemistry and Physics. Deap's results in the mock exams at the end of the first year were very, very bad. "As a result," she says, "my parents agreed to pay for me to continue my A-level studies in a private college. I completed the course in a year, took the exams and still did badly." Despite this result, she managed to get onto a course at Nottingham Trent University to study Pharmacology.

"University was really the first time I had lived away from home and I went wild!" Deap recalls. "Drinking, parties, generally having a good time, but not studying. And then, in the second half of the first year, our course included experiments on live animals and I just couldn't do it." Deap stuck the year out and then went home and confessed to her parents that she couldn't face working on animals and did not want to finish the degree course. This step was very, very difficult for her because she didn't want to disappoint them. "Up until this time," she says, "I never really thought for myself or about myself, I always followed what my parents wanted me to do."

Her parents wanted her to go back to university, so she found the 'clearing list' of places still on offer at UK universities for the following year, closed her eyes and stuck a pin in the list. She didn't know what she wanted to do, so she just trusted her luck. The pin stuck on a degree course in Textile Technology and Management at UMIST (now University of Manchester). Ironically, a lot of the course involved maths, physics and chemistry, especially the subjects focusing on Textile Technology. "I didn't enjoy the work," Deap remembers. "But I carried on regardless and finally finished with a good degree from a good university. I also learned something about myself - if I don't like something, I don't engage with the subject - a lesson I was to learn over and over in the years to come."

Starting out in the business world

Deap used all her energies to graduate, so when the time came, she had made no plans and had no idea what job or career she wanted pursue. Throughout university, she worked in retail sales during the holidays, so with a relevant degree and job experience, she applied for a job in a department store as an allocator. The job seemed easy and Deap wasn't challenged, so she became distracted and bored. After a year she left to take a job at a TV shopping channel working in the planning department. This work involved the hour by hour allocation of 'slots' during which various products would be sold. Soon, Deap began to produce all the management reports as well. Unfortunately, once she mastered these tasks, Deap once again became bored. She stayed with the business for 18 months, but she wasn't happy and didn't fit with the culture, so she started to look around for another position.

"I was in a 'lost' state,' Deap explains. "I still didn't really know what I wanted to do or what would make me happy. Up until now, I kept leaving situations because I never found what I was looking for, but then, I got a lucky break."

Deap applied for a position at *Timberland*, then a family owned business with a big commitment to 'green' issues. The CEO was an environmental activist and regularly spoke to all the employees, not only about the business, but also about environmental issues, social issues and the company's activities. Deap, who took a job as a buying assistant, was delighted. "That man inspired me," she explains, "and I was suddenly very, very happy. The company opened my eyes to what was possible in a business."

In addition to her work, Deap took part in company-sponsored activities that had a socially or environmentally beneficial impact. *Timberland* gave each employee 40 hours per year to use in this way, and two days of this time had to be as part of a larger *Timberland* team. Deap loved these activities with her colleagues, but her job soon became tedious, so she applied for another position within the company. Her new role was in product development, and was located in a different part of London with a new group of people.

Timberland took its supply chain very seriously and didn't consider 'ignorance' a sufficient excuse for causing social or environmental harm. One of the things that Deap learned while working at the company was how to investigate and analyse the complexities and impact of the supply chain. She had the opportunity to travel to the Dominican Republic (the location of a factory fully owned by *Timberland* at the time) and learnt how social audits of *Timberland* suppliers were conducted. "I think this activity was my 'ah ha!' moment," she confesses. "I finally realised what I wanted to do. I need to work with people and make a social impact." Deap began to do personal research on the impacts of fashion on people's lives along the supply chain. "It's not always straightforward or obvious," she explains.

At the same time, Deap remembers "the atmosphere in this office was dismal. It was 'every man for himself' trying to promote personal efforts and careers. I didn't fit in." Deap carried on doing her job, but she began to withdraw, becoming isolated in the office and slowly sinking into depression. Finally, she was asked to be a Global Steward, a *Timberland* function that involved her heading up the volunteering efforts at her work location. That particular office had a very low level of engagement in the company's volunteer programme and it was Deap's role to inspire these employees to join in.

Finally Deap called a meeting of the whole office and asked what was important to them. The people began to lighten up and the atmosphere around the office became more positive. Unfortunately, it was too late for Deap who had slipped ever deeper into depression. She even tried to see if working with those in worse shape than she was would help, and volunteered with a charity that provided a helpline for troubled, often suicidal individuals. Deap worked as a volunteer, but found that listening with empathy only made her own state of mind worse. Finally, Deap quit her job.

The glimmer of an idea

So at the age of 29, Deap was without a job, living at home and facing the possibility of having to be financially supported by her parents. She didn't immediately tell them that she had resigned from *Timberland.* While she was working out her notice, she rang a good friend and explained what she had done, saying that she now had no idea what she would do next. Her friend replied, "Every time you talk about corporate social responsibility, you seem to come alive. Have you thought about a job in CSR?" This statement set Deap in motion. First she 'googled' the words 'corporate responsibility' to see what appeared and near the top of the list were three different universities offering master's degrees in the subject.

Immediately, Deap applied to De Montfort University in Leicester, which was offering the programme that appealed most to her, and was accepted. The timing was good, as the course started just three weeks later. To raise money to pay for her degree, she sold all of her belongings including her car, and went to live with her grandmother in Leicester. Money was still short, but fortunately her parents were supportive and made up the difference.

"I was the biggest geek there!" Deap remembers. "I absolutely loved the subject. I got to the library first thing in the morning and was always the last to leave at night. It was food for my soul and my mood began to lift a bit." After a year, she got her degree and was almost disappointed to have to leave. She returned to London to her parents' house, overqualified, under experienced and without a job. She applied for positions but had no luck, so she decided she would try to find an intern position in order to get the necessary experience.

Her first internship was a six-month post in London, working for *EIRIS*, a research company whose clients were ethical investors. The organisation screened companies for social and environmental impact. Deap worked on one aspect of impact - water usage - examining how companies used water and how they returned any water output back into the environment. She enjoyed the work initially, but it was very repetitive and she was happy when the internship ended.

A second internship took her to Belgium, working within the services team of *CSR Europe*, a network organisation made up of a number of multinational organisations. Deap was involved in a number of research projects there.

Deap came to realise that whatever job she eventually found, she absolutely needed to work with people. While investigating options, she went through a parallel exploration in her personal life. Soon after leaving *Timberland*, she connected with a friend of the family who was a spiritual healer. This woman became a mentor who coached her and taught her to meditate. "Really, she saved me," Deap explains. "And I am very grateful. I continue to work with her and she is even involved in my current business."

Ethical Value

One day, in 2011, during a meditation, the name and concept for a new business came to Deap - *Ethical Value*. She immediately searched the register in Companies House, found that the name was available, and registered the company (although she kept it dormant).

While looking for jobs and doing internships during 2011, Deap volunteered to help at a variety of conferences that interested her. She was keen to attend the conferences but didn't have the money, so she 'worked' her entrance by helping out the conference organisers. Most of the conferences focused on Corporate Social Responsibility and most of the companies who sent attendees were very, very big businesses. However, one company stood out as different, *Ethical Goods*. It was very small and its objective was to bring together charities and large businesses in order to create cause-related marketing campaigns.

Deap made an appointment to meet the managing director of *Ethical*

Goods and during the course of their discussions asked the question, "What would I have to do to get a job at this company?" After serious discussion, the MD hired her as a consultant to work on developing a service offer for SMEs (small and medium businesses), an area he was interested in exploring. Deap liked working for *Ethical Goods* and enjoyed the atmosphere at the small office.

Deap worked on this project for many months and came up with a value proposition that she felt was robust and valuable. The offering was a methodology to screen small and medium companies on their contribution to social and environmental impact - both positive and negative. Furthermore, the output of the study provided next steps for these SMEs to build on their positive initiatives. Unfortunately the MD could not manage to integrate SMEs into his business strategy, so there was no more work for Deap at *Ethical Goods*.

By now, it was 2012. Deap asked if she could keep the proposition she had developed and was told 'yes'. As a result, she dusted off her dormant brand name and resurrected her company - *Ethical Value*. She called on many associated and part-time workers to get started and before long, Deap was running her own consultancy. She took many part-time positions in order to fund her company and keep things going, but she was determined. Over the next three years she began to shape the company, and to develop contacts and additional service offers.

Ethical Value offers four main products:

1. "Bridging the Gap" - providing assistance to the HR department by creating 'safe spaces'
2. "Stakeholder Dialogues - creating Stakeholder Dialogues between companies or between individuals or departments within companies.
3. Stakeholder relationship and reputation package
4. Retail Process optimisation package

Ethical Value was officially launched as a business at the end of 2014. Deap used crowdfunding in an attempt to fund her website. It raised some funds, but not enough, so instead of paying someone else she created the website herself.

"I'm not making money yet, but I will," Deap says confidently. "I have to. The tables have turned and, after many years of supporting me, now I have to help my parents. It will work out. I don't see the detail yet, but I know I'm getting somewhere. I feel like someone on an airplane which is speeding through the sky, but I don't know where the plane will land. I keep the faith."

"I'm happy that I have finally found something that I love and want to do. My dream is to help other people and to help them realise their full potential." She concludes, "I guess the journey I have taken was necessary to get me to where I am today."

Deap describes the outcome of her personal journey well. Like all the stories, hers was as much a story of her own growth as well as the story of her career search - the two became intertwined. Has she now created an organisation that can provide a living and support her personal values? It's too early to be certain, but her career to date has been a natural progression toward this goal. Her timing is good. There are now many businesses willing to employ organisations such as *Ethical Value*. Deap has certainly created something that is in tune with current business trends and now it's up to her to run her company well.

Elizabeth's story, which follows, takes a very different turn. Elizabeth Grier-Menager works in financial services and has done so for most of her career. She likes her work but has always sought to balance her professional life with volunteering activities. Through overwork, she discovered just how crucial these 'good works' are to her ability to maintain a healthy, balanced life. When she moved to London, she discovered that part-time volunteering was virtually impossible to integrate into her working pattern, so she left her profession and did something radical; she created a charity that would enable her - and others like her - to fit meaningful volunteering efforts into their professional lives.

Elizabeth's story – Helping busy Londoners to volunteer

Volunteering started young

Elizabeth has always enjoyed volunteering and even as a teenager she sought out opportunities to help teach disadvantaged children, raise money for the church or work in soup kitchens. Where she grew up in Virginia, USA, these opportunities were plentiful so she could fit these activities between her schooling and other commitments. "My parents both worked for the Government," she explains, "and their jobs meant they both travelled significantly." In fact, during her elementary education, the family travelled together and Elizabeth and her three siblings lived in Jakarta for three years. They also moved around while she was in high school and she visited such countries as Mexico and Venezuela.

"This travel exposed me to all kinds of living conditions," Elizabeth says. "I was exposed to many types of hardship and poverty that I would never have seen had I stayed in the United States. I think this broader view gave me a desire to help others less fortunate than I." This international experience also prompted her to study International Politics at Georgetown University. It was a busy time, studying, working, holding internships but still finding time to volunteer whenever she could. Her internships spanned a range of government positions from the Ecuadorian Embassy to the CIA.

"I thought that law might be a good career for me," Elizabeth recalls. "So after graduation in 1999, I moved to New York City to take up a job as a paralegal in a large firm which specialised in securities Law. I was right 'on track'. Most of my friends decided to study law or take a job in consulting or finance." So Elizabeth was on the trajectory of a well-educated young professional launching herself onto the career ladder. Her work experience helped her to refine her ideas. After less than a year as a paralegal she knew that she definitely did <u>not</u> want to study law, so she found a job in a small consulting firm that focused on the finance sector.

Elizabeth had another motive for selecting this next job. The company had offices in London and she hoped she could arrange a transfer. Her language skills - she is fluent in Spanish, French, Italian and Portuguese as well as English - helped her and she soon arranged to move to London. The work Elizabeth did in London enabled her to broaden the knowledge of the finance sector that had begun when she worked as a paralegal. Unfortunately, less than five months into her London job, the company began to experience difficulties. As the business declined, Elizabeth took action.

A career in finance

Her experience up until that time led her to believe that she wanted to work in the finance sector so she did some research and drew up a list of the top investment banks in Europe, finding out the names of nine heads of Pan European Equity Sales desks. With this list, Elizabeth sent out an unsolicited email to each of them and asked for a job. Five senior executives from this list responded and finally, she took a sales job in convertible finance (selling convertible bonds) at *Credit Suisse*. This position offered her further training and she soon became an equities sales trader for Southern Europe.

Now 25 years old, Elizabeth threw herself into her new job, which was very, very stressful. She worked so hard that she kept getting sick and, as the illnesses became more frequent and severe, she decided to quit. A month later, she was suffering from a severe case of shingles - a condition that often occurs when individuals are under extreme stress. Deciding that her health was more important than the job, Elizabeth returned home to the USA to live with her father in Virginia and to 'take stock'.

While exploring her options, Elizabeth, once again, spent a lot of time doing volunteer work, helping language challenged children with their English studies and new immigrants who were learning English. She also volunteered at an after-school club helping Latino middle and high school kids with their homework.

Finally, Elizabeth decided to apply for an MBA at University of North Carolina at Chapel Hill. She also did an MBA exchange programme for three months in Shanghai at CEIBS (The China-Europe International Business School). It was at this point that she began to study Mandarin to add to her list of linguistic accomplishments. Healthy once again, Elizabeth finished up her MBA and received a phone call from her old boss at *Credit Suisse*, inviting her to come up to New York to meet with him.

When Elizabeth met him in New York, he revealed that he was quitting *Credit Suisse* to start up a hedge fund and he wanted her to help him set up the business. "This was my first entrepreneurial experience," Elizabeth explains. "I had to learn everything about how to set up a business from the ground up, office space, contracts, finding staff - everything! It was exciting and I worked all the time, seven days a week." But working these long hours, Elizabeth began to feel isolated. "It felt like something was missing," she summarises.

Gradually she cut back to working six days a week and then five days, and as she decreased her hours at her hedge fund job, she began to do more volunteer work. She approached a nonprofit organisation called *New York Cares* which had been set up to make volunteering easier. Using this organisation, she could select different activities to suit her availability and she took part in a wide range of events from helping at soup kitchens to teaching computer skills and even helping out during the *New York City Marathon* marathon.

Volunteering fills a need

"Helping people fulfilled a need in me," Elizabeth reflects. "I still worked very, very hard, but now I felt more connected."

Elizabeth stayed in this job, balancing her life with volunteering efforts, for two and a half years, but more 'foreign experience' still beckoned her. She wanted to move back to London. So, once again, she quit her job without having found a position in the UK. This time, her objective was clear; she wanted to work for a hedge fund in London, and she quickly found employment. Fortunately, she did manage to secure a job offer before she moved to London in August 2007. As she started her new job, Elizabeth looked for volunteering opportunities in London, just as she had in the USA, but she was soon to discover that in London, it was not easy to volunteer.

"I was desperate," she explains, "I had a demanding job where I travelled a lot, but I knew I needed to balance it with volunteer work. I had already discovered in my career how so many people just work, work, work and get on that treadmill and run, run, run. They end up just 'doing the process' and making money, but it's really a superficial life. I felt like I had to do something more, or something was missing in my life."

Elizabeth describes the difficulty, "I had just assumed that volunteering in the UK would be the same as in the USA, but it wasn't. It was as difficult as applying for a job. Many volunteer organisations have 20 page applications and then there is the vetting process - it was lengthy and complex. Furthermore, many were poorly staffed and often failed to respond to emails and phone calls on a timely basis. And most wanted a regular commitment during a week day - something that was impossible with my job."

Finally, in the last quarter of 2008, the bottom dropped out of the finance market and Elizabeth was made redundant. She took this opportunity to explore the UK voluntary sector while she looked for new employment. After a few failed attempts to volunteer, she approached the *American Women's Club of London* - an organisation loosely associated with the US Embassy - known for doing a lot of volunteering. Elizabeth was surprised to find that even the *American Women's Club* struggled to find UK volunteering activities for their members. They offered one activity - a monthly helping day at *Ronald McDonald House* in London Bridge and Elizabeth grabbed this opportunity and began to cook for families who used the facilities. While working at this charity, she asked, "What other groups come to help out?" and was told by the CEO of *Ronald McDonald House* that the *American Women's Club* was the only one.

"I was shocked," says Elizabeth. "I thought 'enough is enough!' This situation just isn't good enough!" At that point in 2009, she conceived the idea of setting up a nonprofit organisation to make volunteering easier in England, and specifically in London. Her earlier experience setting up a hedge fund in New York and her MBA prepared her for all the complexities of starting an organisation from scratch. "I never intended to run this organisation full-time forever. I just wanted to volunteer and knew that there were other people with busy lives out there just like me who were frustrated at how difficult it was to volunteer!"

Hands On London

As part of her research, she contacted the executive director of *New York Cares* and he put her in touch with an organisation called *The Hands On Network* (now called *Points of Light*). With the help and advice she received, Elizabeth set up *Hands On London* in 2010. "Interestingly, the whole process was more difficult in the UK. It's much, much harder to set up a charity in the UK - or it was in 2010. I understand that there are more options available today," Elizabeth explains. "And *pro bono* legal help was slow and the scope of work performed was so specific, it wasn't very helpful. Thank heavens for my paralegal experience! I ended up doing 85% of the work myself and finally found someone to look over what I had done." Elizabeth was helped a great deal by the *Hands On Network* in the USA which gave her advice, some skills and made helpful introductions to other foreign affiliates.

"Another obstacle was startup funding," says Elizabeth. "In the UK a charity needs £5,000 in gross annual income or in donations in order to set up. I finally ended up begging for funds from a hedge fund manager I knew who donated the £5,000 seed money." She then began to identify a variety of volunteering opportunities and organised them by type of activity, location and times that volunteers could work. The locations were vital if *Hands On London* meant to service the whole city, which is large and geographically dispersed. Elizabeth began by co-opting a group of her friends who also wanted to volunteer and the inaugural event with her team was held at *Ronald McDonald House*. In the meantime, she found another job with a hedge fund.

For the next year, Elizabeth worked flat out, writing grants, fundraising, meeting with institutions and recruiting volunteers as well as volunteering herself and, at the same time, working full-time at the hedge fund. Once again, her employer started to suffer difficulties in the challenging marketplace and in February 2011, she left her job. From this time, she lived off her savings, sold her expensive watch to pay her rent and worked to grow *Hands On London*.

"The first year, we had no office, I took no salary and had no staff, yet still, the new organisation made an impact," she recalls.

Although *Hands On London* has done many things, it is probably best known for its drive to collect winter coats in an annual campaign called *Wrap Up London,* which Elizabeth started in the autumn of 2011. Volunteers work in London Underground stations around the city and collect donations of warm coats from rush hour commuters to be passed on to asylum seekers, the fuel deprived, domestic abuse victims, the elderly and the homeless. In the most recent campaign there were more than 800 volunteers working throughout London, collecting, sorting and dispensing the coats. Fortunately, the *Metro* - the free newspaper distributed throughout the Greater London transport system - ran articles as did *Time Out* magazine, so the campaign was very well-publicised.

After the first year, the initiative grew. The charity found a great company, *Safestore*, who donated the use of a few storage units for one month so the volunteers had a place to store and sort the coats before distribution. By the second year, *Hands On London* also had some interns who could help as well as more permanent volunteers. Today, the organisation has grown to a list of 4,500 registered volunteers who work in a variety of activities. There are also now more than 100 corporate partners who have worked with *Hands On London* in order to give back to the community via volunteering, service days out, and/or donating coats. At the last *Wrap Up London* in 2014, the charity distributed coats to more than 170 shelters and refuges. The coat drive has now become an annual event and, to date, the coat collection campaign has collected and redistributed more than 42,000 coats to people in need.

Unfortunately, Elizabeth's punishing work schedule meant she became ill again, first suffering from another bout of shingles during the stress of the first *Wrap Up London* campaign, and then becoming severely ill in 2012. Fortunately by this time, there was someone else in the organisation who could step into her shoes while Elizabeth was in hospital and recuperating over the months that followed. This volunteer worked three to three and a half days every week, without pay, to keep things going.

"I tend to overwork," Elizabeth says simply. "And getting the balance right is something I have to work on. But, in a way, stepping away from the full-time management was a good thing. I never intended to work for a charity full-time. I did it to solve a problem! I wanted to volunteer and to enable others like me to have the opportunity too. I set up *Hands On London* to solve a problem so that busy Londoners like myself could volunteer around their schedules while at the same time increase the pool of volunteers who could help our fellow charity partners maintain, if not increase, their services to beneficiaries. What is great is that we also have enabled many companies to better engage with the community."

By the summer of 2013, *Hands On London* had two full-time workers and two part-time staff, plus part-time student volunteers from the USA. In July of that year, Elizabeth accepted the position of Executive Director within investor services in an international investment bank. Today, Elizabeth carries on with her job in financial service and as chair of *Hands On London*. Her employer knows she is still involved with the charity and as a senior managing director and US expat, is highly supportive of her efforts. In fact, he encouraged lots of co-workers, including other senior managing directors in the bank, to take part in various volunteering activities.

"For the last *Wrap Up London* Campaign," Elizabeth says proudly, "I recruited over 100 volunteers from the bank and people really enjoyed it! I am pleased to say that the company fully embraces and supports *Hands On London*. The experience has also changed some of the people who were previously very cynical about volunteering opportunities. My own manager told me it was the most fun he had experienced over the course of the year."

And back in the bank while people carry out their 'day job', Elizabeth explains, there is something extra in the atmosphere, extra team cohesion between staff, and an extra depth to the working environment that reaches all levels. "I believe it's opened up people, changed their perspective," she says. "I'm not sure what words to use to describe it, but it's made the work environment richer."

"I am now very happy - in my job, with my volunteering activities and living in England," she concludes. "And very important to me, I think that *Hands On London* is now independent of me - of course I'm still very involved, but it's taken on a life of its own and will continue to provide volunteering opportunities for Londoners."

So Elizabeth has now returned to her profession in the finance sector – but she also has a means of pursuing volunteering efforts. In addition, she has taken small steps to transform her working environment by engaging her colleagues in voluntary work. Elizabeth's journey was extreme - not everyone has the drive or opportunity to create an organisation and then return to a previous career - but as a result of her efforts many professionals in London will not have to take such drastic measures because they can volunteer through *Hands On London*. And Elizabeth continues to 'put the soul back' into her business life by involving her work colleagues in her efforts.

The last story in this chapter illustrates how some individuals can successfully travel a truly unique path. Neil Seligman's journey is unusual and he is definitely pioneering his approach into a solidly traditional profession - the law. His story is also a little different in that he always felt that there was something special he should be doing, but he just couldn't figure out what it was. Perhaps that's true of everyone's journey, it's just that Neil was conscious of this mission while others were not.

Despite the unusual twists and turns in his path, his story begins in a typical English family in a prosperous village in the Home Counties - the semi-rural suburbs of London.

Neil's story – Finding his purpose

Following parallel paths

Neil grew up in a traditional English village, the son of an airline pilot father and a mother who had been an air hostess. He did well academically and attended a prestigious local private school. But this summary of his youth omits a very important component of his life and mindset. Neil explains, "From an early age I felt the world to be a system of intertwined energies constantly in motion. I didn't have the language to express it at the time but I was already fascinated in human potential and the pursuit of excellence. Although I grew up in Waltham St Lawrence, in the heart of the Home Counties, I was fascinated by the 'New Age'. I followed the two paths simultaneously - being Head Boy at a private school in Reading while following and exploring my own path."

So what did Neil mean by 'his own path'? An explanation begins to emerge from his description of his time in the United States. In his late teens, Neil went to the USA where he worked as a tennis coach in a summer camp. It turns out that his bunkmate was a Reiki Master. Upon making this discovery, the two engaged in lengthy discussions. While they talked, something 'clicked' for Neil with the idea of Reiki, and he began to study it further with his bunkmate.

"I think I was open to Reiki because it was 'experiential', something I could explore for myself rather than someone else's belief system," Neil explains. "Reiki was something I could feel and share." In fact, Neil went on to explain that when he looks back, he always felt attuned to energies, but had no language to express that way of perceiving the world. A musician from a young age, he used the piano to express energies, as a tool to produce vibrations.

While Neil studied law at the University of Bristol, in parallel he began a serious study of Reiki. He soon achieved the first and second degrees of attainment and began to do Reiki healing 'on the side' while he completed his education. After his initial experience in the United

States, Neil carried on with his studies and travelled to the Pacific islands to train with the same Reiki Master who was now doing missionary work in Kiribati. After several months he was initiated to Reiki Master level in both Usui and Karuna Reiki.

A career in law

After completing his law degree, Neil continued to bar training at the Inns of Court School of Law in London, and then went on to practise as a barrister for eight years. Neil's area of expertise was personal injury and clinical negligence and he worked hard in this capacity. Neil explains, "I was a rising star - just in the wrong profession! While I enjoyed using my barrister skills, I had always thought of the law as my 'plan B' until the right thing came along. While practising I saw that, while I was very good at what I did, there were others who could perform as I did. I wanted to find something for which I was uniquely skilled."

During this time he also continued to explore different spiritual practices. Neil explained that his training has included many and diverse activities from one-to-one work with teachers, healing workshops, meditation retreats and even a three-week residential 'clowning course' in Canada, an experience which continues to underscore his mindfulness practice and art process. Neil came to understand that, "…spirituality is a function of our humanity. Everyone has it and if you listen to it, great! But it's there even if you don't use it. I like to use the analogy of wheels on a car - they are there whether the car is moving or not, but you don't have to use them, the car doesn't have to move."

As part of his personal journey, Neil travelled to Vancouver, Canada in 2008 where he found his present spiritual teacher. She set him many tasks and stimulated his introspections and insights, helping him immensely.

So, in May 2009, Neil left the bar to go on a sabbatical from which he never would return.

When trying to figure out his next move, Neil had a wide range of skills and inclinations from which to choose. He had continued his Reiki practice even after he became a barrister. He explains, "Reiki became entwined in my life. It just became a part of how I operated. I loved being a barrister, but I think it was the intellectual challenge and the skills of advocacy that appealed to me more than the law itself. My fulfilment came from the healing and coaching practice that I continued to build up on the side. This activity was genuinely precious to me." Neil's challenge was to craft a career that enabled him to express his passion around witnessing the unfolding of human potential and the pursuit of excellence.

Today, Neil has emerged from his long transition. His consultancy, *The Conscious Professional*, is winning praise from top-tier firms as he delivers resilience and mindfulness training to help individuals increase professional capacities and wellbeing. What started as a small drop-in class for judges, barristers and solicitors at *The Law Society* in 2013 is now growing into an exciting business through which Neil strives to bring together the emotional, rational and spiritual to enhance professional excellence.

Neil also offers an alternative viewpoint. "Many people feel that if they are doing something good, it means that they have to 'downscale' their lifestyle. That might be the right choice for a particular individual but it doesn't always have to be that way. When one is on the right track in life and one is really following his or her path, the natural outcomes are abundance, joy and thriving. The 'conscious business' movement presents an opportunity for us all to create, develop and grow with greater compassion, integrity and clarity. I would encourage all social entrepreneurs to start small but dream big."

And dream big is what every individual in this chapter tried to do, regardless of background or personal challenges. Although none of these individuals has yet made a global impact, they have made a big difference to the people they help. All of them had to carve a unique niche where none had existed before - whether creating a social business or a new charity, helping the population at large or employees in large corporates. These individuals had no help or guidebooks to lead them on their journey, but tomorrow's social pioneers will have more help. The next chapter focuses on stories of people who set up businesses, charities and social networks to enable others to follow an easier path.

Chapter 9

SUPPORT ORGANISATIONS

"Thousands of candles can be lighted from a single candle, and the life of the candle will not be shortened. Happiness never decreases by being shared."
Buddha

Social business, charity, 'for profit, for good', transforming a large corporate one department or event at a time - not everyone has taken one of these direct approaches. This grassroots movement of individuals trying to build social impact into their jobs has left a gaping need. Until recently, there has been no one to help, advise or guide the myriad of social pioneers who form this movement. There were no guidebooks, websites or networking groups to provide advice and guidance. But the situation has changed. Another route taken by social pioneers has been to provide this support and over the past few years, organisations, books and networks have popped up all over the world.

The first journey chronicled in this chapter illustrates how an individual came to a crossroads where she felt certain that her next contribution would be to help others on their journeys. Like many others who are searching for a more meaningful and holistic approach to work and life, Maggie De Pree's life to date can be viewed as a 'quest' - a quest that she continues up to the present moment.

Maggie's story – Helping others find their path

Values from an early age

Maggie was born and grew up in Portland, Oregon a city in the Pacific Northwest of the United States. This region has always fostered an ethos of individual responsibility and sensitivity to the environment, and Maggie's upbringing instilled in her the importance of community as well as the environment and how the two were interconnected. As a result, she grew up surrounded by a strong sense of civic responsibility.

When Maggie went to university, she decided to attend Scripps - a respected women's liberal arts college in Southern California - and Maggie suffered a bit of culture shock when she moved south. "When I arrived in California," she recalls, "I was shocked at the 'disconnect' between people and the environment. Growing up where I grew up, I assumed it would be the same everywhere - but my eyes were opened to a different truth. It was clear that in Southern California there had been no real urban planning. There were miles and miles of freeways, strip malls and smog littering the landscape." This awakening made her realise that not every place was like Portland.

While at university, Maggie wrote a thesis that focused on the connection between childcare and women. From her studies it became clear that no matter the intention between couples, the woman was typically the 'default' when childcare issues arose. The inequity intrigued her - it didn't seem fair. She studied one of the national programmes - *Head Start* - to obtain data for her thesis. The *Head Start Program* was originally launched in 1965 in order to give pre-school children from poor families a better chance of succeeding when they entered the school system. The programme worked not only with the children, but also with their families to help provide them with skills and a more stable home environment.

The data revealed that the programme wasn't fulfilling its intended function, but it continued to be kept in place and funded for political reasons. In other words, the presence of the programme gave the illusion of solving a problem that wasn't actually being solved. The government money could have been better spent. But, no politician wanted to be seen to be the one that stopped *Head Start*.

However, because Maggie's own family worked in local Portland government she grew up with a fundamental belief that government could be effective and get things done. The insights she took from investigating the *Head Start Program* led her to ponder, "What is the best way to get stuff done?"

"I don't really remember the belief I held at the time," Maggie explains. "I was just very curious that politicians weren't actually pursuing outcomes and impact, but rather, were pursuing votes and dollars. It led to more disillusionment with government at that time. Though I also simultaneously was learning in my economics degree studies about market failures - major failures of the market to take account of social issues like gender and environment. I think together these insights led me to question about how systems work or, in other words, 'how to get stuff done."

Starting a career

After graduation, Maggie headed to Washington DC where she found a job with *Arthur Andersen* as a research analyst. She worked in the Office of Federal Tax Service, Economic Analysis Division, where her role was to look for ways that *Arthur Andersen* clients could minimise their tax liabilities. In fact, the whole purpose of the group was to save money for clients by reducing their tax liability. The work was an important learning experience for Maggie, not only from an analytical point of view, but also in terms of seeing how big organisations worked. Culturally, she found the whole experience very depressing.

At *Arthur Andersen* everyone worked long days and for what? To get promoted and continue to work long days and long weeks. "There was only one woman partner," Maggie recalls, "And no minority partners at all. It was all 'white men', aged, tired and worn down."

Maggie goes on to describe her 'ah ha!' moment, "I looked up one day and saw many tired people, aged before their time and managed by tired, pre-aged managers and I thought 'What am I doing here? Why am I doing this?'"

Maggie began to question her whole pathway, and the underlying assumption that her next step in life was to get a good job in a big company, make money and build a career in an organisational hierarchy. She quit *Arthur Andersen* and moved to Boston, where she embarked on a quest to find meaning in her life and to try to map out a path for herself. Working in a variety of temp jobs and then in government, she discovered that work alone was not enough. Boston's lack of 'personal community' led Maggie to introspection and eventually, to a move back to Portland.

Once back in her home town, Maggie quickly found a job as an office manager for a city councillor and then, moved to a job at *Portland Energy Conservation* (now *PECI*), a not-for-profit. In her role, Maggie was frequently faced with the issue of 'sustainability'. Her work for *PECI* led her to understand that it is possible to leverage the private sector to make energy conservation and move toward energy efficiency.

In 1997-98, Maggie's boss at *PECI* left to work for another environmental startup called *ECOS*, and Maggie soon followed and became *ECOS*' first employee in Portland. The focus at *ECOS* was energy efficiency consulting and the typical project was to design and implement large-scale energy efficiency projects which they termed 'Market Transformations'. These projects covered a wide range of businesses that spanned from manufacturers of items as small as light bulbs to larger appliances such as washing machines. *ECOS*, in effect, worked as a catalyst between companies and consumers, and consulted with the whole supply chain around energy savings, including policy makers.

From her work at *ECOS*, Maggie developed the view that for anything to succeed, one must view entire systems. So, for example, to answer the question: "Why are people buying energy efficient products?" one needs to look at 'the whole', from development, cost, legislation, marketing, sales and disposal. As a natural 'systems thinker', this approach excited and energised Maggie and she saw it as a method for actually accomplishing change.

She elaborates, "One of the biggest blocks to sustainability is short termism - the short termism driven by the stock market and quarterly reporting of company profits as well as the short-termism of elected government officials and policy makers."

At the time, Maggie began to consider going to business school. So, after four years at *ECOS* she left to study for an MBA at The University of California Los Angeles (UCLA). At business school she pursued her interest in entrepreneurship and studied it from a number of different perspectives. Maggie explains, "At business school I did two different internships that were very, very meaningful for me: one at *Nike* and the other at *Johnson & Johnson*. From these projects I observed how corporates made decisions to invest in sustainability."

After graduating, Maggie was asked by *ECOS* to return to Portland to take up a more senior role. It took her another two years to she realise that she had 'moved on' and needed something different in her career. She had developed a taste for the 'international' - having studied in Paris during both her MBA and at university, and was once again drawn to the energy and excitement of a more global city. She worked with a life coach to help her identify her own tensions and aspirations. Should she stay in Portland where she had a community, or was she now ready to move out into the wider world? Did she want to be an entrepreneur or did she want to pursue her personal goals by working in a large corporate environment?

Europe beckons

Maggie began applying to and was interviewed by various organisations to enable her move to Europe. Her sister was in London, so Maggie headed for England. She managed to get a job using her *Nike* connections, at a consultancy called *SustainAbility*, a business that advised large corporates on sustainability issues. She was assigned a research role that focused on 'social entrepreneurship', in other words, entrepreneurship that was concerned with social issues, with a purpose beyond just making money. Maggie worked in this role from 2006 to 2009 where she gained both experience and the perspective to understand what 'worked', and began to get a broader view of what was happening in the world.

The cultural perspective also increased her learning. Maggie explains, "I found the willingness to critique businesses, and even the capitalist business model, was far stronger in the UK than in the USA. Professionals were more willing to question the fundamentals of market systems and this openness led me to consider a broader range of options or potential solutions in consulting situations."

While at *SustainAbility*, Maggie collaborated with the company's founder John Elkington, a thought leader in the field. Together, they discovered that social entrepreneurship wasn't just limited to the fringes of society, but was actually being pursued within the heart of some of the biggest companies. They started referring to these corporate innovators as 'social intrapreneurs', and authored a report on the topic called: *The Social Intrapreneur: A Field Guide for Corporate*

Changemakers. In 2008, John left to set up a new business, *Volans*. After his departure, some of the energy disappeared from Maggie's work environment, so she decided to leave as well.

With a colleague from *IDEO* and another partner, she set up a business called *Imaginals*, named after the cells in caterpillars that are responsible for the transformation from caterpillar into butterfly. *Imaginals* was a design and innovation consultancy that focused on sustainability and social intrapreneurship.

However, in 2013, tensions between the business partners surfaced. As Maggie worked to balance her role as an entrepreneur with her role as a mother (her daughter was born in 2010), her business partners pursued a vision to transform *Imaginals* into a fast-paced, global technology company. This tension eventually led to a splitting of the partnership, and Maggie left *Imaginals* and set up her own company, *The Human Agency*.

The League of Intrapreneurs

At the same time, Maggie was contacted by a woman she knew from *SustainAbility* who had moved to *Ashoka*, a nonprofit organisation whose broad mission is to support social entrepreneurs who are leading and collaborating with change makers. This woman wanted to work with Maggie on a project to identify corporate change makers. From these initial discussions, *The League of Intrapreneurs* was born. The goal was to:

1. Raise awareness of social intrapreneurship
2. Empower individuals with a sense of personal responsibility

Ashoka had already created a web platform to enable an 'open source competition' called *Changemakers*. Maggie and the rest of the team decided to use this tool to try to identify intrapreneurs. They posted the question: "Are you a social intrapreneur - working within a large corporate to drive transformative change around social and/or environmental challenges?"

They launched this initiative in September 2012, calling it *The League of Intrapreneurs Competition*, and received over 200 entries from around the world. Of these, four finalists were selected as winners, receiving six months of *pro bono* consultancy from *Accenture Development Partnerships*. The team also created a 'toolkit' to help aspiring social intrapreneurs.

When asked about the responses, particularly whether there were differences in approach between the UK and USA, Maggie noticed that the USA tended to focus more heavily on technological innovation. She also discovered that, in all cases, the intrapreneurs had to be comfortable with challenging the *status quo*.

The Human Agency

Today, Maggie carries on with *The Human Agency* and other work.

This organisation is about:

1. 'Agency' or the capacity of a person, a lone individual, to act in a world by his/herself, without looking to others to do so.
2. Being human - being a whole individual at work and removing the masks that we so often wear to ask "What's the right thing to do?" "What is the right way to show up" in any given instance.

Rather like a 'think tank', *The Human Agency* is a 'think/do tank'. As an organisation it looks for funding via crowdsourcing, and/or from foundations and business sponsorship.

Returning to her strength - holistic systems - Maggie observes, "All around us the systems are constantly changing. What I have tried to do is create a 'space' - a virtual space - where we can all learn together." She continues, "With the benefits of a learning culture we can ask: How should we organise? What's the least bureaucratic structure we can build that will yield the greatest result?"

In addition to these initiatives, Maggie continues to do consulting work for businesses and organisations seeking answers to questions around sustainability.

Maggie believes this group approach will become more and more critical as the working model shifts. Maggie explains, "In the next generation (new graduates) we can see a shift in assumptions. These workers will not be beholden to a single employer and will begin to describe their work history in terms of 'output' rather than job descriptions. They will aspire to be judged on what they have done rather than on rank in an organisation."

Technology is enabling all these changes and the change itself is a process, not a goal. Explaining what drives her now, Maggie responds, "I cannot, once exposed to these issues, not do something about them. Now I ask myself, where else can I have meaningful impact?"

Maggie is now exploring ways to organise local communities so that they can have a voice in these issues. How much is enough? Her next mission is to create a groundswell among the general population to question these fundamental values.

So, Maggie's journey led her from traditional organisations to startups with a pro-environment agenda, from internships in large corporations to consultancies. Today, she runs a consultancy that helps individuals to drive social change from within traditional employment. In addition *The League of Intrapreneurs* is alive and active, and Maggie is still involved. There is a website which provide contacts, events and inspiration as well as a 'tool kit' for 'cubicle warriors.'

Maggie was determined to help individuals wanting to drive changes within their work environment, but what about businesses that want to do something different? In earlier chapters there were some examples. Erika Uffindell's consultancy helps business leaders. Neil Seligman helps individuals, particularly professionals such as barristers. Lucy Findlay helps maintain the standards of existing social enterprises. But what about someone who wants to set up a social enterprise? Where do they go for help?

The answer is that today there are more and more options, and Craig Dearden-Phillips' organisation, *Stepping Out*, and his book *Your Chance to Change the World* both provide help and guidance to individuals who want to start a small, socially focused business. Craig learned these lessons 'the hard way', through personal experience, but his efforts have eased the path for others who also want to take this route.

Craig's story – Helping others change the world

The early years

Craig was born in the north of England to parents who worked hard and managed to move from their working class origins to a middle class lifestyle. Like many people with similar success stories, they gravitated to politically conservative values and supported Margaret Thatcher. However, Craig took a different political direction. Growing up in the middle of an area affected by strikes, job losses and businesses in decline, he was all too aware of the misery around him. His response was to join the Labour party and he began to take a great interest in politics.

He was the first person in his family to go to university, and became involved in student politics, where he witnessed backbiting, nastiness and bickering amongst the other students - and it troubled him. He considered this behaviour unpleasant and unnecessary. As a result, he soon decided that he did not want to be a politician and although he carried on with his political studies, he had no idea how he wanted to use his education.

Craig graduated with a degree in Politics from Newcastle University and was about to start on an advanced degree course when he had a mental breakdown. "I was about as close as you can get to needing to be institutionalised without it actually happening," Craig explains. As part of his therapy during recovery he did a couple of years of volunteer work and this experience kicked off a new career direction, away from politics and the corporate world. He has never looked back.

As part of his volunteer work, Craig spent some time working with people who had learning disabilities. These interactions, combined with his personal experience, led him to decide that he wanted to concentrate his efforts on helping those with mental and physical health problems. His experience of working in a charity called *Skills for People* kept him interested and he continued to learn about these issues from the age of 21 to 24.

"During this time I realised that the recipients of 'help' had very little control over their help," explains Craig. "They didn't manage the funds allocated for them nor did they have any say in the activities designed to help them. In fact, they had very little control over anything in their lives and neither the charities nor the National Health Service (NHS) were doing anything to remedy the situation."

Craig decided that things should be different. His experience in this small charity provided the inspiration and foundation for his next career move. "What I believe in today is very much based on what I picked up at that time," he reflects. "I identified with what they were trying to do; the lives of the people I got involved with were lives that were 'wanting to be lived' but they weren't being lived."

Speaking Up

Craig realised that these people had no 'voice' in their care, simply by virtue of their disabilities. Furthermore, the care systems weren't working. In general, these systems didn't help disabled individuals to achieve their full potential. So, in 1996, Craig set up a small charity and named it *Speaking Up*.

The goal for *Speaking Up* wasn't merely to provide better services and advocacy, it was also into instil a sense of confidence and aspiration in those who used its services. Craig was frequently quoted as saying that he wanted to "raise the bar" in terms of his constituents' self-belief and ambition. During the first decade of the new millennium both Craig and *Speaking Up* went from success to success. He obtained money from the lottery fund and matching funds from the Government, and set about expanding his offerings and services. In 2002 *Speaking Up* was a winner in *The Guardian's* charity awards.

Unfortunately, this recognition came at the time when funding was drying up, so Craig needed to figure out a new way to fund *Speaking Up* in order to continue and grow both its quality of service and its reach. To this end, he decided to take a completely different tack and approach the business community. Having begun to work on getting his MBA, Craig was becoming well versed in how to do just this, and he realised that he needed to apply many of the same disciplines and structures found in the business world.

After a lot of hard work, he finally found an organisation that would help. A venture philanthropist organisation called *Impetus Trust* gave him £500,000 and helped him to develop a business plan and strategy. Craig brought in directors from the private sector, in particular, a sales director who began to solicit contracts from more and more NHS care trusts and local authorities to provide selected services and advocacy for learning disabled people. *Speaking Up's* success continued and the organisation won a £3m contract from the Government.

Incredibly, during this time Craig also found time to write a book entitled *Your Chance to Change the World: The No-fibbing Guide to Social Entrepreneurship* (Directory of Social Change, 2008), and it does exactly what it says on the cover. The book is a step-by-step guide to setting up a social business and it incorporates much of what Craig learned as he struggled to grow his charity. He sets out a clear list of activities that all businesses should follow to ensure success and does so in a very accessible manner. This approach certainly worked for *Speaking Up*.

As the organisation grew, it acquired a smaller charity and eventually, renamed itself *VoiceAbility*, the name that it still uses today. Craig expanded his role to act as an advocate for this marginalised segment of the population in discussions with the NHS and the UK Government. He wrote articles, appeared before government committees and gave talks all over the United Kingdom. Over time, *VoiceAbility* provided more and more services for its constituency, including NHS Complaints, community advocacy, and training services.

Stepping Out

As the charity got bigger, Craig's role shifted from CEO to Chair. Finally, when it grew to £10m in 2012, he felt he had done as much as he could do and left to start a different venture, which he called *Stepping Out*. Craig's new social business grew out of his experience interacting with government (social services) and the NHS and he set up *Stepping Out* to help public sector organisations to develop and grow successful social enterprises.

Craig credits his success to the social enterprise model that has allowed him to cherry pick from the private and voluntary sectors and combine them to best effect. He says, "I learned very early on that the private sector is good at efficiency and being straightforward and simple, while the public and voluntary sector is prone to inertia, a real lack of 'can do'. I have always wanted social business to be a hybrid, taking the very best of private sector ethos with the best of the public and voluntary sectors." The model sits comfortably with his politics, which he described in a 2008 interview with *The Guardian* newspaper as "having the idealism of the left, while using the methods of the right". During this period, Craig's politics also shifted to a more 'middle road' approach.

So, how does Craig's social enterprise work? *Stepping Out* exists to help the increasing number of private enterprises that are emerging from the public sector. In addition to the good work done by the organisation, Craig takes 15% of any excess earned and puts it into another entity he created, the *Stepping Out Foundation* which, in turn, provides seed money to emerging social enterprises. "Social enterprises are on the rise," explains Craig. "I'm seeing more and more thinking people in the traditional business world who are opting out and trying to create businesses which also address social issues."

Craig's story illustrates how entirely unplanned circumstances can set social entrepreneurs on their path. His first encounter with the NHS and social services was as a user of their services, so he was in a position to observe first-hand how these agencies worked. The voluntary work that was part of his recovery helped him to return to full health, but also launched him into what would become his career path. He was and is a 'doer' and a problem solver and he quickly engaged with trying to solve the problems that he encountered. In doing so, he created his own bespoke career ladder, first working in a charity, then setting up and running a successful charity and finally, establishing a social business which helps others to establish social businesses.

It's not always necessary or possible to follow a career path that leads directly from the end of school or university. For many of the social pioneers in this book, the search for the 'right' job provides them with the experience to step into the role when the opportunity appears. Craig moved from helping individuals in *VoiceAbility*, to helping people who wanted to set up social enterprises by providing both consultancy and, in some cases, the seed money to turn a good idea into a reality.

But what about existing businesses, big and small - is there any place that interested owners and managers can go for help, inspiration and to find a network of like-minded individuals? Gina Hayden provides help for many of these companies by focusing on business managers and executives. Her story is another example of someone who followed a somewhat tortuous journey before finding a comfortable path.

Gina's story – Helping business leaders

A holistic perspective from the start

"Since I was very young, it's always been important to me to feel I had a choice," Gina begins. "I think happiness is, among other things, about believing we have choice and this view has driven my life direction."

In trying to explain how she arrived at this conclusion, Gina started by describing her childhood in South Africa. Her parents were both from a Christian background and she started going to a Methodist church at the age of two. She dutifully attended each week until she was 16 years old and was confirmed in the church. The first Sunday in church after her confirmation she experienced one of those 'ah ha!' moments. As she looked at the minister holding the bible and preaching, she thought, "How does he know his truth and his book is 'the Truth'? After all, there are many other religions which have their books and each believes that they preach 'the Truth', that they are 'right' and that the others are wrong."

From that moment, Gina began to search for an 'umbrella' belief system, a 'book of beliefs' that catered for everyone's religious doctrine with the conviction that there must be one that encompassed all truths. At the age of 19 or 20 she discovered Buddhism and although not a practicing Buddhist, she decided that the Buddhist philosophy came closest to being the 'umbrella' belief system - a unifying system. Gina recalls, "Looking back I realise that the underlying essence of my life has evolved around what I can evolve to be, and how can I build something that unifies things, unifies everything without making others' belief systems wrong."

Gina attended university in South Africa and did a Psychology degree. After graduating, she found a job doing psychometric profiling for a small consulting firm and although she enjoyed this work very much, after a few years she decided to apply to graduate school to obtain a master's degree in Clinical Psychology. Unfortunately for Gina, the Affirmative Action requirement meant that places in the universities where she applied were skewed toward complying with these numbers. (Affirmative Action is the South African policy designed to ensure that the diverse population sectors are fairly represented across companies and organisations, a kind of positive discrimination.)

This situation brought Gina to a key branch point in her life journey. She realised that, in the foreseeable future, she would never be able to obtain the degree and the future she wanted as long as she remained in South Africa, so she took a giant step into the unknown. She packed her bags, left her family, friends and native country and moved to London to look for opportunities to study in the UK.

A voyage into the unknown

"There I was, aged 29, with suitcase in hand and ready to start over," remembers Gina. "But there is something great about being in a foreign country, especially the UK, you can 're-form' yourself." Gina went on to explain how she used her move to do just that. In many ways, she found the British culture enabled her to do more things and do them comfortably. "England feels more organised and safe to me, while Africa feels more brutal, life is cheaper," Gina says. "And this brutality permeates everything in the culture, both private and business life. In the UK, there are rules that you can rely on, so it's easier to build something new. You can trust the rules and work within them."

Gina obtained her master's in Counselling Psychology, working for low wages in market research and secretarial jobs while she completed her studies. She found a job doing psychometric profiling at *PricewaterhouseCoopers* (*PwC*) and within that organisation her career developed and grew. Her next role at *PwC* was as a leadership development consultant. "I was very fortunate," she explains. "I had a boss who was innovative, experimental and encouraging." Things seemed to click and Gina's career prospered and advanced.

After five years, she left *PwC* and set up her own consulting business to focus on leadership development and business consulting. "I was very interested in how to get people to relate to each other authentically in the workplace. A lot of what I did was about getting people to step out from behind their corporate masks and connect to each other, as people," Gina explains. "Very often in teams, relationships can get stuck, which gets in the way of the productivity of the team. When team members stop defending their positions on some issue and get behind a common goal, and understand each other as humans, connection can happen."

Gina had always been intuitive, and when she hit 39 years old, she sensed that her 40s would be a different time for her. Her 30s were a decade when she was experimenting with her power to be expansive and creative in a business environment. It was a time in which she established her career. Now, she felt that when she turned 40, there would be a shift in her life that would force her to focus inwards. As events would prove, Gina was right.

In 2008, at the age of 40, she fell pregnant and found that her partner, also originally from South Africa, was not supportive. Realising that she would soon be a single mother in an impending recession, she was vulnerable as a consultant and on her own in London, so she returned to South Africa for what she planned to be a period of maternity leave. While initially attempting to maintain the relationship with the father of her child, she realised after a time that this would not work out and she moved to be closer to her family in another town.

"I realise now that it was a necessary 'breakdown' of my identity so that I could undergo another period of personal growth," Gina explains. "I didn't know what to do and couldn't figure out how to work my way out of it, how to escape." Luckily, a friend who understood the situation and sensed that something was desperately wrong, helped out by organising the move within South Africa to where Gina's family lived. In the end, Gina remained living in South Africa for a further three years.

Next, a few key events propelled Gina into a new phase of life. The first happened when she discovered the website for *Creative Consciousness,* and the messages on it struck home. She signed up for a Consciousness, Awareness and Development course and began to get involved. She had a revelation during the first four days of the course when the discussion focused on the question 'Who am I?' The participants spent a long time trying to describe who there were and, after some discussion, the facilitator finally revealed, "'I' is a letter. That means that 'I' am a movement of language in time." This exercise was intended to show everyone how each person had been constrained by their own personal construction of self.

Gina explains, "I realised that how I saw myself was just a construction, a bundle of thoughts that I had been taking as the truth about myself. These thoughts had also been limiting me. With this awareness came a fantastic sense of freedom - the freedom to be a creator of my own life rather than be in reaction to my beliefs or views of yourself, or be a victim of these." She started to wonder how this approach could be applied to business life. Gina began writing, and researching on the internet to find out more.

Conscious Capitalism/Conscious Leadership

On the web, Gina discovered work that existed around the Consciousness Quotient, Conscious Leadership and Conscious Capitalism, learning more and more as her exploration progressed. She was drawn to Conscious Capitalism and had a strong feeling that she needed to be in the same room as two of the co-founders of the movement, John Mackey (*Whole Foods Market* co-CEO) and Raj Sisodia, but with no idea about how this would happen. She started a blog on these topics and created a following, slowly building up a network of like-minded individuals. Finally, in 2012, she travelled to the US to attend a Conscious Capitalism Summit and from this event, got on its mailing list.

As a result of being on this mailing list, and living back in London, Gina found herself invited to lunch by Raj Sisodia, one of the people she was trying to meet. He wanted to link up with several interested people to see about the possibility of setting up a UK chapter for Conscious Capitalism. She became involved in the activities around forming a UK chapter, and helped to arrange a dinner for John Mackey to meet with about a dozen UK CEOs in order to promote Conscious Capitalism. Sitting at the dinner table at one point in the evening, she looked around her and thought, "This is exactly what I envisioned two years ago and it has come true."

"I have real passion for promoting Conscious Leadership," Gina explains. "The way I see it, businesses are very powerful change agents - in some ways, more powerful than governments. I share the view of Conscious Capitalism that businesses cannot evolve further than the level of consciousness of their leader." Gina believes that business leaders have the power and a chance to impact the culture of their company and their employees' lives. Now that big businesses are global and the business network - assisted by technology - extends around the world, these leaders are well positioned to make a major impact. "But they need to get past their egos first. We all have egos, and this separates us and makes us conduct business by trying to get the most for ourselves."

New ways of doing business include collaboration, rather than competition, with former competitors, and looking for ways to maximise the benefit for all stakeholders involved in a business.

What does Conscious Leadership look like? *The Global Centre for Conscious Leadership* has worked extensively to try to begin to map an answer this question. The group has developed a blueprint, a map so that business leaders can use it as a mirror in which to view themselves. The blueprint then becomes a leadership development tool.

So what is Gina's next step? She is now doing what she always aspired to do. In many ways all the different jobs, moves, education and experience in her life have led her to this point. She wants to continue to work with and help business leadership develop to be more conscious in its actions. Gina believes that everyone benefits: the leader, the company, employees, customers, and society. "I believe that this work is my way of contributing to the world," says Gina. "And it's extremely important to me to feel like I am making a contribution."

"I have always looked for unifying principles in all the important aspects of life. There is a 'oneness' or 'wholeness' about humanity, but business has generally keep itself outside of this unity - at least in recent decades. Business can be inclusive. It employs people and serves people. Many businesses now have a global reach, so they could truly act as a unifying force, but only if the leaders are engaged in such a mission." Gina focuses on business because, in today's world, it is a useful portal to increase connectedness and unity in the world and it's vitally important to her to contribute to building this connectedness.

Gina concentrates on helping business leaders, primarily in large and international corporations, by providing tools and information for those ready to make a change. But what about smaller companies - not social enterprises, but small and medium-sized national businesses. How are they being encouraged in their social efforts and 'doing good'? Kay Allen's story is one answer to this question.

Like many of the individuals in earlier chapters, Kay chose to work with business leaders to achieve significant social benefit, yet in the end, this work was not enough to satisfy her urge to 'give back'. She moved on to take direct action, in both creating her own small business and working with government initiatives to encourage others to contribute to society.

Kay's story, which follows, starts off in the traditional business world where Kay was lucky in that she found herself working at a senior level with sympathetic bosses. These individuals enabled her to find her feet in establishing socially beneficial programmes. As part of this work, she became involved with large charities and government initiatives, and was soon taking part in a variety of activities concerned with helping socially disadvantaged individuals. From these roles she segued into setting up her own socially beneficial small business, as well as taking on consulting work in order to 'pay the rent' and fund her various activities.

Kay's most recent activity is an organisation called *Trading for Good*, which helps to promote and publicise 'good works' and 'social contributions' made by SMEs (Small and Medium Enterprises) who cannot afford to pay for such publicity and rarely get the accolades they deserve. Kay's story illustrates the path she took and demonstrates how it is possible for individuals to make a contribution as intrapreneurs, running small businesses and working with government.

Kay's story – The business benefits of 'doing good'

A traditional start

Kay Allen started her business life in HR. "I didn't have a particularly good education, wasn't sure what I wanted to do, so I just bumbled into a career," she explains. "I joined *B&Q* (a major UK retailer) in 1989 and was lucky. I worked for a fabulous Managing Director (MD) - Martin Toogood - a man who believed in sustainable business practices; as part of his management team, I took part in creating strategies to support these practices." In this position, Kay put together strategies for employment of over 50s and disabled individuals at a time when few businesses focused on these employee groups.

In researching her strategy, Kay became involved in many activities outside work and she was fortunate that her efforts were supported by the MD of *B&Q*. As a result, she was appointed as commissioner on the UK Government's *Disability Rights Commission*. She also got involved with the charity *AgeUK*, plus various other charities and groups representing disabled people. Kay soon learned that it could be straightforward, and often cost no extra, to make business environments accessible. Kay also played a role in setting up training programmes that taught employees to be more customer-oriented, another key prong of a sustainable business strategy.

The best approach

Kay stayed at *B&Q* for about five years and then left to take a job at *BskyB*. "It was the right moment for me to make a change," Kay explains. "It opened up and taught me a new business area, communications and technology, both critical in the increasingly technological world of the 1990s." At *BskyB*, Kay set up an 'accessibility team' and was instrumental in improving communications for people with a hearing impairment. *BskyB* started using sign language interpretation on some programmes and the quality and frequency of subtitling improved dramatically. Kay attributes much of her success to being able to put together a cogent business argument for making these changes.

"What many CSR professionals fail to do is to get inside the head of the CEO," Kay reveals. "The way to describe what they should be thinking is with an 'and'. For example, I want my business to be a huge corporate success. How do I do that and be socially responsible?"

"I understood what kept the executives up at night. What their problems were. And I knew that if I could explain what I wanted to do in terms that helped them solve their problems, we would have a 'win/win' situation." Kay explained how her first steps in a new job would be to thoroughly understand the business. Next, it was necessary to understand the business plan. "After all," she concludes, "business does have to be sustainable."

After around three years at *BskyB*, Kay was headhunted for a job at the *Royal Mail Group* (the UK postal service). "Working at the *Royal Mail Group* was phenomenal and a real eye opener for me," says Kay. "Postmen and women are some of the kindest people in the world. Most of them do significant work outside their jobs, for charity." From her time at the *Royal Mail Group*, Kay's experiences began to crystallise and she realised that, "Leadership is everything!" Kay understood that she had been extremely fortunate and privileged to have worked for many excellent leaders, who truly inspired people.

As *Royal Mail Group* underwent various reorganisations, Kay decided it was time to leave. She didn't have a job when she made this decision so she set up her own business and called it *Really Useful Stuff*. The business, which is still going strong, is a not-for-profit social enterprise that sells products designed to make daily life easier for disabled and older people. At the same time, Kay wrote and published a book entitled *Corporates are from Mars, Charities are from Venus* (Diverse Advice Limited, 2012). This book consolidated Kay's experiences and learning from working with both charities and large businesses in the UK. It was fortunate that her book was completed by the end of 2011, because in December of that year she received a call from Steve Hilton, an adviser to Prime Minister David Cameron's Government.

A call from the government

"I'm 'the Queen of networking' and I suppose that's how I came to be rung," Kay explains. "I was posed the question 'How do we get the 'Big Society' ethos into small businesses? In fact, how do we get a feeling for what small businesses are doing now?"

As a first step, Kay went off and did some research on small businesses in the UK. Up until that point there had been an enormous amount of anecdotal evidence that small businesses were very involved in their communities, but there was no consolidated, hard evidence for the Government to examine. Another issue that emerged was that small businesses found it difficult to publicise their activities - even if they wanted to do so - because they have neither the infrastructure nor the resources to broadcast their good works.

Kay determined that a platform on which SMEs could publicise their good works should be created. Such a platform could provide multiple benefits. For example, during her research, Kay determined that SMEs tend to learn 'peer to peer', so if another SME does something clever, a small business is more likely to identify with these efforts and try it. Thus, *Trading for Good* was born.

Five key insights that shaped the platform:

1. SMEs learn peer to peer
2. SMEs need quick access to relevant information

3. It should let proud businesses 'shout about' their achievements
4. It should allow the SMEs to share stories and learning
5. It should be quick, simple and easy

Kay explains, "The philosophy underpinning *Trading for Good* was not about telling SMEs what they must do, rather it was about them 'telling us what they are already doing.' We hope that this 'show and tell' approach might nudge businesses to do a little bit more by sharing best practice with others."

The beta-site was launched in July 2012 and was met with a positive response. By the end of 2014 approximately 19,000 SMEs had registered, and Kay has plans to grow the network still further on a region by region basis. Today, *Trading for Good* is a not-for-profit that relies on contributions and support from larger businesses and it is moving from strength to strength. So far, it has acted to facilitate relationships and smooth out interactions between SMEs and large corporates, particularly in their role as purchaser or prime contractor with SMEs. The organisation has also helped SMEs work better with young people and the environment.

How does Kay measure her success at *Trading for Good*? Her answer: the number of SMEs who have signed up for *Trading for Good*, and the quality of their activities.

Always busy, today Kay divides her time between growing *Trading for Good* by engaging regional organisations, growing her social enterprise *Really Useful Stuff* - now a family run business - and running a boutique consulting business, *Diverse Advice Ltd* to share her business skills and experience with other businesses.

Kay's experience illustrates that someone with determination can develop a programme for social benefit no matter what the legal entity. Furthermore, with such a strong business background and experience working with government, she is well connected and understands how to influence both these types of organisation in order to support her efforts. None of her experience was 'lost', rather she used it to build charities and a public platform to publicise and encourage small businesses that make social contributions.

So, far this chapter has told the stories of people who help different constituents to 'do good', whether these are individuals in large corporations, social businesses or just small businesses who want to give back to the communities. There are many such groups springing up all over the world. The strength of this movement is growing and new connections and networks are forged daily, both locally and internationally. Mark Stevenson's activities - his speaking engagements, his writing and his establishment of a global network to deal with social issues - illustrates yet another approach.

Mark S's story – Changing Corporate Culture & Mobilising People

An unusual start

Mark Stevenson was the first in his family to attend higher education when he went to University of Salford, Manchester, to study business computing. Even then, his ambitions were divided. He understood the importance of getting a formal education but his first love was music. A Manchester-based university offered a thriving music scene and throughout his education, he remained a part-time musician, playing, writing and performing.

He continued to straddle both these worlds after he graduated and moved to London. He took various 'proper jobs' - such as computer industry analyst and helping to set up a technology PR firm, before finding that a freelance life, working as a writer, cryptography consultant and general 'brain for hire' suited him better as he continued to try to carve out a music career. He carried on working in this manner for the next ten years. His band, *Clear*, was the first UK band ever to 'crowdfund', having never reached agreement over contractual terms with a record company. They released an album in 2003 that spawned two singles but failed to raise their profile much above their existing fan base. Eventually, the group disbanded in 2005 and Mark took stock of his situation.

Hitting his early 30s caused Mark to think about his future - marriage, a family, a house with a mortgage. He felt he might never be able to take on these responsibilities if he continued along the career path he had been following. Mark decided that his next step should be a role in the corporate world so he found a job as Marketing Director in a financial transactions company. Although he performed well in the role, the environment didn't excite him and his indifferent attitude began to show. Eventually, this proved his undoing and after 18 months, he and his employer parted ways.

A new perspective emerges

It was then that Mark realised that the lack of wife, family or mortgage wasn't a problem, but a liberation. "There was no one waiting for me to put food on the table, so I asked myself what I really cared about - because I realised there was very little stopping me dedicating my life to whatever that was." He continues, "I knew what I didn't like: the atmosphere of fear and cynicism that pervades society and so much of our culture, politics and economics. I also got annoyed by the anti-intellectualism that was present, and felt frustrated by the general resistance to new ideas that might make the world better. So, I decided to dedicate my life to spreading a movement around what I call 'Pragmatic Optimism' - being unashamed to dream big and then bring our best creative and critical skills to realising those dreams"

Mark spent the next year working as a stand-up comedian. "I thought that being a stand-up would help me distil my thoughts and ideas," he says. "It forced me to deliver ideas succinctly. It was excellent training." And while Mark worked, he thought about what he wanted to do next; it wasn't entirely clear.

Mark also wrote and published a book called *An Optimist's Tour of the Future* (Profile Books, 2012) in which he tours around the world looking at cutting edge innovations in science and discusses how these might impact the environment and the world. With his background in performance, particularly stand-up comedy, Mark's initial book tours were the beginnings of the speaking career he now enjoys. This activity has also given him direct feedback on the impact of his writing and philosophy, and an insight into people's typical reactions to his views. "Most people would read the book or hear me speak," he remembers, "and they were lovely - very flattering, until they asked me - as many, many people did: 'What can I do?'"

"I discovered that if you give people hope or scare them about the future, and I do both," Mark continues, "but then, give them no answer, no roadmap for the way forward, they feel disempowered."

The League of Pragmatic Optimists

Struggling to figure out a response, Mark decided to set up a meeting of a group he called, *The League of Pragmatic Optimists*. It was to be a simple networking group in which people could meet in a room to 'work' ideas about how to solve a particular issue. Individuals could attend or not, as they wished. They could bring a topic to be 'worked', give feedback or join in a cause and become more involved elsewhere.

There were only 8 guiding principles to which any group had to adhere:

1. Have an unashamed optimism of ambition
2. Involve yourself in projects that are bigger than you
3. Engineer serendipity
4. You are what you do, not what you intend to do
5. Making mistakes is ok, but not trying is irresponsible
6. Commit to evidence – also known as 'Think like an engineer, not like a politician.'
7. You will lose a lot (in the beginning) – also known as 'Play the long game'
8. Police your own cynicism

Essentially, the *League* acted as a catalyst, to bring together like-minded individuals with the hope that some of them might go off and actually do something positive.

"The idea took hold," says Mark, "and there are now six chapters of the *League* around the world, in addition to one in the UK, there is one in New Zealand, one in Costa Rica, one in Finland and three in Spain. Each group has its own character. In the UK, it serves more of a networking role, while in Spain the participants are far more action-oriented."

His workload running a change consultancy and writing his next book has diminished some of the driving force in *The League of Pragmatic Optimists*, so it now meets more irregularly, but Mark hopes to find someone to take over the helm of the UK branch to ensure that it continues to meet more often.

The new book, *We Do Things Differently* (Profile Books, 2016) and

Mark's consultancy are both focused on the same topic: cultural change. The book shines a spotlight on individuals who have caused successful and positive change in human systems such as education and health care. Mark's consultancy (also called *We Do Things Differently*) aims to help large corporates get fit for a different future.

"The problem with large corporates is that they become institutionally complacent," Mark explains. "They reward mediocrity rather than innovation or excellence. To get employee engagement you need to shift the existing culture, and that's a big job."

"Not every business has the same issues. Our first step in helping is to diagnose the underlying problem and then agree a process for change. In a great many corporates a big problem is that the formal company values are not reflected in their actions. I tell them 'You are what do you, not what you say you do.'"

All in all, Mark has managed to fashion himself a career that uses his skills and experience and, at the same time, embodies his personal values. He has now found a way to marry, take on a mortgage (and hopefully have a family) while working in a role which is meaningful to him and which he believes makes a difference.

While speaking to Mark for this book, he kept saying, "You really must speak to Rob Symington. He's doing great things!" And indeed, Rob's is yet another story of an individual who jettisoned his traditional career in order to set up an organisation for others who want to leave the traditional business world. Rob, like Mark, began his work in London but is now setting up networks around the world to support professionals fleeing from their traditional jobs. Rob's organisation is called *Escape the City* ('the City' being the English expression for the traditional financial district in London).

Rob's story – Assisting 'Corporate Refugees'

A traditional start

Rob Symington's family has been in the wine business for many years and has a vineyard in Portugal dedicated to making port. Therefore, though English, his early years were spent in Portugal until, at the age of eight, he was sent to England to school. He stayed in the UK for higher education, studying History at the University of Edinburgh, although his course included a year of study in France. Rob explains that, like others from a similar background, he did 'the milk round' after graduation - a process whereby large prestigious corporations interview the graduates of top universities with an eye to giving them their first job. Rob reminisces, "Like others, I headed onto the corporate 'gravy train', not sure exactly what I wanted, but certain that I wanted to do something commercial."

In 2007, *Ernst and Young* offered Rob a job in its business consulting group. He describes himself at that time as 'business green' or 'wet behind the ears' but keen and eager to learn. Rob eagerly threw himself into his job, working hard and feeling excited to be a part of change projects in other large corporations. He desperately wanted to see the positive impact that a well thought out and implemented change programme could have on improving a business. Initially, Rob worked as a junior member of a consultancy team, working late most nights and often going into the office at weekends; he was undaunted because he longed to see results.

Rob himself describes this time by saying, "There was a gradual unravelling. I was working typically 70 hours a week in big corporates. I was so eager to see what changes our team could bring about… and then, it began to dawn on me that, in reality, nothing was changing." Rob continues, "I began to feel like I was on the 'outside' of some inside joke shared by the large businesses. I just didn't get it. There was, in fact, no significant change happening as a result of our consulting work, we were just helping individuals in personal power plays within corporate politics. The primary driver for all the work and the expense was some individual's personal advancement. Advancement meant more power and more power meant more money."

Realisation dawned

As this realisation dawned, Rob became introspective. He began to understand how important 'meaning' and 'purpose' was to him and in the work he pursued. As his understanding solidified, Rob realised, "Damn! There is nothing in this for me. Chasing money isn't enough for me." And Rob saw lots and lots of corporate money wasted as individuals pursued personal ambition. Although well launched up the career ladder, Rob felt he couldn't continue to work in this environment. "I was externally very successful, but I felt like a fraud," he recalls. "None of my accomplishments felt real or meaningful. I felt like I was missing the whole reason for my existence."

Reviewing his life up until that point, Rob realised that he had spent most of his time in 'institutions' - either educational establishments or well respected corporations. Yet, the only moment he felt that, "the story was as good as it felt" was when he took a road trip to Africa when he was 21 years old. It was challenging, fun, interesting and hard work and he was fully present. In other words, he was genuinely engaged in what he was doing and understood why he was there. He thought deeply, trying to understand what it was that seemed so engaging about that time, so that he could figure out what he needed in his working life.

"Freedom" was a word that popped into his head - the freedom to figure out what to do and how best to do it. As he developed this idea Rob realised that he liked problem solving, having an idea about a solution and turning it into a reality. "I had a hunch that I could build something of substance," he explains. "I played with lots of ideas and read widely. As I did, I began to wonder if my frustration at working in large corporations might be the basis of a business." Rob discussed his ideas with friends and decided to 'test the waters' while he was still employed, by writing an anonymous blog.

Escape the City

The response to his blog was tremendous. Inspired by the feedback from his readers, he and a friend, Dom, decided to take a risk and start a business. In 2010 he resigned from his traditional job and set up *Escape the City Ltd.* Together, Rob and Dom decided on a strap-line that reflected their own actions and came up with 'Do something different!' Rob describes the 'problem' he was trying to solve with his business, "People's aspirations are changing, but the structures in which they are working are not. It's those people, the 'escapees' from this traditional work environment, who are my primary customers."

Escape the City encourages those of a mindset similar to Rob's to leave 'the system' so that they can change it. He firmly believes that if enough good people leave, then it will impact business's bottom lines and those remaining will feel compelled to change the culture. "At first, people laughed at what I was doing," Rob says. "But now they are contacting me so that I can tell them what's happening to their companies."

So what does *Escape the City* do? It has evolved. Initially Rob had to figure out how to generate enough revenue on which to live so he set up a 'job book', essentially creating a recruitment agency of sorts. This bureau focused on companies who wanted to employ the type of person who shared the values of *Escape the City*. Rob also raised money by putting on selected events. Finally, over time, the business has developed a global social networking campaign as well as training for aspiring escapees.

Rob uses the language of a book by Seth Godin called *Tribes*, a book he read while he was figuring out how to 'escape the City' himself. *Tribes* resonated with him and he uses many of its principles in the way he has set out his business. "People are basically tribal," he says. "They need social validation. That's one of the reasons why those very individuals who once scoffed at me now ask for my opinion."

Escape the City goes from strength to strength. "I don't see other similar movements as competitors, but as allies in a similar movement," says Rob. "And the more of us that exist, the stronger the movement will be. We are all activists and I see *Escape the City* as one brand of activist."

And *Escape the City* is a popular movement. Although working with only a small group of 11 people based in London, the team feed a global network of more than 200,000 individuals. Rob now worries about how they will build a company that can be scaled up in size without falling into the trap of behaving like the very large corporates he was trying to escape. "I want to build 'escape schools' around the world," Rob explains, "and build all the activities around a distributed, global network."

The London team currently offer two different, intensive three-month courses called:

1. Startup Tribe
2. Escape Tribe

These are essentially 'how to' courses focused on helping individuals who want to create their own businesses or networks based on the values espoused by the *Escape the City*. In fact, Rob and *Escape the City*, hope to fish in the pond created by these individuals in their specialist recruitment function.

"One big difference," says Rob, "between our approach and those of traditional businesses, is that we espouse the entrepreneurial, 'can do' mind set. Such an approach recognises that 'failure' is a part of the process. For the traditional corporate, this philosophy is heresy. Failure is not acceptable and I believe that this attitude stifles creativity and growth and generates a 'fear' and 'blame' culture."

Rob concludes with the thought that perhaps his views come from his experience of the family business, in which the family view themselves as caretakers for the next generation rather than businessmen determined to extract maximum profit from their assets, year on year. He recognises that there are a few individuals in large corporations who are trying to shift their businesses toward a similar philosophy, but these individuals are still rare.

Escape the City provides yet another option for professionals who are dissatisfied in their current, traditional employment and Rob is trying to offer this support on a global scale. In fact, from reading these stories one could take the view that the whole movement began in the UK, but that's because these stories merely represent a snapshot of one region on the globe. A scan of the internet suggests that this movement covers the Americas and parts of Asia as well as Europe. To give a flavour of a US version of this movement, Aaron Hurst has shared his story and tells how it led him to create a business called *Imperative*.

Aaron's story – Helping others find 'purpose'

An entrepreneur with a social mission

Aaron Hurst has experienced a varied career history. Educated at the University of Michigan, he has held a wide range of posts since college, including entrepreneurial positions in various tech startups in Silicon Valley, California. He also spent a lot of time in teaching and worked in curriculum development for intercity schools in Chicago. Even in the early days of his career he tried to balance his natural entrepreneurial skills with his desire to work in the community, a desire met by his teaching and educational positions.

Finally, in 2001, Aaron founded the *Taproot Foundation*, an organisation that aimed to build a network of *pro bono*, professional volunteers. It was during his involvement at the *Taproot Foundation* that he noticed something intriguing. When interviewing volunteers it soon become clear that volunteering represented the most 'successful' and rewarding activities of many of the professionals who took part. For these individuals, the unpaid work they did was far more rewarding than their paid career. This observation led Aaron onto a new pathway that was to eventually lead him to creating *Imperative* in December 2013.

What was his idea? What was he trying to accomplish with *Imperative*?

"I wanted to figure out how to make all work feel as good as *pro bono* work," explains Aaron.

Working with an academic partner, Aaron started out by developing a psychological assessment, a ten-minute questionnaire designed to discover what it is that gives a person a sense of 'purpose'. It was this sense of purpose that he believed provided the 'feel-good' factor in the volunteer activities.

Next, Aaron and his business partner developed an organisational assessment so that companies could understand their workforces and what motivated them. Today, *Imperative* also does a lot of advocacy consulting with HR (Human Resources) leadership to help them understand the importance of individual and corporate purpose. "For example," Aaron explains, "there is research which shows that people who find great meaning in their work use job descriptions as a starting point, rather than a boundary, to delineate their jobs. I refer to this activity by individuals as 'job tailoring' and explain the positive impacts for organisations in which employees act in this way."

Aaron went on to explain how he tries to assist in the alignment of individual and corporate purpose for the benefit of both constituents. In his work, Aaron has identified 24 different 'purpose patterns' and has even published a book entitled *The Purpose Economy* (Elevate, 2014).

In this book Aaron explains why he believes that the economy is shifting to a purpose economy and attributes much of the current trend toward doing meaningful work to this shift. "The information economy has been the third economy," he states. "But now, with extended life spans and affluence, society and the individuals within society are looking to expand their need for satisfaction by seeking purpose in their work."

Today, *Imperative* is prospering. Aaron has raised a seed round of funding and now maintains a staff of 12 people. This solid foundation is important because Aaron has an ambition to connect people to their purpose, on a massive scale. He hopes to help many by connecting them to jobs with content that provide fulfilment. "I see this activity as vital to helping to make the shift from the information economy to the purpose economy," he says. He has affiliates around the globe and has formed a partnership with the *BMW Foundation* to promote his work and messages.

"Most companies do have good intentions, but they don't understand their employee behaviours," Aaron explains. "Others, while they may believe in values, are not willing to 'fall on their sword' for them. And not all companies or organisations behave in a homogeneous manner." He spoke of his experience of finding 'pockets of purpose' and micro cultures within larger organisations, which are not aligned with corporate values.

"Sometimes the difficulty is not in the intent, but in the successful implementation within a company," Aaron declares. "Individuals are my ultimate customer and businesses are really the means to that end."

When asked why he believes that purpose has become so important for professionals today, Aaron suggests that much had to do with the state of the world and world events as 'Millennials' entered the workforce. In the USA and much of Europe, these years were a time of recession and jobs were difficult to find. At the same time, environmental issues appeared prominently in the news. For many this would be the first generation that would probably not earn as much as their parents. All in all, life prospects for these young professionals looked 'darker' than those of proceeding generations.

Aaron has developed a methodology for helping these individuals. "The first step is for them to understand themselves," he explains. "And then, they should try to figure if they can do something to satisfy their purposes where they are currently working. Typically, the route to discovering an individual's purpose has more to who with 'who he or she is, rather than where they are working."

It's not unusual for this process to take some time. Aaron estimates that the average 30 year old urban professional is probably in his or her second or third job before knowing what 'they want to be when they grow up'. Today, with the tools and methodology available from *Imperative*, there is help at hand.

Aaron's approach has been a combination of academic and pragmatic - combining both the individual and social perspective in trying to design a service that addresses the single large issue that preoccupies many people - the desire to have 'purpose'. Whether the drive to find purpose is the cause or the effect of an economic shift, the individual sits at the heart of this dynamic. Aaron is trying to help people, one at a time, to find the right job role. He has discovered this need by working with businesses and individuals throughout the United States over the last decade. His findings show that the 'snapshot' of activities already described for the United Kingdom would likely find traction in the rest of the world as well.

Returning from the global perspective back to the United Kingdom, this chapter ends where the idea for the book began, with the *Harvard Oxford Alumni Social Business Group* which was founded in late 2012, with its inaugural event early in 2013.

The Harvard Oxford Alumni Social Business Group

This section does not focus on an individual story. Maya Mehta, an Oxford alumna co-founder of this group has already told her story in Chapter 5. The Harvard alumna is the author of this book and a biography may be found in the front. Both these individuals joined forces to set up a networking event. They started out by focusing on these alumni communities but it soon expanded beyond this small group to include people from all educations and backgrounds. The original concept was to provide a venue for individuals who were determined to make a social impact in their job, and who wanted to meet others with similar objectives in order to exchange ideas. The networking evening hosts four or five panellists whose activities embody the spirit of the group.

Typically the panel is composed of:

- a social entrepreneur
- an intrapreneur from a large corporate
- a person who left the business world to set up or work for a charity
- a panellist who has established some kind of support organisation to enable this movement.

The idea behind this panel composition was to provide an activity that would spark interest in every member of the audience and demonstrate examples of the options available to them. The panellist discussion is followed by an open question session and then, less formal questioning over drinks. Most of the stories in this book come from panellists at a *Harvard Oxford Alumni Social Business Group* event.

As of 2015, this event, currently held twice a year, is another example of a 'support organisation'. So far, it has successfully linked up like-minded individuals, provided connections between attendees for resources and inspired many of those attending into taking action. One woman breathed a sigh of relief at the end of the first event, saying, "Until I came here, I thought I was all alone. Now I know that there are lots of others who feel the way I do!" For others, attending the event was the final push they needed to leave their unsatisfying corporate career and move to a social business.

All the activities are volunteer led. No one gets paid. To date, the *Harvard Club of the UK* has provided the administrative services, sending out many of the invitations and tracking registration. Locations in central London have been kindly donated by Harvard and Tufts University alumni so that the cost of the event merely covers drinks and nibbles. The two founders carry out all the activities in their own time while working in full-time jobs. So, although this network provides a useful service, inspiring and connecting individuals who are social pioneers, there is a limit to its reach. It is hoped that this book will extend that reach and provide insights, inspiration and information to its readers so that others who cannot attend the event can also benefit.

The collection of stories shows a movement that exists and is growing. Many individuals, those already in work and those just starting their careers, are searching for something more than they currently experience in their jobs or see in job advertisements. What they seek is greater social involvement in their day to day activities - whether this involvement is helping people or the environment. The 'what' is clear.

What isn't obvious is 'why'? Why now? What is different today from 30 or 40 years ago that has prompted this wave of social involvement?

Chapter 10

WHY AND WHY NOW?

"Today, for me, the biggest thing is to make an impact and change things for the better. I now see things differently than when I began this journey. I don't believe that most individuals, all by themselves, can expect to change the world. However, individuals who support and encourage businesses to make change can do a great deal. It may not be everyone's passion to change workplace culture but to me, it's very important."

Participant, Harvard Oxford Alumni Social Business Group

The contributors to this book aren't saints; they are a selection of ordinary people, all of whom have managed to do extraordinary things. Some of their activities were big and some were small, some were local and some, international. To these social pioneers, fame wasn't the driving factor nor was 'fixing the world' in one fell swoop. The motivation was to make a personal difference to someone else's life or to the planet. Although this chapter concludes the book, it doesn't end the story. Their journeys continue and the overall social movement is growing. Indeed you may be inspired by them to start a journey of your own.

These stories chronicle the attempts of individuals to define their own role in making a positive social impact. As one contributor expressed it,

"I believe that what's important for people who want to change things is to decide where they want to be. A big organisation? A small one? Banking? Technology? Retail? Charity? It doesn't matter. What matters is how they behave within that role and the impact they make on the company culture. For example, perhaps a banker could decide to concentrate less on money and focus some effort and resources on people rather than profits. It really doesn't matter where a person works, a person can do what he loves as a profession and still make a positive personal impact on improving the world and society. For me, the journey is about awareness and defining the potential social impact within any role."

These personal explorations raise many questions: What's happening? And why now? This trend among today's professionals is widespread and continues to grow in strength. It's not confined to one market sector or one geography in the Western world. Although the stories in this book focus on the UK, one could fill another book with similar interviewees from the United States or other European countries. This trend has been observed by many and incorporated into mainstream business thinking - it's now possible to take a class in social entrepreneurship at university or business school, and terms like 'conscious leadership' and 'mindful business practices' are entering the mainstream.

Even conservative businesses like *PriceWaterhouseCoopers* (*PwC*) have taken note. In an article written for *Harvard Business Review* in November 2014, *PwC*'s US Chairman, Rob Moritz explains, "When I was coming up, we knew what we were doing, but we didn't ask why we did it. We didn't give much thought to our, or the firm's role in society. For me, that point crystallises the generational issues that *PwC* and many other organisations are facing." Later in the article he goes into more detail when he concludes, "Businesses need to create an environment that allows people to give back and excel both at the office and outside it… Millennials are quick to react negatively to any perceived disconnect between the firm's words and its actions. If they don't believe us, they leave." (see References).

Is technology responsible?

There are, no doubt, many factors driving this shift, but the increased sophistication and prevalence of technology, especially the internet and mobile technologies, have certainly acted as a catalyst. In fact, technology has provided two drivers: first, its widespread use by large organisations has reduced direct human interaction and facilitated global growth of such corporations, while at the same time, the increased 'connectedness' of individuals by internet, networks and mobile phones has opened up information sources and increased an individual's ability to reach many others with new ideas. So today's growing use of technology may be both a cause and an enabler of this trend.

First, let's look at how companies have adapted technology to see how these changes might have contributed. Computers and later, mobile phones, were deployed first as tools and eventually evolved to become the fundamental infrastructure which underpins and drives a business. The evolution of corporate adoption of computers, networks and smartphones, shows how technology has come to isolate individuals within the large corporate workplace and instead of merely replacing boring tasks once performed by employees, has reduced highly skilled jobs to automaton-like, repetitive activities. A quick look at the last 40 to 50 years of Western corporate history illustrates how things have changed.

In the 1970s computers began to automate clerical functions, replacing staff in many organisations. Despite this loss of personnel, the company structure remained similar. In the 1980s, new applications were developed, and more and more activities became computerised. In addition, networking technology began to advance and many large corporations could afford to link up their various locations around the world. Finally, although not widespread, this decade also saw the beginning of commercial mobile phone technology.

By the 1990s, the internet was taking off and the prevalence of mobile phones rapidly increased. With this growing take up of technological innovation, businesses began to replace more and more functions, and, more importantly, they reorganised and started to work in completely different ways - outsourcing the work of entire divisions to specialist providers and thereby replacing whole departments and functions. Overall, more and more functions formerly carried out by people were now carried out by machines. In the UK, even the ubiquitous 'tea lady' was replaced by automated coffee and tea dispensers.

The deregulation of financial services and the stock market may have played a role

At the same time, technology and the tools it offered were not the only the only factors at play. Large corporations became increasingly focused on the bottom line to the exclusion of all else. Up until the 1960s or 1970s, professionals expected to have a job for life in their chosen company. In some businesses during those decades, computers began to replace human clerical functions - some jobs were lost, although many of these workers were redeployed in other areas. However, beginning in the 1980s with the liberation of financial services from prior regulatory restraints, the pace of change accelerated and performance on the stock market - hence, share price - started to call the shots in businesses around the planet.

So, by the mid-1980s, there were two forces at work, the computerisation of business functions and increased pressure from shareholders to drive profits up on a regular basis. As a result, businesses changed. Not all businesses, and not overnight, but slowly many began to focus less and less on the long-term and more and more on the quarterly or annual profit report for shareholders. Nothing else matched profits in terms of importance and not just profits, but ever-increasing profits - quarter after quarter, year after year, companies tried to improve performance at the expense of - well, basically everything. In the drive for profits, customers, employees, suppliers, the environment all suffered so that profits could be driven ever higher.

So, what has been the typical course of action in businesses faced with this pressure?

Large businesses exhibited a characteristic response. First, they installed computers to achieve reduced costs. Next, employees were sacrificed as the businesses 'downsized' or 'rightsized' in an attempt to feed that starving monster - the shareholders. As time progressed, product quality and/or size was 'managed' to allow for more profit and finally, customers were sacrificed too. Anyone who has played close attention to consumer brands over the years will have observed the reduction in package size of some products without the concomitant reduction in cost.

Customer service and the customer experience also suffered in many instances as computers replaced people as a customer interface. Call centres and automated answering systems illustrate two examples of this trend. Meanwhile in some types of businesses, like the growth of consumer computing, large international businesses outsourced the sales and servicing of all but its largest clients to agents, distributors or retail outlets. In many ways, as these businesses grew ever larger, they became perceptibly less people-oriented.

The 'tea lady' was one example, and another is PAs (personal assistants) and secretaries whose jobs have, more and more, been replaced by technology so that only the most senior directors have a human being to help with mail or to screen phone calls. For everyone else, phone calls go directly to a voicemail system and mail is now email and goes directly to the individual(s) via the computer system - now there is no need to speak to a human being to leave a message or organise a meeting. In some businesses these behaviours have become so ingrained that, even in small offices of four or five people who sit together in one room, it is not uncommon for an individual to send an email rather than speak directly to a colleague.

Computerised phone answering systems replaced personal contact between employees and customers. The majority of customer service activity was placed firmly into the hands of the customer, who is now forced to fill out forms online and repeatedly provide information when once, someone in the business would have done this work. In many large consumer focused companies, it's impossible for customers to speak to a human being without making a colossal effort. Today, many customer interfaces - ATMs for banks, airline and other travel check-in and ticketing services, even some checkout areas at stores - have removed the human employee and replaced it with a computer.

Do people need people?

All of these examples were once opportunities for human to human interaction. People might have known their regular bank teller or checkout clerk, and exchanged personal information along with 'good mornings'. This interaction has been lost. Even in large office businesses, many activities that were formerly face-to-face are now automated. Computerised training has now replaced classroom training in many large corporates. This training was once a vehicle, not only for learning but for growing a network of colleagues elsewhere in the business, exchanging ideas and best practice, and for building company 'spirit' and reinforcing company values.

Robert Reich, a well-known US political commentator, professor and author, places much of the blame on the corporate leaders. In his article (see References) he states,

"…A half-century ago, CEOs typically managed companies for the benefit of all their stakeholders - not just shareholders, but also their employees, communities, and the nation as a whole.

"The job of management," proclaimed Frank Abrams, chairman of *Standard Oil of New Jersey*, in a 1951 address, "is to maintain an equitable and working balance among the claims of the various directly affected interest groups… stockholders, employees, customers, and the public at large. Business managers are gaining professional status partly because they see in their work the basic responsibilities [to the public] that other professional men have long recognized as theirs."

This view was common among chief executives of the time. *Fortune* magazine urged CEOs to become "industrial statesmen." And to a large extent, that's what they became. But starting in the late 1970s, a new vision of the corporation and the role of CEOs emerged - prodded by corporate "raiders," hostile takeovers, junk bonds, and leveraged buyouts. Shareholders began to predominate over other stakeholders. And CEOs began to view their primary role as driving up share prices. To do this, they had to cut costs - especially payrolls, which constituted their largest expense."

Is profit a bad thing?

While nothing is wrong with a business making a profit, it is not healthy for a business and everyone involved in its supply chain to chase a never-ending growth in profits - especially if these profits are often made at the expense of smaller suppliers further down the supply chain. The environment also pays a price in the quest to drive a never-ending increase in production, distribution and profits. The question to ask is: how much profit is enough?

Similarly, in terms of the role of the stock market, there is nothing intrinsically wrong with a business seeking outside investors so that it can grow. Sadly, in recent years, the 'tail has been wagging the dog'. The short-termist approach to profits appears to have inhibited many companies from taking a longer term and more holistic view of their businesses. Profit is not an infinite commodity and a continuous increase in profits is, ultimately, not a sustainable strategy. A similar issue arises in all democracies in which politicians, fearing that unpopular, long term decisions might negatively impact their chances of re-election, fail to undertake key investments.

So why have so many large businesses fallen into this trap? Much can be explained by the changes over this same time period in how top executives are paid. Typically, the salaries of CEOs and other top directors were linked to this increase in productivity, measured as 'profits'. Shares and share options continue to make up a percentage of most of the executives' pay packets, so it has been in their personal interest to keep share prices growing. Thus, personal remuneration drove these behaviours and profits became more and more important to the exclusion of other measures. It is also interesting to note that during this time the link between productivity and earnings for all workers began to move apart. (see References)

It is precisely this sort of mindset that drove many executives to commit illegal acts. Scandals such as *Enron* and a myriad of banking crises reflect how this compulsion to grow profits can change a whole business culture and nudge otherwise law-abiding citizens toward criminal activities. In fact, there are studies that suggest that the ideal profile for today's corporate executives matches the behaviours documented for psychopaths. Paul Babiak and Robert Hare, leading experts in psychopathic behaviour and diagnosis, (*Snakes in Suits: When Psychopaths Go to Work*, HarperCollins 2006) claim that a disproportionate number of psychopaths easily succeed and prosper in the current large corporate environment.

Where does that leave us?

So, a picture comes into focus of today's workplace - an environment that's heavily computerised and measured for efficiency, with each employee, no matter how senior, carrying out a specific function. The workplace feels driven and the atmosphere is competitive. Each worker is isolated from significant face-to-face interaction with colleagues, customers, even suppliers, and because each role is well defined, the employee is easily replaceable. The whole environment contributes to making workers feel that they are merely a cog in a large machine, a machine whose output solely benefits the shareholders.

Office workers and professionals have become today's 'factory workers', but their output is knowledge and data, rather than manufactured goods. People look back on the early days of industrialisation - factory workers doing the same activities over and over, often working 12 hour days - and disparage the cruelty that forced employees to work under these conditions. Working conditions might be physically safer now, but, otherwise, how different are they? Are our working days actually shorter or any less boring than the factory worker of 200 years ago? Is physical safety 'enough' in a job or should mental and emotional factors be considered as well?

Today's workers in large bureaucratic organisations often feel like they are running on a treadmill and many of the stories in this book used this term, or a similar description. The individuals felt like they were going faster and faster, their energy going toward driving the corporate machine, but their efforts getting them, personally, nowhere. Thus, in many large organisations, the working life has become 'soulless'. What about home life? Private life? Does it or can it make up for what's missing at work? Has anything changed?

Again, the answer is 'yes', much has changed. Since the 1960s and 1970s, the shape of the nuclear family has altered. Fewer and fewer children escape living in a household which has experienced divorce and many live in one-parent families. Furthermore, families are far more mobile. Many children no longer grow up in neighbourhoods surrounded by lots of relatives and close friends. More and more, people scarcely know their neighbours. In addition, while not true of all religions, in general, fewer and fewer individuals regularly attend places of worship.

Attending Church, Temple, Synagogue, Mosque - any place of worship - whether one was religious or not, played a part in creating a close community. Charitable activities, social events and helping others in the community were fundamental to the experience, whatever the religion. What has replaced this sort of interaction for those individuals who no longer attend a place of worship? Schools can create a community too, of course, but sadly schools have also become big and impersonal. Furthermore, children often travel long distances from their home to attend school, making socialising of whole families and meeting with school friends more difficult.

In effect, for many people the sense of community that once existed, while not entirely absent today, has certainly diminished. This loss can serve to isolate the individual who now may have little sense of community or close family ties. The question is then: can internet communities replace face-to-face communities? Are they enough? Do people really have to see each other and speak voice-to-voice to feel part of something? Looking at the psychological element in a bit more detail, this globalisation and other changes within society may have left some basic human needs unfulfilled.

There is no clear answer, but a recent online article by Chandra M Johnson (see References) attempts to address this question and has come up with some interesting conclusions. We human beings are primed to take in information from a variety of sources to form a complete picture of any social interaction. Smell, touch, facial expressions, voice, body stance, even invisible chemicals secreted in small amounts - pheromones - all play a part in forming a meaningful interaction. Most of these added cues are lost when people limit their communication to text or the internet.

Chandra makes a good case for balancing what she terms online learning and experiential learning. She describes it as, "...the difference between looking at a picture of cool, green grass and actually walking barefoot in it. The problem is that the more people and children interact with a person or the world through a screen rather than in real life, the less emotion is attached to the exchange." She quotes many leading experts who have looked into the question, and concludes that that emotional intelligence does not develop normally in children who spend extensive time online and communicate predominantly via texts. She goes on to suggest that when people eschew face-to-face contact for communication, particularly for personal issues, it doesn't satisfy an intimacy need.

Perhaps it's this unsatisfied need that is driving the quest for greater 'meaning' in job roles. Evidence also suggests that employees who believe in the values of an organisation work together more effectively and can be more successful. Even small social enterprises follow this trend with a recent article in *The Guardian* newspaper (9 July, 2013) claiming "New survey suggests social enterprises out-performing mainstream businesses." Thus, one great fear, a loss of profits, need not be a problem in a well-run social business. In earlier chapters, there were examples of how employees, managers and directors actually improved the productivity of their department or division. All it took was a novel approach and effort on behalf of the individual to change the way activities were carried out.

Large corporations should not be written off.

Despite all the issues that beset today's corporate environment, businesses do play a crucial role in supporting society. Without the money generated by business there would be far less money for charities, which is to a great extent provided by employed individuals and corporates through their CSR (Corporate Social Responsibility) programmes. Without money, there wouldn't be the tax revenue to pay for government, so government assistance would dwindle. In today's world, successful businesses of all sizes are critical to providing support for social programmes, but the philosophy and values of the business should be in line with providing this support. For example, the fact of giving money to good causes while simultaneously destroying or polluting the environment does not offset the negative environmental impact. Profits need to be balanced with social values in a more sustainable fashion than is generally practiced today.

Maybe what's needed is a shift from an obsession with ever-increasing profits to a drive 'for profit, for good', with leaders of these businesses taking a more holistic view of the business activities. Perhaps, as Béla did in his businesses, the executives should set up a system which balances the needs of shareholders with those of its customers, employees, local community, suppliers and the environment. Such an approach does not need to mean 'no profits', but it might reduce the level of profits reported each quarter - sometimes only in the short term, sometimes, an overall reduction in profits. Is that bad? How much profit is enough? Are ever-increasing profits a realistic aspiration? Is it sustainable?

This book chronicles the stories of some individuals and organisations whose values genuinely do encourage social betterment. As one of them explained, "People want to be a part of something bigger than themselves, something they can believe in... It has become commonplace to assert that organisations need shared meaning, and this is surely so. But shared meaning is about more than fulfilling your mission statement - it's about forging and maintaining powerful connections between personal and organisational values."

In fact, evidence from the stories in this book and from mainstream business publications suggests that a shift is occurring. In *Harvard Business Review*, Rob Goffee and Gareth Jones (see References) two academics from London Business School and IE Business School in Madrid, sum up their findings as follows, "What is the organisation of your dreams? In a nutshell, it's a company where individual differences are nurtured; information is not suppressed or spun; the company adds value to employees, rather than merely extracting it from them; the organization stands for something meaningful, the work is intrinsically rewarding; and there are no stupid rules."

This quote sounds great, but how close is it to reality?

Looking at the bigger picture, there are still many, many large corporations that focus exclusively on ever-increasing profits. Profit has become the sole value to these organisations. Customers, employees - everything else is reduced to numbers and statistics, specific individuals no longer matter. Someone leaves, or there is customer churn, no problem, as long as the overall numbers tally and support the business's profit objectives. The result is inevitably that customers leave, as well as good employees, and they leave with a bad feeling about that particular business.

One contributor summed up the situation very well when she explained, "Many large companies express values that don't reflect corporate behaviours. You have only to look at the retention rate of new graduates. Most of these young, idealist individuals believe what they are told at the job interviews, accept a job and then discover that the company didn't practice what it preaches. This story is an old one, and I kept looking for a company that 'walked the walk' and behaved according to the values it advertised."

The important shift in values does not start with businesses, rather, it begins with the people who work in them as well as the leaders who lead them. It doesn't matter whether they are entry-level employees, senior managers or business leaders, each can play a part. And what seems to be happening today is a mind shift in which each individual tries to make a personal impact on improving the world in some way. As one contributor sums it up, "At its most basic, the world depends on people just living their lives, going to work, doing their jobs. But these same people can affect many, many small changes, just by being conscious of their own impact on everything - at work, at home and in between. And it's important that they give themselves credit for this consciousness and the behavioural changes that it elicits. These smaller, individual impacts are also important. I don't believe that most individuals all by themselves can expect to change the world. However, individuals who support and encourage businesses to make change can do a great deal."

Technology has also played a positive role, acting as a low cost enabler for people all over the world to communicate and investigate. With this facility, more and more ideas are exchanged and virtual and face-to-face networks formed. Individuals can make their contributions, large or small, and feel part of a larger movement. And people, in their desire to connect directly with others and to find meaning in their work and life, will, little by little, address some of society's issues.

And now, a call to action.

As Mark Stevenson noted in his story in Chapter 9, people aren't happy when you get them excited about an issue and then can't tell them what to do. Hopefully, having read many different people's journeys, the reader feels inspired to set out to discover his or her own path. The individuals in the book come from diverse backgrounds, educations, countries and religions. The only common threads that bind them all together is that each has a desire to put 'soul' back into their working life. There is no reason why the reader who has sufficient passion and a desire to take action cannot do the same thing. It may not be easy, but it can be done.

This book has told the stories of many people who have tried and succeeded to put meaning into their work life. All of them struggled to a greater or lesser degree until they became aware of what it was that was missing, and then figured out what it was they sought. The awareness typically started as a vague unease and then dissatisfaction - in most cases a dissatisfaction in spite of what appeared on the surface to be a good job or a successful career. With this awareness, these individuals first looked within themselves to work out what to do and then looked around to see what wasn't right about their situation. Finally, each searched to understand what else what happening in the world. The journey was neither obvious nor easy.

Each of the pioneers described in this book was brave and all were special people who carved out routes that others may now follow. One lesson is clear for those who follow. The first step is to become 'aware'. But awareness alone is not enough; an individual needs to feel enough passion to want to take action. It's this awareness, plus action, that leads to change.

So, how does one become aware? Many of the stories describe using meditation and mindfulness and that is certainly an approach that is growing in popularity. But it is important to take care in selecting a supplier for mindfulness training - not all suppliers are equal. As one attendee of the *HOASBG* explained, "There are more and more people who now take a six-week course and get a certificate who consider themselves able to teach 'mindfulness' and 'meditation'. The whole approach is more than just a process to be followed or a course to be taken and then you are fixed. True mindfulness is about following a path. Meditation, properly done, can be a tool to help on that path, and the whole route is underpinned by ethics and values."

"A good way to think of the different impact is to consider a 'rose' analogy.' If someone gives you a bunch of roses and you put them in a room, they look lovely and smell nice, but only for a short time. True mindfulness is like planting a rose bush. You have to prepare a hole for it, water it, prune it and give it attention, but then, you have roses year after year."

Getting started...

So, an essential first step is awareness. Look within and analyse your values and what motivates and makes you happy. If you need help, there are many companies who can help and there are tools available on the website. Aaron Hurst in Chapter 9 provides tools to help people clearly identify their purpose. Neil Seligman in Chapter 8 offers a different approach to introspection and mindfulness and others, like Gina Hayden and Erika Uffindell, both mentioned in earlier chapters, focus on business executives in particular and some of their initial steps focus on mindfulness and gaining an insight into personal values and motivation.

These examples are just that - no doubt a scan of the internet will yield many, many more.

Having become aware - a process that might take weeks, months or even years - what comes next? Well, having a clearer picture of personal values and an increased understanding of self and of the surrounding environment, the next step is to work to gain insight, create a vision of 'what good looks like'. This stage involves exploring options and putting together a plan. This book has illustrated a number of directions that such plans may take.

For some, this plan meant 'fixing' the organisation in which they worked - either overtly or covertly. For others it meant creating a new business or charity in which they could pursue their personal values while at work. Finally, there were others who decided to leave the commercial world entirely and work for a charity or not-for-profit. So, the next step was making a plan, perhaps many plans, because the first one didn't succeed. But awareness and a mindful approach combined with passion enabled these individuals to plan again, and keep going until each found a suitable route.

The final step is the most difficult, because it involves taking action and possibly stepping out into the unknown. There are five stages to the journey and each should be attempted before moving on:

1. AWARENESS
2. CLEAR PERSONAL VALUES
3. INSIGHTS
4. A VISION
5. A PLAN

Then, DO IT!

For success, it is necessary to go through each of these steps before one can take ACTION. Both the plan and action may have to be repeatedly refined before achieving success, but no activity is ever wasted. In all the stories where the individuals took a long and winding road (Chapter 8), they built on previous actions and, because their awareness increased, they were able to use these experiences to help them in their ultimate plan.

A road map makes a journey easier, but a guide makes it easier still. Some of the individuals in this book have set up enterprises that try to help individuals and businesses through this process. Vari McLuskie in Chapter 6 is one example. Vari and her team can provide the tools and guidance to both individuals and businesses. Then there is Rob Symington's story in Chapter 9, with *Escape the City* plus others already mentioned, who offer support at key stages of the journey. And of course, there are many others not included and more emerging every day. So, if the passion to do so is there, an individual can bring meaning to his or her job.

But what about businesses?

So, how do we get this army mobilised? All the individual stories build a great narrative, but large corporations, in many ways responsible for the current situation, can play a major role in 'putting the soul back' into corporate life. But why should these businesses change?

There are two key reasons: customers and employees. Today, more and more people and corporations make buying decisions that take into account the ethics and corporate behaviours of a business. The failure of a business to ensure a more balanced approach can negatively impact its bottom line as discerning customers migrate to more socially aware and involved suppliers. In addition, large businesses now have to work harder to retain the best and the brightest employees. This younger generation has a different rule book and is driving employers to think very differently about how to recruit, retain and grow their workforces. The change in attitude is happening. Businesses can stand apart and try to ignore the change or they can embrace it, and enable and encourage their employees to 'do good' as part of their daily job.

In the end, despite the rise of technology, businesses are still composed of people. The personal stories in this book clearly illustrate that for more and more employees, the 'hands off' contribution that a business makes through Corporate Social Responsibility is not enough. Many employees want to feel that they make a difference while doing their day-to-day jobs, or as an embedded part of their business environment. As Aaron Hurst suggested in Chapter 9, people are looking for 'purpose' in their work and when they have purpose they tend to work more productively, and most of the stories support this hypothesis. Almost everyone disclosed that he or she now worked harder and longer hours than in previous jobs, but that each was now happier to do so.

Peter Maxmin and Steve Turpie whose stories were told in Chapter 2, both found different ways to incorporate 'giving back' and 'doing good' into the work environment and both found that these activities made their people happier and more committed to the company. It didn't stop everyone from doing their jobs, but it did take a bit of effort on the part of Peter and Steve to think in a slightly different way. In Steve's case, he used a typical business activity - the departmental offsite meeting - and invested time and effort to deliver it in a different way so that it accomplished two goals: its original business purpose and a socially beneficial purpose.

In the same chapter, Jean Ward also managed to mobilise an entire company around the building of a school as a fitting memorial to a work colleague killed in the 2004 tsunami. And in another story, Andrew Warren clearly demonstrated that mobilising his diverse work force around supporting the UK Volleyball team for the 2012 Olympics not only made for a happier workforce, but a more profitable business.

Paul Lomas' experience, described in Chapter 5, illustrates that business partnerships too, can prosper when incorporating *pro bono* work into their standard way of working. Paul followed the advice given by Kay Allen in Chapter 9, when she said, "I want my business to be a huge corporate success. How do I do that and be socially responsible?" Kay managed to provide good arguments for supporting social programmes within a number of large UK corporations, and did so successfully. It can be done. It has been done.

Everyone can make some contribution, just as the security guard mentioned in Chapter 5, who played his role in giving to a local homeless shelter. His small gifts made a big difference in the lives of some of the local homeless population. While some people can play a bigger role in putting the soul back into the working environment - particularly owners and top executives - everyone can make a difference, step by step, one person at a time.

REFERENCES

Chapter 5

Reference 1

Peck Christen, R., Rosenberg, R. & Jayadeva, V. (2004) Financial institutions with a double bottom-line: implications for the future of microfinance. *CGAP* [online] Available from cgap.org [accessed 23 August, 2015]

Chapter 6

Reference 1

Biztaxlaw.about.com (2013) *What is a Disregarded Entity - Disregarded Entity Definition,* July 2013 [accessed 10 August, 2013]

Reference 2

Ridley-Duff, R. J. and Bull, M. 2011. *Understanding Social Enterprise: Theory and Practice.* London: Sage Publications

Chapter 7

Reference 1

Moro, D. & McKay, S. Briefing Paper 28 - The Growing workforce in the voluntary and community sectors: analysis of the Labour Force Survey 1993-2009. *University of Birmingham, Third Sector Research Centre* [online] Available at Birmingham.ac.uk [accessed 23 August, 2015]

Chapter 10

Reference 1

Moritz, R. (2014) The Chairman of PwC on Keeping Millennials Engaged. *Harvard Business Review* [online] November 2014. Available from Hbr.org [accessed 23 August, 2015]

Reference 2

Reich, R. (2014) How Business Schools Can Help Reduce Inequality. *Harvard Business Review* [online] September 12, 2014. Available from Hbr.org [accessed 23 August, 2015]

Reference 3

Lazonick, W. (2014) The Big Idea - Profits without Prosperity, *Harvard Business Review* [online] September 2014. Available from Hbr.org [accessed 23 August, 2015]

Reference 4

Johnson, C.M. (2014) Face time vs. screen time: The technological impact on communication, *Deseret News National* [online] August 29, 2014. Available from deseretnews.com [accessed 23 August, 2015]

Reference 5

Goffee, R. & Jones, G. (2013) Creating the Best Workplace on Earth. *Harvard Business Review* [online] May 2013. Available from Hbr.org [accessed 23 August, 2015]